KV-147-737

Microprocessor Interfacing

Microprocessor Interfacing

R. E. Vears

Newnes
An imprint of Butterworth-Heinemann Ltd
Linacre House, Jordan Hill, Oxford OX2 8DP

A member of the Reed Elsevier group

OXFORD LONDON BOSTON
MUNICH NEW DELHI SINGAPORE SYDNEY
TOKYO TORONTO WELLINGTON

First published 1990
Reprinted 1992, 1994

British Library Cataloguing in Publication Data
A CIP catalogue record for this book is available from the British Library

ISBN 0 7506 0883 8

Printed in Great Britain by Redwood Books,
Trowbridge, Wiltshire

Contents

Preface vii

1 **Signal conditioning** 1
Need for signal conditioning 1
Amplification 1
Operational amplifiers 2
Filtering 11
Problems 20

2 **D to A conversion** 23
Signal conversion 23
Types of digital to analogue converter 24
DAC characteristics 27
Interfacing DACs to a microcomputer 29
DAC applications 33
Problems 45

3 **A to D conversion** 48
Types of analogue to digital converter 48
ADC characteristics 52
Interfacing ADCs to a microcomputer 54
Voltage measurements 63
Scaling 63
Problems 68

4 **Data transfer techniques** 70
Synchronization of data transfers 71
Direct memory access 74
Electrical buffering 76
Serial/parallel and parallel/serial conversion 80
Multiplexing 81
Standard buses 85
Electrical isolation 89
Problems 91

5 Parallel I/O controllers 93
Need for I/O controllers 93
Simple parallel I/O ports 93
Hardware/software for general purpose interfaces 104
Programmable parallel I/O controllers 108
Problems 142

6 Serial I/O controllers 145
Serial data transfers 145
Baud rate 146
Software UART 147
Shift register (in VIA) 154
Dedicated serial I/O controllers 157
Software routines 160
EIA RS-232 standards 164
TTL/RS-232C interfaces 167
Problems 170

7 Dedicated I/O controllers 171
Keyboard encoding 171
Hex keyboard interface 171
ASCII (QWERTY) keyboard interface 176
VDU interface 177
Forming characters on the CRT screen 179
Cathode ray tube controller devices 179
Floppy disk controllers 183

Index 191

Preface

This book provides coverage of the Business and Technician Education Council (BTEC) level NIII unit in Microprocessor Interfacing (syllabus U86/335). However, it can be regarded as a textbook in interfacing for a much wider range of studies.

The aim of this book is to provide the reader with a foundation in microprocessor interfacing techniques, hardware and software, so that interface problems may be identified and solutions devised. Each topic in the text is presented in a way that assumes in the reader only the knowledge attained inb BTEC Microelectronic Systems NII/III, Electronics NII and Electronic Principles NII.

The text concentrates on the widely used 6502, Z80 and 6800/02 microprocessor families, details of which are contained in Heinemann's Checkbook Series, *Microelectronic Systems NII/NIII* by the same author. Most of the hardware circuits and software routines are readily adaptable for use with any available microcomputer system based around these microprocessors. Basic details of typical interfacing devices for each of these microprocessors are included in the text, but the reader is encouraged to obtain complete manufacturer's data sheets whenever attempting to solve an interface problem.

Finally, I wish to express thanks to colleagues who have provided the necessary encouragement, and to my wife, Rosemary, for her patience during the preparation of this book.

R. Vears
1989

Chapter 1

Signal conditioning

Need for signal conditioning

The signals obtained from transducers and sensors are rarely suitable for direct processing by a microcomputer, and in addition to analogue to digital conversion, some form of pre-processing or signal conditioning is usually required. Signal conditioning may consist of simple amplification or scaling, but often takes the form of shaping and 'cleaning' of signals prior to processing. Hardware alone may be used for this purpose, but often a purely software solution is applicable. Many signal processing problems may consist of a mixture of hardware and software. Simple signal conditioning may involve the following processes:

1 Amplification.
2 Linearization.
3 Offsetting.
4 Filtering.

Amplification

Many types of sensor generate a very low amplitude output signal, perhaps only a few millivolts. Such a low level of signal is insufficient to directly drive an analogue to digital converter. An ADC requires typically a change in input signal level of 20 mV in order to step to the next digital output value. Clearly a sensor which generates a maximum output of, say, 5 mV, would be unable to cause any noticeable change in output from the ADC. It is therefore necessary to amplify the output signal from such transducers to obtain a sufficient signal level to operate an ADC.

Operational amplifiers

While it is possible to design small-signal amplifier circuits using discrete components (transistors, resistors and capacitors), for all but specialist applications, integrated operational amplifiers provide a convenient solution to the problems associated with increasing the amplitude of signal levels from sensors.

An *operational amplifier* (or op-amp) consists of an integrated circuit (IC) package which contains a multiple transistor high gain differential amplifier circuit. The symbol used for an op-amp is shown in Figure 1.1.

It can be seen that an op-amp has both inverting and non-inverting inputs, and it amplifies the difference between its two input signals. Differential inputs are useful for use with sensors which produce very low levels of signal amplitude.

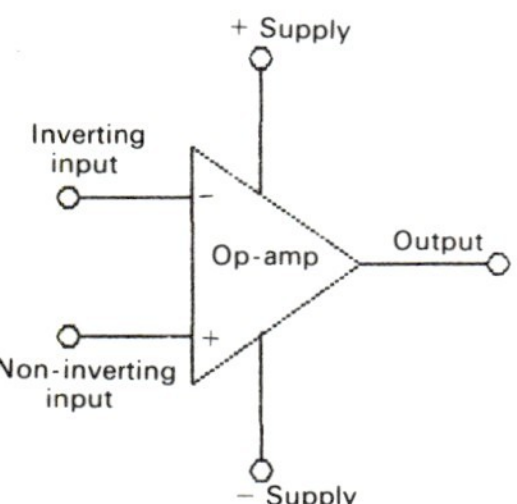

Figure 1.1

Operational amplifier characteristics

Open-loop gain: This is the gain of a basic op-amp before the application of negative feedback (NFB) and is commonly in excess of 10^6 (120 dB).

Closed-loop gain: This is the gain of an op-amp after application of NFB. It is usually considerably less than the open-loop gain, and is almost entirely determined by the values of the feedback components.

Input impedance: With one of the op-amp inputs connected to ground, the input impedance is the impedance presented between ground and the other input. This is typically 0.5 MΩ for a general purpose op-amp, but is modified by the application of NFB, reducing it towards zero for an inverting amplifier and raising it to several MΩ in the case of a non-inverting amplifier.

Output impedance: This is the impedance measured between ground and the output terminal of an op-amp. A typical figure for open-loop output impedance is 100 Ω, but this is reduced considerably by the application of NFB.

Bandwidth: The bandwidth of an op-amp is determined by its frequency response and is the difference between the upper and lower cut-off frequencies, i.e., the frequencies at which the output falls to 0.707 (− 3 dB) of its mid-point output. Since the frequency response of an op-amp extends down to DC the bandwidth equals the upper cut-off frequency. The application of NFB to an amplifier reduces the gain but increases the bandwidth such that the gain-bandwidth product is a constant. The actual bandwidth for different values of gain may be determined from Figure 1.2 which shows the open-loop characteristics of a 741 op-amp.

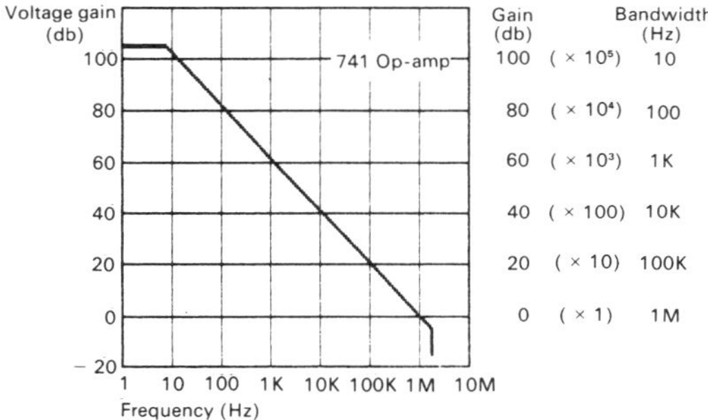

Figure 1.2

CMRR: The common mode rejection ratio (CMRR) of an op-amp may be defined as the ratio of common mode input voltage (identical + and − input signals) to differential input for the same change in output voltage.

The ideal characteristics for an op-amp are as follows:

1 Infinite open-loop voltage gain.
2 Infinitely high input impedance.
3 Zero output impedance.
4 Infinite bandwidth.
5 Infinitely high common mode rejection ratio.

Voltage gain

The voltage gain of an amplifier circuit, A_v may be expressed as:

$$A_v = V_o/V_i$$

where V_o = output voltage, and
V_i = input voltage.

An op-amp circuit for simple voltage amplification is usually connected as shown in Figure 1.3 which is an inverting amplifier configuration.

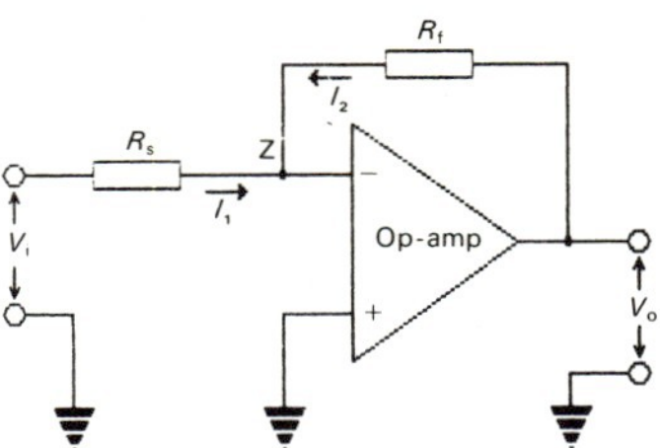

Figure 1.3

It can be seen that the circuit contains a series input resistor R_s and a feedback resistor, R_f. Assuming that the op-amp has the ideal characteristics stated, then the following conditions are true:

1 For *any* output signal level, the input to the op-amp at point Z is zero (virtual earth), since the op-amp has infinite gain.
2 The current flowing into the op-amp at point Z is zero since the input impedance is infinitely high (open circuit).
3 The gain of an op-amp with feedback may be determined as follows:

$$I_1 = -I_2 \tag{1}$$

$$I_1 = \frac{V_i}{R_s} \tag{2}$$

$$I_2 = \frac{V_o}{R_f} \tag{3}$$

Substituting (2) and (3) in (1) gives:

$$\frac{V_i}{R_s} = \frac{-V_o}{R_f}$$

Evaluating for V_o:

$$V_o = \frac{-R_f \times V_i}{R_s}$$

But since:

$$V_o = -A_v \times V_i$$

$$\boldsymbol{A_v = \frac{-R_f}{R_s}}$$

Therefore it can be seen that the gain of an op-amp with feedback may be determined by the ratio of R_f to R_s. In practice, ideal characteristics are not obtainable, but provided that the required gain is considerably lower than the open loop gain, the resultant error is acceptably small.

Example: Design of an inverting amplifier with a voltage gain of 50 and an input impedance of 10 kΩ

$$R_s = 10\,\text{k}\Omega$$

$$\text{Gain} = R_f/R_s$$

Therefore

$$R_f = 50 \times 10\,\text{k}\Omega$$

$$= \mathbf{500\,k\Omega}$$

The circuit required is shown in Figure 1.4.

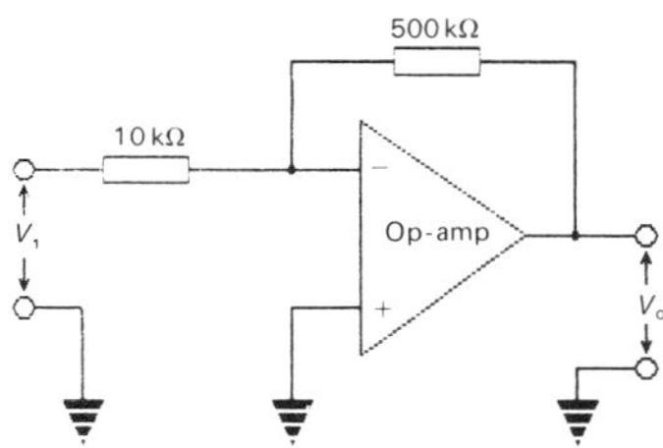

Figure 1.4

A non-inverting amplifier may be constructed as shown in Figure 1.5.

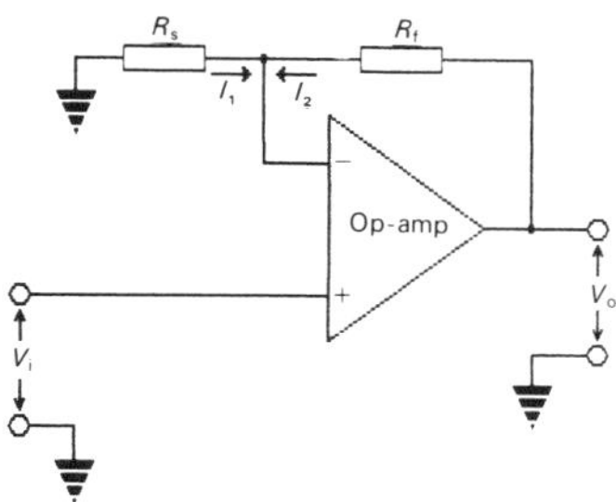

Figure 1.5

The gain of a non-inverting op-amp with feedback may be determined as follows:

$$I_1 = I_2 \tag{1}$$

$$I_1 = \frac{V_1}{R_s} \tag{2}$$

$$I_2 = \frac{V_o - V_i}{R_f} \tag{3}$$

Substituting (2) and (3) in (1) gives:

$$\frac{V_i}{R_s} = \frac{V_o - V_i}{R_f}$$

Evaluating for V_o

$$V_o = \frac{V_i \times R_f + 1}{R_s}$$

But since

$$V_o = A_v \times V_i$$

$$A_v \simeq \frac{R_f}{R_s}$$

For certain applications, impedance matching rather than amplifiction may be required. An op-amp may be configured as a unity gain non-inverting amplifier by using a circuit of the type shown in Figure 1.6.

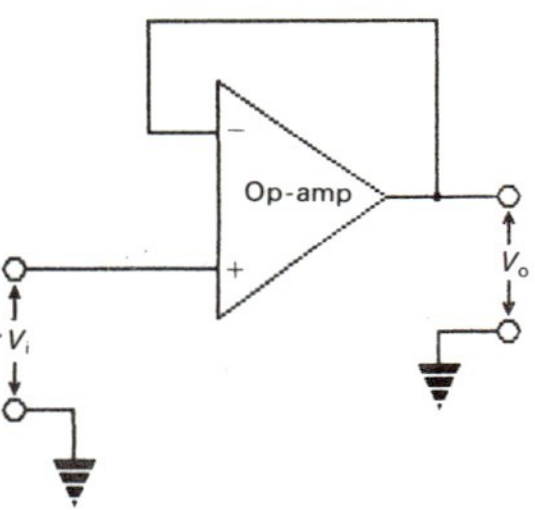

Figure 1.6

Example: Design of a non-inverting amplifier with a gain of 25 and an input impedance of 5 kΩ

$$R_s = 5\,\text{k}\Omega$$

$$\text{Gain} = R_f/R_s$$

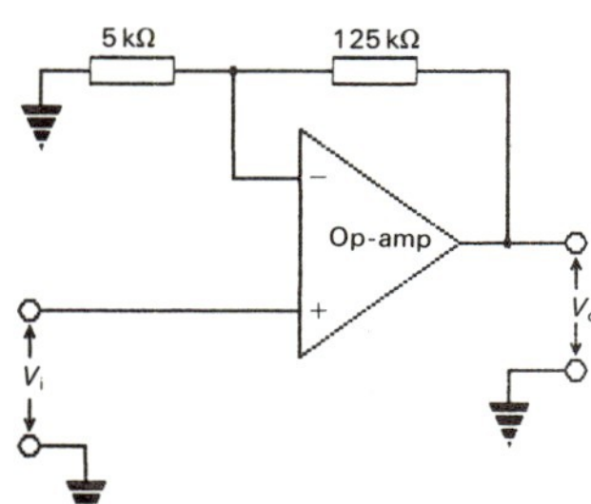

Figure 1.7

Therefore $$R_f = 25 \times 5\,\text{k}\Omega$$
$$= \mathbf{125\,k\Omega}$$

The circuit required is shown in Figure 1.7.

Practical guidelines

When designing amplifier circuits using op-amps, it is advisable to adhere to the following guidelines:

1 The value of R_s determines the input impedance of a single stage inverting amplifier circuit, and this should be at least ten times the source impedance of the input signal to avoid loading effects.
2 The value of R_f should be no greater than 1 MΩ.
3 The gain of a single stage should not exceed 500.

High-gain amplifiers

The theoretical gain of an op-amp, R_f/R_s, is only true if the open loop gain is infinite. As feedback is reduced, and gain approaches the open loop figure, the difference between theoretical and practical values of gain widens. It is therefore good practice to limit the gain expected from a single stage to around 500 (typical open loop gain figure = 10^6). When gains greater than this figure are required, then two or more single amplifier stages should be cascaded, as in Figure 1.8.

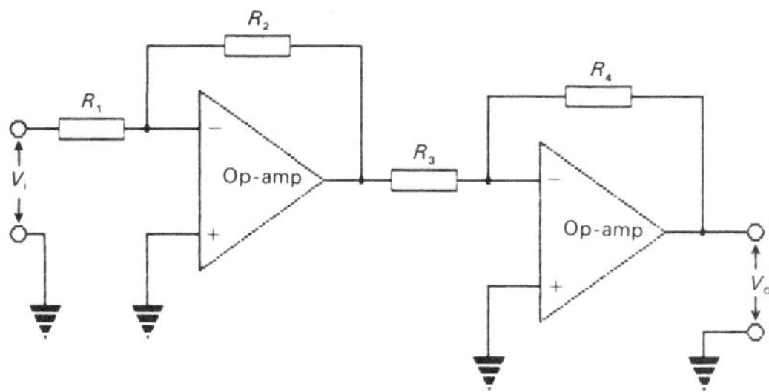

Figure 1.8

The overall gain of this circuit may be expressed as:

$$A_v = \frac{R2}{R1} \times \frac{R4}{R3}$$

Example: Design of a non-inverting amplifier with a gain of 1000 and an input impedance of 10 kΩ (assume that Z_{out} of each stage is 75 Ω)

Since the required gain is greater than 500, two cascaded inverting stages are required to obtain a non-inverted output. Possible combinations to obtain a gain of 1000 are:

1 2×500
2 4×250
3 5×200
4 8×125
5 10×100
6 20×50
7 40×25

Of these combinations, 6 and 7 provide the best distribution of gain between the two stages. Therefore design for a gain of 25 in the first stage, and 40 in the second stage.

First stage:

$$R_1 = 10\,\text{k}\Omega \text{ (input impedance)}$$
$$\text{Gain} = R_2/R_1 = 25$$
$$\text{Therefore} \quad R_2 = 25 \times 10\,\text{k}\Omega$$
$$= \mathbf{250\,k\Omega}$$

Second stage:

$$R_3 = 1\,\text{k}\Omega \text{ (at least } 10 \times Z_{out}\text{)}$$
$$\text{Gain} = R_4/R_3 = 40$$
$$\text{Therefore} \quad R_4 = 40 \times 1\,\text{k}\Omega$$
$$= \mathbf{40\,k\Omega}$$

Slight changes may have to be made to the gain of each stage, or redesign using 6 in order to obtain resistors of preferred values.

Differential mode

A differential amplifier has two inputs, as shown in Figure 1.9. The amplified output signal, V_0, is proportional to the *difference* between two ground relative input signals, V_1 and V_2 which are applied to the inverting and non-inverting inputs. The actual differential input is therefore $V_1 - V_2$, and it follows that if $V_1 = V_2$, then the amplifier output is zero. Thus signals which are common to both inputs, e.g. noise, are rejected and this is known as *common mode rejection.*

The arrangement is very useful where sensors with a very small output voltage are used in conjunction with very high gain amplifiers, since otherwise it could be difficult to differentiate between signal and noise.

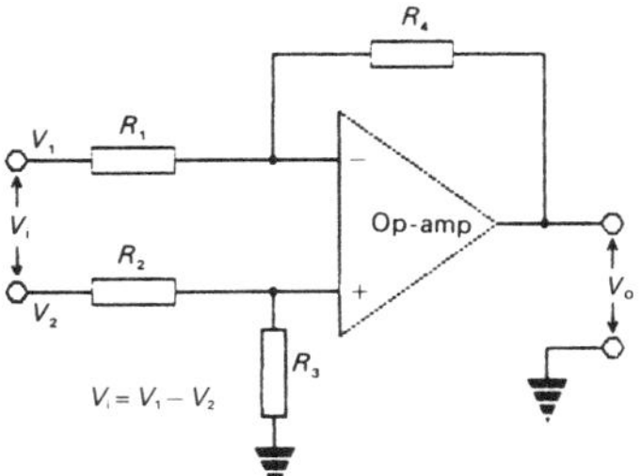

Figure 1.9

Example: Design of a differential amplifier with a gain of 10 and a differential input impedance of 20 kΩ (10 kΩ per input relative to ground)

$$\begin{aligned} R_1 &= 10\ \text{k}\Omega \\ R_2 &= 10\ \text{k}\Omega \\ \text{Gain} &= R_f/R_s \\ \text{Therefore } R_3 &= 10 \times 10\ \text{k}\Omega \\ &= \mathbf{100\ k\Omega} \\ R_4 &= 10 \times 10\ \text{k}\Omega \\ &= \mathbf{100\ k\Omega} \end{aligned}$$

The circuit required is shown in Figure 1.10.

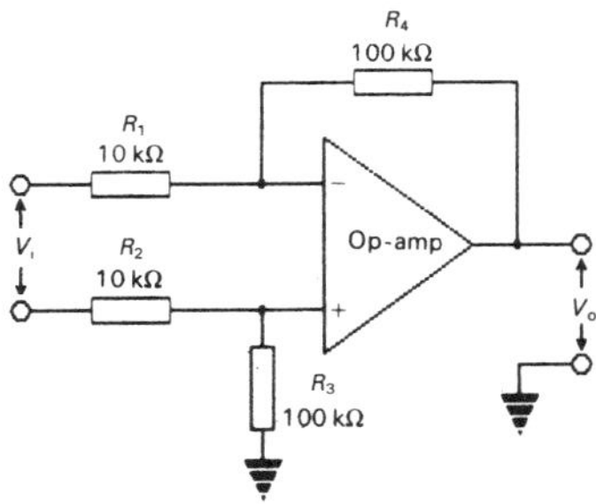

Figure 1.10

Offsetting

An op-amp should deliver an output voltage of zero when its input is zero, i.e., inverting and non-inverting inputs at the same potential. This is often not the case, however, and an 'offset voltage' is generated. Two main causes of offset errors are:

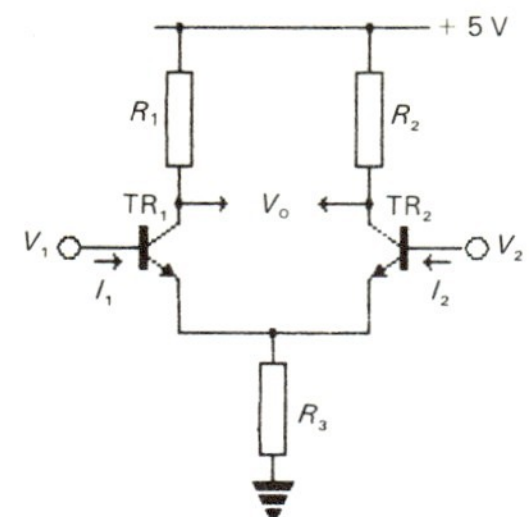

Figure 1.11

1 The input stage of an operational amplifier consists of a differential amplifier (see Figure 1.11).

Each transistor in the differential pair requires bias currents I_1 and I_2. In theory, I_1 and I_2 are identical, but in practice, there is always a small difference called the *offset* current (I_{off}).

$$\boldsymbol{I_{\mathrm{off}} = I_1 \sim I_2}$$

This offset current produces an output voltage equal to $I_{\mathrm{off}} \times R_{\mathrm{f}}$.

2 An internally generated 'input offset voltage' which occurs when both inputs are zero and there is no resistance to cause volt-drops due to base bias currents. This form of offset is usually caused by manufacturing tolerances and differences in gain of the input transistors.

Offset-null

It may be necessary to cancel offset errors (offset null) in an op-amp circuit, perhaps for calibration purposes. Many op-amps are provided with *offset-null* inputs (e.g., 741), and a circuit similar to that shown in Figure 1.12 may be used.

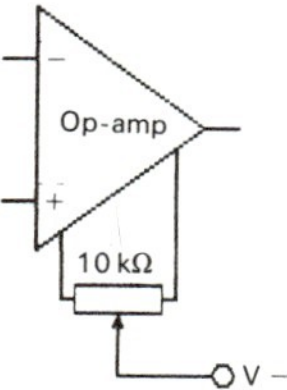

Figure 1.12

Linearity

The output signal from a sensor should be directly proportional to the applied stimulus, resulting in the ideal 'straight-line' characteristic shown in Figure 1.13(a).

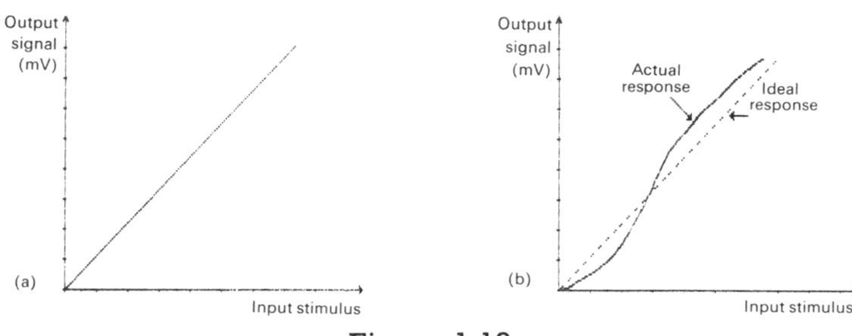

Figure 1.13

Frequently, however, sensors do not possess ideal characteristics and departure from the straight line is called 'non-linearity' (see Figure 1.13(b)). If the degree of non-linearity is small it may often be ignored, but where unacceptable errors would result, linearizing processes must be incorporated into the system. This may be achieved by the use of hardware such as an op-amp with feedback arranged to provide equal but opposite non-linearity. Alternatively, software routines may be used to provide similar compensation.

Filtering

Unwanted frequencies are often introduced into analogue signals from a variety of sources, e.g. noise or switching signals. Filtering is a process which rejects all unwanted frequencies from the entire spectrum, thus selecting only the wanted range of frequencies for further processing. The analysis of filter circuits can often involve complex mathematical processes which are outside the scope of this book, therefore only basic filtering techniques are considered here.

Filters may be described as *low-pass*, *high-pass* or *band-pass* and typical filter response curves are shown in Figure 1.14.

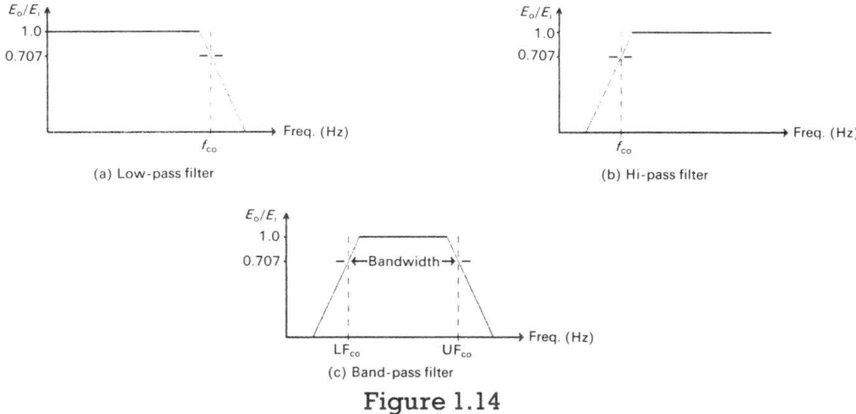

Figure 1.14

The low-pass filter is often called an *integrator*, and the high-pass filter is known as a *differentiator*.

Passive filters

Simple filters may be constructed using only resistor-capacitor networks. These are known as *passive filters* and rely upon the change of capacitive reactance (X_c) with frequency to cause them to be frequency selective. They may therefore be regarded as frequency selective potential dividers. An increase in frequency causes the value of X_c to decrease, thus producing a smaller volt drop across C, while a decrease in frequency has the opposite effect. A low-pass filter uses the voltage across the capacitor as its output, while the high-pass filter uses the voltage across the resistor (see Figure 1.15(a) and (b)).

Figure 1.15

Cut-off frequency

A simple filter cannot suddenly cut off at a specified frequency, but slopes away at a rate determined by the filter design. For example, the output from a simple low-pass filter slopes away such that its output is halved for each doubling of the input frequency. The filter is therefore described as *first-order* and has a slope of 6 dB/octave. A high-pass filter requires a halving of frequency for a similar reduction in output.

The cut-off frequency is therefore defined as the frequency at which the values of X_c and R are equal, i.e.

$$R = X_c$$

$$R = \frac{1}{2\pi fC}$$

$$\text{Therefore} \quad f = \frac{1}{2\pi RC}$$

At this frequency, due to the phase difference between the voltages across R and C, the output is not 0.5 but 0.707 of the maximum, and a phase difference of 45° occurs.

Example: Design of a low-pass filter with a cut-off frequency of 250 Hz and an input impedance of 8 kΩ at this frequency

$$\begin{aligned}
\text{At cut-off frequency } Z &= 8\,\text{k}\Omega \\
\text{Therefore } R^2 + X_c^2 &= 8000^2 \\
\text{but at cut-off frequency } R &= X_c \\
\text{Therefore } 2R^2 &= 8000^2 \\
\boldsymbol{R} &= \mathbf{5656\,\Omega\,(5.6\,k\Omega)}
\end{aligned}$$

$$\text{Capacitive reactance } X_c = \frac{1}{2\pi fC} = 5656\,\Omega$$

$$C = \frac{1}{2\pi \times 250 \times 5656}$$

$$\boldsymbol{C} = \mathbf{0.11\,\mu F}$$

A suitable circuit for this filter is shown in Figure 1.16.

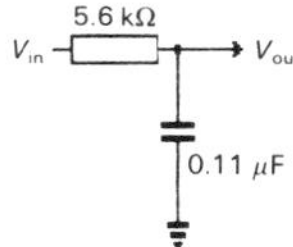

Figure 1.16

Note that the values of components in this example assume that both source and load impedances may be ignored. Appropriate buffer circuits may be used to ensure that this is the case, otherwise these impedances must be included in the calculations.

Active filters

It is possible to obtain steeper slopes in filter cut-off characteristics by cascading passive circuits, but this inevitably causes a reduction in amplitude of the wanted frequencies. A better solution is provided by making use of an operational amplifier circuit, possibly with frequency selective feedback, to form an active filter.

Active low-pass filter

An example of an active low-pass filter is shown in Figure 1.17. This is a second order filter which has a slope of 12 dB/octave. The cut-off frequency

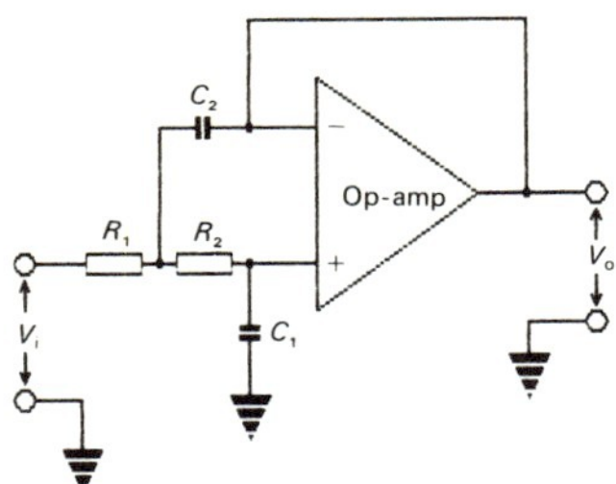

Figure 1.17

may be expressed as:

$$f = \frac{1}{2\pi \times R_2(C_1 C_2)^{\frac{1}{2}}}$$

where C_2 equals $2C_1$ and R_1 equals R_2.

A high-pass filter may be constructed by reversing the positions of R and C in the low-pass filter circuit, as shown in Figure 1.18. In this case, the cut-off frequency may be expressed as:

$$f = \frac{1}{2\pi \times C_1(R_1 R_2)^{\frac{1}{2}}}$$

where C_1 equals C_2 and R_1 equals $2R_2$.

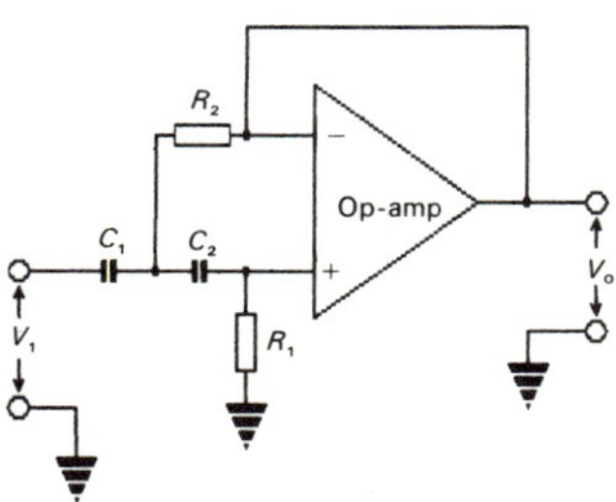

Figure 1.18

Example: Using a circuit of the type shown in Figure 1.17, with $C_1 = 0.01\ \mu F$, design a low-pass filter with a cut-off frequency of 500 Hz

---

Value of C_2: since $C_2 = 2C_1$, and $C_1 = 0.01\ \mu F$

$$C_2 = \mathbf{0.02\ \mu F}$$

Value of R_1,R_2:

$$R_1 = R_2 = \frac{1}{2\pi \times f(C_1C_2)^{\frac{1}{2}}}$$

$$R_2 = \frac{1}{2\pi \times 500\,(2 \times 10^{-16})^{\frac{1}{2}}}$$

$$\boldsymbol{R_1 = R_2 = 22.5\,\text{k}\Omega}$$

Example: Design of a high-pass filter circuit of the type shown in Figure 1.18, with $R_2 = 15\,\text{k}\Omega$ and a cut-off frequency of 1 kHz

---

Value of R_1:

$$\text{since } R_1 = 2R_2, \text{ and } R_2 = 15\,\text{k}\Omega$$

$$\boldsymbol{R_1 = 30\,\text{k}\Omega}$$

Value of C_1,C_2:

$$C_1 = C_2 = \frac{1}{2\pi \times f(R_1R_2)^{\frac{1}{2}}}$$

$$C_2 = \frac{1}{2\pi \times 10^3\,(3 \times 15 \times 10^7)^{\frac{1}{2}}}$$

$$\boldsymbol{C_1 = C_2 = 7500\,\text{pF}}$$

Band-pass filters

Band-pass filters may be constructed by cascading high- and low-pass filter circuits of the type already described, the cut-off frequencies being calculated to give the required bandwidth.

Software filtering

Filtering of signals may be performed by processing the digitized version of an input signal with the aid of appropriate software. As a simple exmple of this form of signal filtering, a system which filters an input square wave may be considered. Suitable hardware is arranged as shown in Figure 1.19(a). An input square wave signal (approximately 5 V p-p) for processing is applied to bit 7 of port A of the parallel input/output (PIO) of a microcomputer. A digital to analogue converter (DAC), connected to port B of the PIO, is used to convert the processed digital output signal back into analogue form. The software which processes the input signal provides an output which varies according to the following equation:

$$\boldsymbol{V_{\text{out}} = 0.5 \times C + 0.75 \times P}$$

where C = current input from port A bit 7, and
P = previous output to port B.

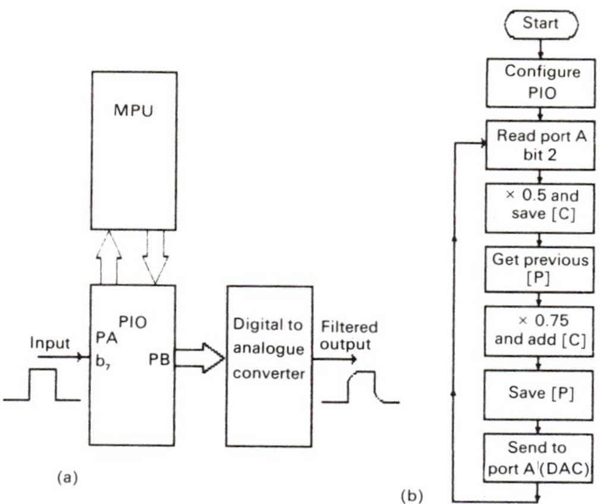

Figure 1.19

For input signals other than square (or pulse) waveforms, an analogue to digital converter (ADC) is required to convert the analogue input signal into digital form prior to processing. In such cases the software must also be modified in order to operate the ADC. A flowchart for the basic processing system is shown in Figure 1.19(b).

Sample program listings for the 6502, Z80 and 6800 microprocessors are provided so that the filtering process may be studied. An input signal frequency of approximately 500 Hz to 1 kHz should prove suitable for testing this sytem provided that clock frequencies similar to those indicated in each program are used. A double beam oscilloscope may be used to compare input and output waveforms, and experiments may be conducted using various input frequencies and different filter constants (0.5 and 0.75 in the sample programs).

Minor adjustments to the port configuration may be necessary in each case in order to accommodate input/output (I/O) devices different to those used by the author.

(a) 6502 – clock frequency 1 MHz

```
0000                    ;*****************************
0000                    ; Software low-pass filter
0000                    ; program for a 6502 based
0000                    ; microcomputer with 6530/32
0000                    ; PIA
0000                    ;*****************************
```

```
0000                    ;
0200                   *=   $0200
0200           CURRENT =    0
0200           PREV    =    1
0200           TEMP    =    2
0200           OUTPUT  =    $FF
0200           INPUT   =    0
0200           PORTA   =    $1700
0200           PORTB   =    PORTA+2
0200                    ;
0200                    ;configure 6530/32 PIA
0200                    ;
0200 A9 00              LDA     #OUTPUT         ;Port A dir byte
0202 8D 01 17           STA     PORTB+1         ;send to DDRA
0205 85 01              STA     PREV            ;clear previous
0207 A9 FF              LDA     #INPUT          ;Port B dir byte
0209 8D 03 17           STA     PORTA+1         ;send to DDRB
020C                    ;
020C                    ;calculate 0.5 of current input
020C                    ;
020C AD 00 17 CYCLE     LDA     PORTA           ;read input signal
020F 29 80              AND     80H             ;mask unused bits
0211 4A                 LSR     A               ;divide by 2
0212 85 00              STA     CURRENT         ;and save
0214                    ;
0214                    ;calculate 0.75 of previous output
0214                    ;
0214 A5 01              LDA     PREV            ;get previous output
0216 4A                 LSR     A               ;divide by 2 (=0.5)
0217 85 02              STA     TEMP            ;and save
0219 4A                 LSR     A               ;divide by 2 (=0.75)
021A 18                 CLC
021B 65 02              ADC     TEMP            ;calculate 0.75
021D                    ;
021D                    ;calculate current output and send to DAC
021D                    ;
021D 65 00              ADC     CURRENT         ;next output to DAC
021F 85 01              STA     PREV            ;save for next calc
0221 8D 02 17           STA     PORTB           ;send to DAC
0224                    ;
0224                    ;repeat cycle
0224                    ;
0224 4C 0C 02           JMP     CYCLE
```

(b) Z80 – clock frequency 2 MHz

```
                        ;****************************
                        ; Software low-pass filter
                        ; program for a Z80 based
                        ; microcomputer with Z80 PIO
                        ;****************************
                        ;
1800                    ORG     1800H
000F =          OUTPUT  EQU     0FH
00CF =          INPUT   EQU     0CFH
0080 =          PORTA   EQU     80H
0081 =          PORTB   EQU     PORTA+1
0082 =          CTRLA   EQU     PORTA+2
0083 =          CTRLB   EQU     CTRLA+1
                        ;
                        ;configure Z80 PIO
                        ;
1800 3ECF               LD      A,INPUT         ;Port A dir byte
1802 D382               OUT     (CTRLA),A       ;input mode 1
1804 3E0F               LD      A,OUTPUT        ;Port B dir byte
1806 D383               OUT     (CTRLB),A       ;output mode 0
1808 1600               LD      D,0             ;clear previous
                        ;
                        ;calculate 0.5 of current input
                        ;
180A DB80       CYCLE:  IN      A,(PORTA)       ;read input signal
180C E680               AND     80H             ;mask unused bits
180E CB3F               SRL     A               ;divide by 2
1810 4F                 LD      C,A             ;and save
                        ;
                        ;calculate 0.75 of previous output
                        ;
1811 7A                 LD      A,D             ;get previous output
1812 CB3F               SRL     A               ;divide by 2 (=0.5)
1814 57                 LD      D,A             ;and save
1815 CB3F               SRL     A               ;divide by 2 (=0.75)
1817 82                 ADD     D               ;calculate 0.75
                        ;
                        ;calculate current output and send to DAC
                        ;
1818 81                 ADD     C               ;next output to DAC
1819 57                 LD      D,A             ;save for next calc
181A D381               OUT     (PORTB),A       ;send to DAC
                        ;
                        ;repeat cycle
                        ;
181C 18EC               JR      CYCLE
```

(c) 6800 – clock frequency 1 MHz

```
0000                    ;****************************
0000                    ; Software low-pass filter
0000                    ; program for a 6800/02 based
0000                    ; microcomputer with 6821 PIA
0000                    ;****************************
0000                    ;
0200                    ORG   $0200
0200            CURRENT EQU   0
0200            PREV    EQU   1
0200            TEMP    EQU   2
0200            OUTPUT  EQU   $FF
0200            DRA     EQU   $8004
0200            DDRA    EQU   DRA
0200            CRA     EQU   DRA+1
0200            DRB     EQU   DRA+2
0200            DDRB    EQU   DRB
0200            CRB     EQU   DRB+1
0200                    ;
0200                    ;configure 6821 PIA
0200                    ;
0200 4F                 CLRA
0201 B7 80 05           STAA    CRA             ;select DDRs
0204 B7 80 07           STAA    CRB             ;and make Port A
0207 B7 80 04           STAA    DDRA            ;all inputs
020A 97 01              STAA    PREV            ;clear previous
020C 86 FF              LDAA    #OUTPUT         ;Port B all
020E 8D 01 17           STAA    DDRB            ;outputs
0211 86 04              LDAA    #4              ;select I/O regs
0213 B7 80 05           STAA    CRA             ;of Ports A & B
0216 B7 80 07           STAA    CRB
0219                    ;
0219                    ;calculate 0.5 of current input
0219                    ;
0219 B6 80 04 CYCLE     LDAA    DRAA            ;read input signal
021C 84 80              ANDA    80H             ;mask unused bits
021E 44                 LSRA                    ;divide by 2
021F 97 00              STAA    CURRENT         ;and save
0221                    ;
0221                    ;calculate 0.75 of previous output
0221                    ;
0221 96 01              LDAA     PREV           ;get previous output
0223 44                 LSRA                    ;divide by 2 (=0.5)
0224 97 02              STAA     TEMP           ;and save
```

```
0226 44          LSRA                  -;divide by 2 (=0.75)
0227 9B 02       ADDA    TEMP          ;calculate 0.75
0229             ;
0229             ;calculate current output and send to DAC
0229             ;
0229 9B 00       ADDA    CURRENT       ;next output to DAC
022B 97 01       STAA    PREV           ;save for next calc
022D B7 80 06    STAA    PORTB          ;send to DAC
0230             ;
0230             ;repeat cycle
0230             ;
0230 20 E7       BRA     CYCLE
```

Problems

1 (a) Define the term 'signal conditioning'.
(b) Name three processes which may be used for signal conditioning when interfacing an electrical sensor to a microcomputer.

2 With reference to an operational amplifier, define the following terms:
(a) Open-loop gain.
(b) Closed-loop gain.
(c) Input impedance.
(d) Output impedance.
(e) Bandwidth.
(f) CMMR.

3 (a) With the aid of a diagram, show how the gain of an operational amplifier is set to its required value.
(b) Explain what is meant by the term 'virtual earth'.

4 Design an inverting amplifier with a voltage gain of 100 and an input impedance of 5 kΩ.

5 Design a non-inverting amplifier with a voltage gain of 50 and an input impedance of 3 kΩ.

6 Design a non-inverting amplifier with a gain of 2000 and an input impedance of 20 kΩ (assume that amplifiers with an output impedance of 75 Ω are used).

7 (a) Explain the main advantage of using a differential amplifier when interfacing devices with a very low level of signal output to a microcomputer.
(b) Design a differential amplifier with a gain of 200 and an input impedance of 5 kΩ.

8 Explain why 'offset voltages' occur in amplifier circuits and describe how the effect of offset errors may be removed.

9 (a) Explain why it may be necessary to filter a signal before it can be processed by a microcomputer.
(b) List three types of filter and, with the aid of typical filter response curves, describe the effect of each type of filter upon a signal being processed.

10 With reference to filter circuits, define the following terms:
(a) Passive.
(b) Active.
(c) Slope.
(d) Cut-off frequency.

11 Design a passive *low-pass* filter with a cut-off frequency of 100 Hz and an input impedance of 10 kΩ.

12 Design a passive *high-pass* filter with a cut-off frequency of 300 Hz and an input impedance of 5 kΩ.

13 A square wave input is applied to bit 7 of port A (address $1700) and a digital to analogue converter is connected to port B (address $1702) of a 6502 based microcomputer which uses a 6530/32 peripheral interface adaptor (PIA). A software filter is required which operates according to the following equation:

$$V_{out} = 0.25 \times C + 0.875 \times P$$

where C = current input from port A bit 7, and
P = previous output to port B.

Write a 6502 assembly language program to implement this process.

14 A square wave input is applied to bit 7 of port A (address 80H) and a digital to analogue converter is connected to port B (address 81H) of a Z80 based microcomputer which uses a Z80 PIO. A software filter is required which operates according to the following equation:

$$V_{out} = 0.25 \times C + 0.875 \times P$$

where C = current input from port A bit 7, and
P = previous output to port B.

Write a Z80 assembly language program to implement this process.

15 A square wave input is applied to bit 7 of port A (address $8005) and a digital to analogue converter is connected to port B (address $8006) of a

6800/02 based microcomputer which uses a 6821 PIA. A software filter is required which operates according to the following equation:

$$V_{out} = 0.25 \times C + 0.875 \times P$$

where C = current input from port A bit 7, and
P = previous output to port B.

Write a 6800 assembly language program to implement this process.

Chapter 2

D to A conversion

Signal conversion

A microcomputer is a digital system which processes data in the form of binary numbers. Each number may represent a physical quantity such as temperature, pressure or velocity and enters or leaves the microcomputer via its input/output (I/O) ports.

If sensors used to monitor external physical quantites are capable of delivering digital signals, e.g. switches, then they may be directly interfaced to an input port. Similarly, if output devices (actuators) controlled by the microcomputer are capable of accepting digital signals, e.g. stepper motors, then these may be directly interfaced to an output port.

Digital signals are discontinuous and therefore change abruptly, in discrete steps, from one value to the next. Intermediate values are therefore represented by the nearest step in the sequence. By way of contrast, however, physical changes in the 'outside world' (i.e., external to a microcomputer) have

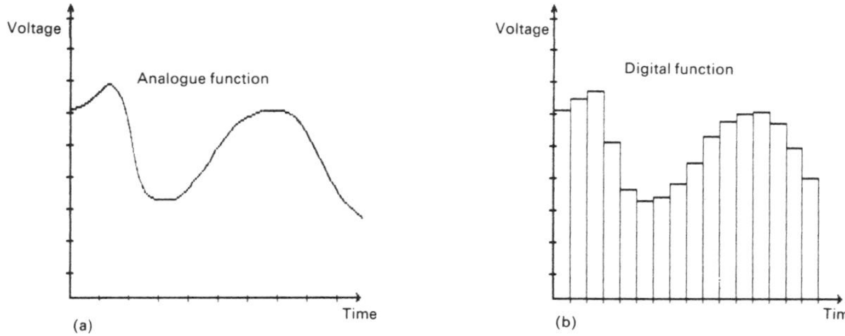

Figure 2.1

infinite variations and change smoothly from one value to the next. The electrical output from sensors which are used to monitor physical conditions therefore also changes continuously, and a system which processes continuously variable signals is known as an *analogue* system. The difference between analogue and digital signals is shown in Figure 2.1(a) and (b).

Consequently, when a microcomputer is used to monitor and control an analogue system, interfaces are required to convert analogue signals into digital form (*analogue to digital converter* or ADC) and digital signals into analogue form (*digital to analogue converter* or DAC). A typical arrangement is shown in Figure 2.2.

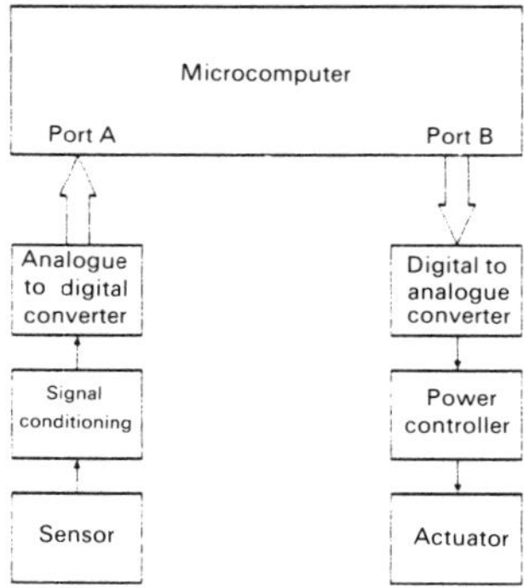

Figure 2.2

Types of digital to analogue converter

A digital to analogue converter (DAC) is a device which converts a multibit digital signal at its input into an equivalent analogue output signal. A digital to analogue converter is actually a multiplier circuit, and has a transfer function which may be expressed as:

$$f = a \times b$$

where a = digital input,
and b = analogue reference I or V

The digital input 'a' is expressed as a fraction of the maximum value obtainable with the number of bits used. The general expression for the digital output is therefore:

$$V_{out} = (a/2^n) \times V_{ref}$$

but since most DAC inputs are 8-bit, this is usually expressed as:

$$V_{out} = (a/256) \times V_{ref}$$

For example, a 'half-scale' digital input of 10000000_2 (128_{10}) produces a value for '*a*' of 128/256 or 0.5. The maximum or 'full-scale' input is 11111111_2 (255_{10}) when using 8-bits, therefore the full-scale output is:

$$V_{out} = (255/256) \times V_{ref}$$

i.e., for an '*n*'-bit input, the full-scale is $(2^n - 1)$ and the corresponding analogue output falls short of V_{ref} by an amount equivalent to that contributed by the least significant bit (see Figure 2.3).

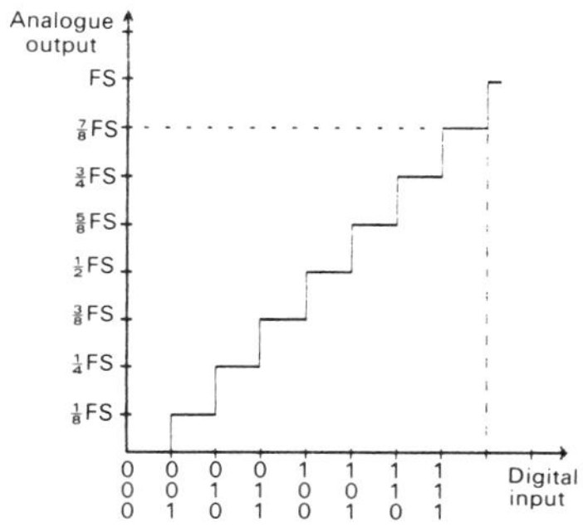

Figure 2.3

Most DAC converters make use of summing circuits, containing either binary 'weighted' or *R*-2*R* resistor ladder networks. Descriptions of the operation of both types of converter are included for reference purposes, but for the average user, the internal construction of a DAC is of little consequence.

Binary weighted resistor DAC

The circuit of a binary weighted resistor type of DAC is shown in Figure 2.4, which for simplicity is restricted to four bits.

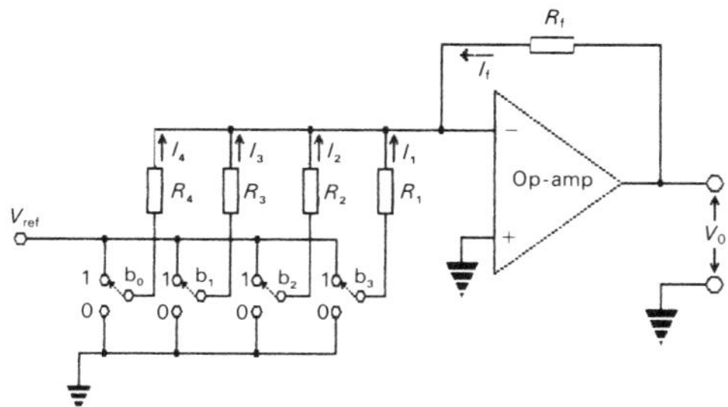

Figure 2.4

Each resistor in the input network is given a binary weighting such that:

$R_1 = 1 \times R$
$R_2 = 2 \times R$
$R_3 = 4 \times R$
$R_4 = 8 \times R$

Each input (b_0 to b_3) may have a value of 0 V or V_{ref} dependent upon the value of the digital input signal, and is represented in Figure 2.4 by the use of switches S_0 to S_3. By reference to the theory of operational amplifiers in Chapter 1, it can be seen that:

$$\boldsymbol{I_f = I_1 + I_2 + I_3 + I_4}$$

Assuming full scale conditions:

$$I_f = \frac{V_{ref}}{R_1} + \frac{V_{ref}}{R_2} + \frac{V_{ref}}{R_3} + \frac{V_{ref}}{R_4}$$
$$I_f = V_{ref} \times (1/R_1 + 1/R_2 + 1/R_3 + 1/R_4)$$
$$I_f = \frac{V_{ref}}{R} \times (1 + \tfrac{1}{2} + \tfrac{1}{4} + \tfrac{1}{8})$$

But output voltage,

$$V_o = -I_f \times R_f$$

Therefore $$V_o = \frac{-V_{ref}}{R} \times R_f(1 + \tfrac{1}{2} + \tfrac{1}{4} + \tfrac{1}{8})$$

If $R_f = R$ $$V_o = -V_{ref}(1 + \tfrac{1}{2} + \tfrac{1}{4} + \tfrac{1}{8})$$
$$V_o = -\mathbf{1.875} \times V_{ref}$$

It can be shown that if the number of bits is increased, then:

$$V_o = -2 \times V_{ref}$$

and the equivalent parallel resistance (R_{in}) of all of the input resistors, R_1 to R_n.

$$\boldsymbol{R_{in} = R/2}$$

R-2*R* resistor DAC

Practical difficulties arise when attempting to construct a weighted resistor network in a DAC. These are:

1 Obtaining resistors which have a precise binary relationship throughout the required range.
2 The very low levels of current associated with the lower order bits of the network.

These problems become greater when the resolution is increased, i.e. more bits are used. For these reasons the *R-2R* network, which only requires two different resistor values, is used in most DAC integrated circuits. The circuit of an *R-2R* DAC is shown in Figure 2.5.

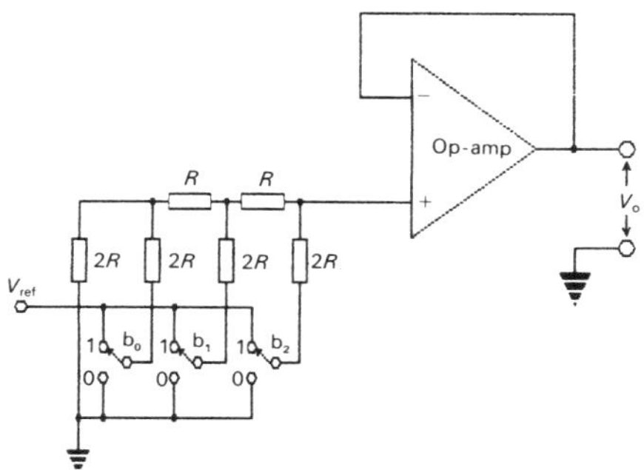

Figure 2.5

An analysis of this type of network is best carried out by the application of Thevenin's theorem, but basic operation may be demonstrated by considering the operation of the *R-2R* network with sample input signal conditions as shown in Figure 2.6(a) and (b).

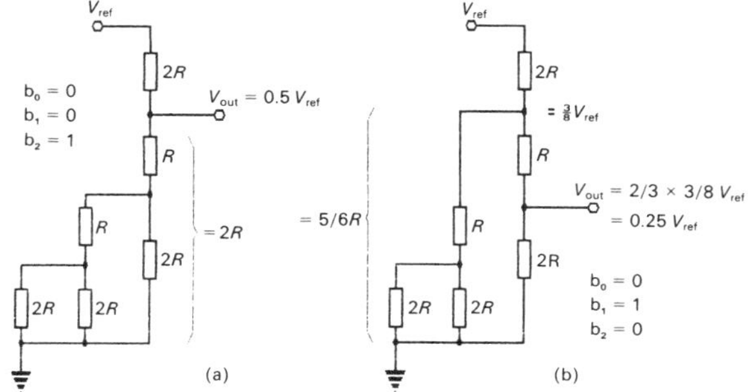

Figure 2.6

DAC characteristics

A large number of monolithic DACs are available from various manufacturers. When selecting a DAC for a particular application, reference should be made to the manufacturer's data sheets to determine its suitability. The following parameters and definitions may need to be considered.

Resolution

The resolution of a DAC refers to the number of input bits it possesses, and indicates the smallest incremental change in analogue output voltage. For example, if a DAC has '*n*' input bits, the number of increments is $2^n - 1$, and the magnitude of each increment is given by the expression:

$$V = \frac{V_{ref}}{2^n - 1}$$

Example: Determining the resolution (in mV) of an 8-bit DAC with a full scale output of 5 V

$$V_{ref} = 5\text{ V}$$
$$2^n = 256$$

$$\text{Therefore, resolution} = \frac{1}{256 - 1} \times 5$$
$$= \mathbf{19.6\,mV}$$

Monotonicity

When the input code to a DAC is increased in steps of one LSB, the analogue output voltage should also increase in steps of magnitude dependent upon the resolution of the converter. If the output always changes in this manner, the DAC is said to be *monotonic* since the output is a single valued function of the input. If any step in this progression results in a *decrease* in the DAC output voltage, the DAC is said to be *non-monotonic* (see Figure 2.7). The monotonicity of a DAC may be expressed in terms of the number of bits over which monotonicity is maintained.

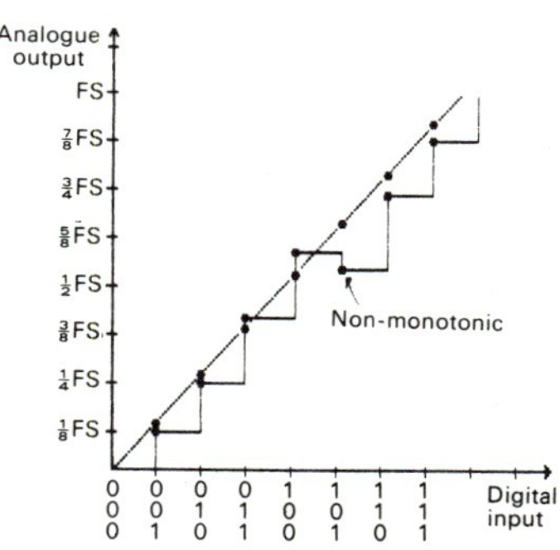

Figure 2.7

Offset (zero scale error)

Assuming unipolar operation and natural binary inputs, an input code of zero to a DAC should produce an analogue output of zero. Owing to imperfections in components and manufacturing techniques, however, a small offset may exist so that the transfer characteristic no longer passes through zero (see Figure 2.8).

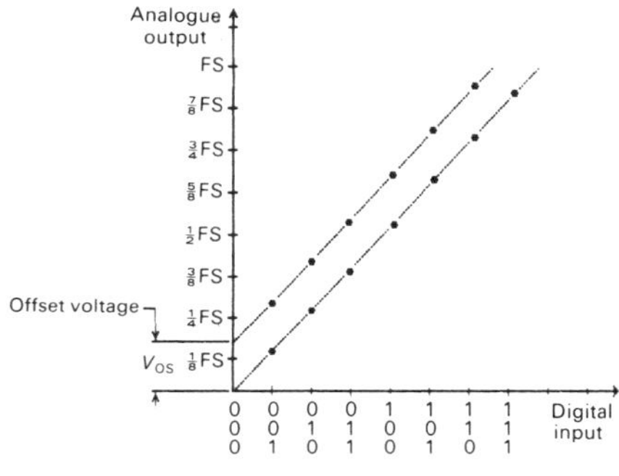

Figure 2.8

Gain

The gain of a DAC is an analogue scale factor that describes the relationship between the converter's full scale output and its reference input (V_{ref}). The gain is usually adjusted by the user to full scale × $(1-2^{-n})$ with all input bits at logical 1. Ideally, the transfer characteristic then progresses linearly from zero to full scale as its binary inputs sequence from minimum to maximum value. Imperfections in a DAC may cause a deviation from the ideal, as shown in Figure 2.9.

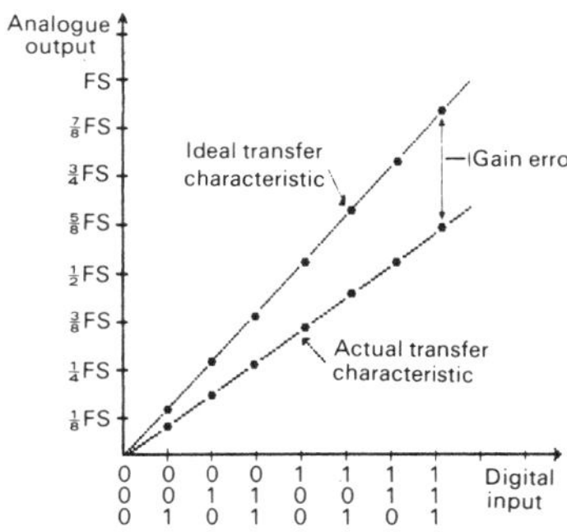

Figure 2.9

The difference in slope between actual and ideal transfer characteristics is known as the *gain error*.

Linearity

Offset and gain errors may be 'trimmed' so that the end points of the characteristic lie on zero and full scale, but this does not guarantee that intermediate points all lie on the ideal line. Linearity is a measure of how closely the analogue output characteristic of a DAC conforms to the ideal. This is usually quoted as a linearity error and is the deviation of the analogue output from an ideal straight line, expressed in percentages or p.p.m. of the full-scale range or as a fraction of one LSB (see Figure 2.10).

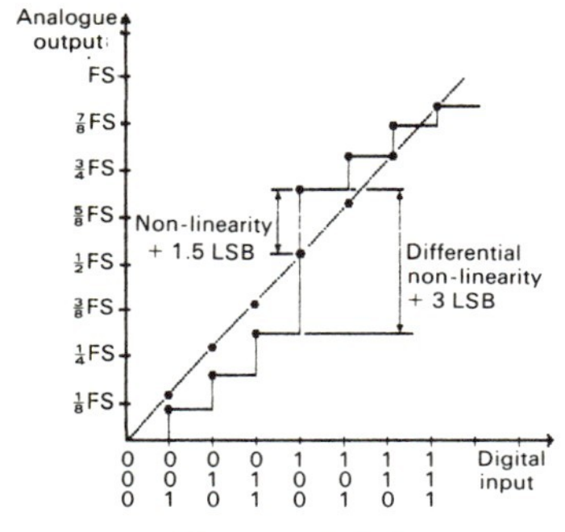

Figure 2.10

A linearity error within $\pm \frac{1}{2}$ LSB assures monotonic operation, although the converse is not true and a monotonic DAC may have large linearity errors.

Settling time

The settling time is the time taken for a DAC to settle to within $\pm \frac{1}{2}$ LSB of its final value after a transition in its input code. This is typically 100 ns, but varies according to the number of bits that change. A single bit change, e.g. 00000000 to 00000001, gives the fastest figure while a transition which results in all bits changing, e.g. 01111111 to 10000000, gives the slowest settling time figure.

Bipolar operation

Previous theory has considered the output from a DAC as being single polarity (unipolar), i.e., the digital input produces an analogue output voltage between zero and some positive value. Some practical applications require a bipolar output voltage, i.e., positive and negative output voltage, and this may be achieved by the application of a negative offset of $V_{REF/2}$ to the analogue output voltage, as shown in Figure 2.11(a) and (b).

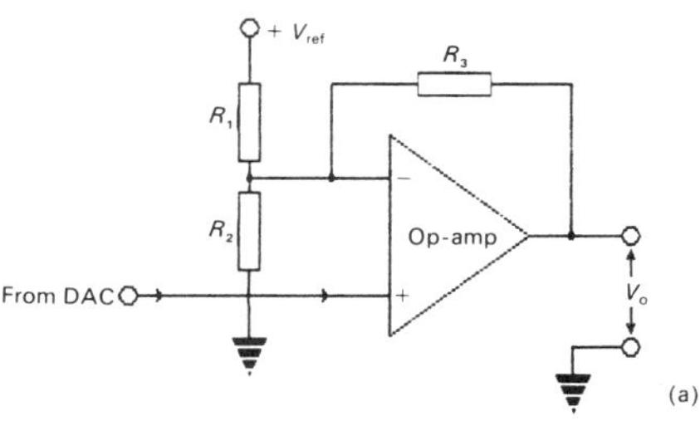

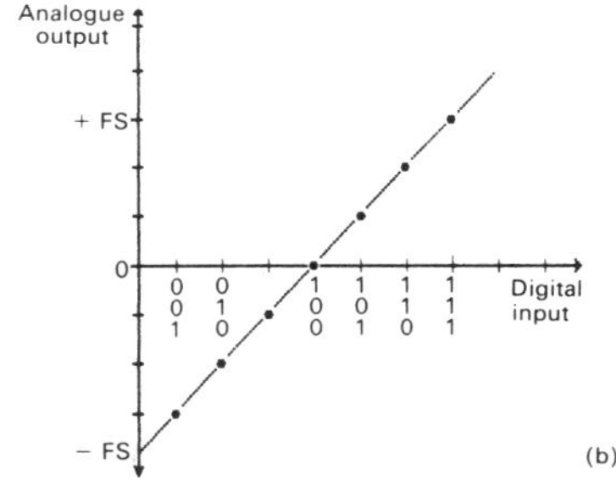

Figure 2.11

Interfacing a DAC to a microcomputer

A DAC may be interfaced to a microcomputer in one of the following ways:

1 Connected directly to the parallel outputs of a PIO or PIA (port interface).
2 Connected to a microcomputer data bus via suitable latches (bus interface).

Both forms of interfacing are shown in Figure 2.12(a) and (b).

Figure 2.12(a) shows the connections required to interface a DAC0800 to a PIO or PIA. This form of connection is simple to achieve where a microcomputer is already fitted with an appropriate parallel interface, since it only involves direct connection of the DAC circuit to a parallel output port. The PIO or PIA must be configured as an output port for this application.

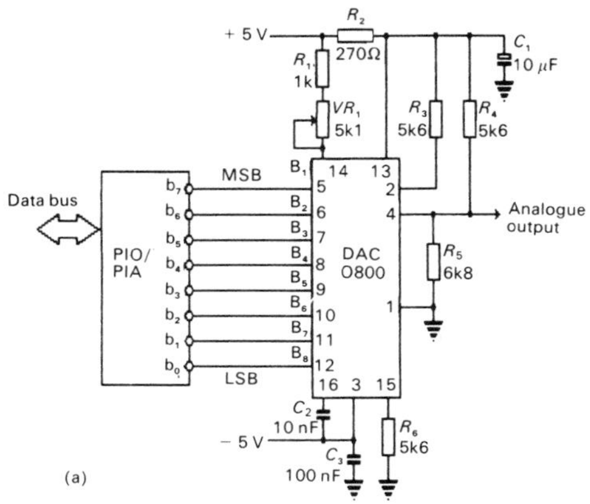

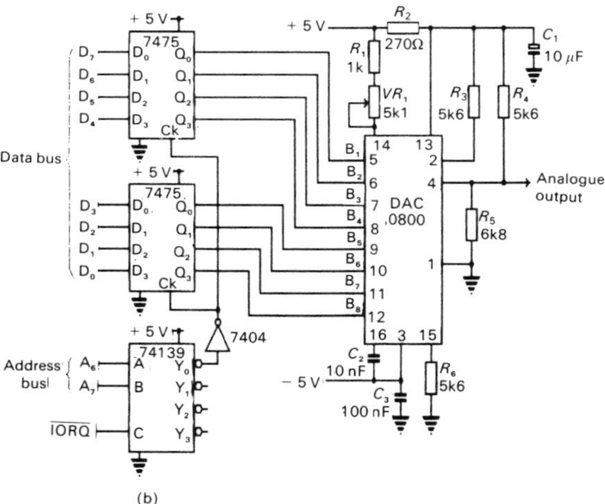

Figure 2.12

Figure 2.12(b) shows how a DAC may be interfaced directly to the data bus of a microcomputer. This method of connection may be preferred where the DAC forms an integral part of a microcomputer circuit rather than being part of an externally connected peripheral. The DAC is assigned an address (I/O or memory mapped), and data for conversion is captured from the data bus at an appropriate time by clocking the 74LS75 latches with a positive pulse obtained by inverting an output from the address decoder (an I/O address in the range 00–$3F_{16}$). No port configuring is required when using this circuit.

DAC applications

The manner in which a microprocessor based system operates is influenced profoundly by the software used. Software is therefore an integral part of the system as illustrated by the following examples.

1 Waveform synthesis

One application of a DAC concerns the use of a microcomputer for generating certain waveforms, e.g. ramp, triangular and sine waves. Essentially this consists of transferring a sequence of digital values to an output port, with an appropriate time delay between consecutive values in order to obtain the correct periodic time. This sequence is then repeated continuously. A suitable circuit for this purpose is shown in Figure 2.13.

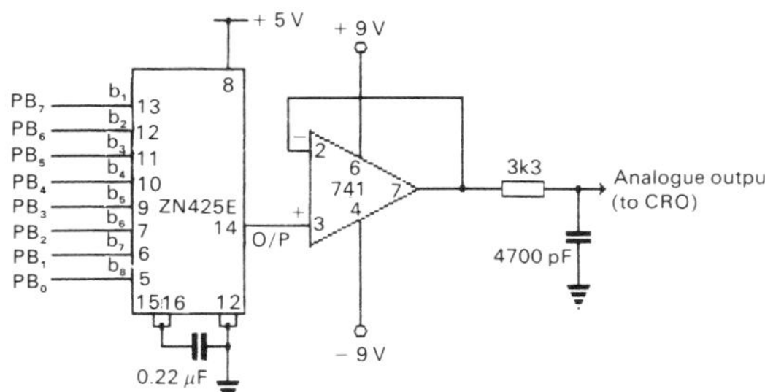

Figure 2.13

The following programs for the 6502, Z80 and 6800 microprocessors enable the operation and limitations of a DAC to be studied when generating common waveshapes.

Ramp waveshape

A ramp (or sawtooth) waveform is the simplest shape to generate, it being only necessary to increment a register repeatedly and output the contents of this register after each increment. A flowchart for the required software is shown in Figure 2.14.

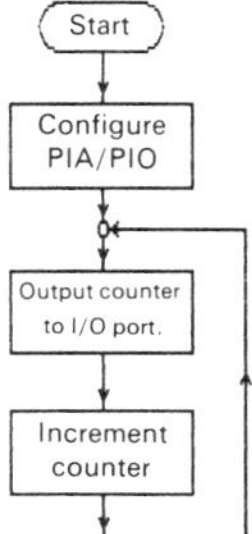

Figure 2.14

(a) 6502 ramp waveshape

```
0000                    ;*********************************
0000                    ; Ramp waveform generator for 6502
0000                    ; with DAC0800 connected to 6530/32
0000                    ; PIA
0000                    ;*********************************
0000                    ;
0000          PAD       =       $1700          ;port A data reg
0000          PADD      =       PAD+1          ;port A direction reg
0000          OUTPUT    =       $FF            ;output control word
0000                    ;
0200                   *=       $0200
0200                    ;
0200                    ;configure Port A of 6530/32 PIA
0200                    ;
0200 A9 FF              LDA     #OUTPUT        ;PA all outputs
0202 8D 01 17           STA     PADD           ;
0205                    ;
0205                    ;generate ramp waveform
0205                    ;
0205 18       RAMP      CLC                    ;adjust ramp slope
0206 69 01              ADC     #1             ;by change of inc.
0208 8D 00 17           STA     PAD            ;output to port
020B 4C 05 02           JMP     RAMP           ;
```

(b) Z80 ramp waveshape

```
                        ;*********************************
                        ; Ramp waveform generator for Z80
                        ; with DAC0800 connected to Z80 PIO
                        ;*********************************
                        ;
0081 =                  PBD     EQU     81H     ;port A data reg
0083 =                  PBC     EQU     PBD+2   ;port B control reg
000F =                  OUTPUT  EQU     0FH     ;mode 0 control word
                        ;
1800                    ORG     1800H
                        ;
                        ;configure Port B of Z80 PIO
                        ;
1800 3E0F               LD      A,OUTPUT        ;select mode 0
1802 D383               OUT     (PBC),A         ;byte output
                        ;
                        ;generate ramp waveform
                        ;
1804 D381     RAMP:     OUT     (PBD),A         ;adjust ramp slope
1806 C601               ADD     A,1             ;by change of
1808 18FA               JR      RAMP            ;increment
```

(c) 6800 ramp waveshape

```
0000                ;*********************************
0000                ; Ramp waveform generator for
0000                ; 6800/02 with DAC0800 connected
0000                ; to 6820/21 PIA
0000                ;*********************************
0000                ;
0000         DRA    EQU    $8004        ;port A data reg
0000         DDRA   EQU    DRA          ;port A direction reg
0000         CRA    EQU    DRA+1        ;port A control reg
0000         OUTPUT EQU    $FF          ;output control word
0000                ;
0200                ORG    $0200
0200                ;
0200                ;configure Port A of 6820/21 PIA
0200                ;
0200 4F             CLRA                ;reset bit 2 of CRA
0201 B7 80 05       STAA   CRA          ;to select DDRA
0204 86 FF          LDAA   #OUTPUT      ;port A all outputs
0206 B7 80 04       STAA   DDRA         ;
0209 86 04          LDAA   #4           ;set bit 2 of CRA
020B B7 80 05       STAA   CRA          ;to select DRA
020E                ;
020E                ;generate ramp waveform
020E                ;
020E 8B 01   RAMP   ADDA   #1           ;adjust ramp slope
0210 B7 80 04       STAA   DRA          ;by change of inc.
0213 20 F9          BRA    RAMP         ;
```

These programs may be modified to demonstrate the effect on analogue output of:

1 Incrementing the output in larger steps.
2 Decrementing the output rather than incrementing it.
3 Incrementing the output between set limits.

The effect of bringing the filter in and out of circuit and change of time constant may also be studied.

Sine waveshape

While it is a relatively simple matter to generate waveshapes such as ramp and triangular by calculation of the value of each sample byte sent to the DAC, generating a curved shape such as a sinewave is much more complic-

Table 2.1

Angle (°)	*Sine*	*Dec.*	*Hex*	*Angle* (°)	*Sine*	*Dec.*	*Hex*
270 (−90)	−1.0000	00	00	5	+0.0872	139	8B
275 (−85)	−0.9962	01	01	10	+0.1736	150	96
280 (−80)	−0.9848	02	02	15	+0.2588	161	A1
285 (−75)	−0.9659	04	04	20	+0.3420	172	AC
290 (−70)	−0.9397	08	08	25	+0.4226	182	B6
295 (−65)	−0.9063	12	0C	30	+0.5000	192	C0
300 (−60)	−0.8660	17	11	35	+0.5736	201	C9
305 (−55)	−0.8191	23	17	40	+0.6428	210	D2
310 (−50)	−0.7660	30	1E	45	+0.7071	218	DA
315 (−45)	−0.7071	37	25	50	+0.7660	226	E2
320 (−40)	−0.6428	46	2E	55	+0.8191	233	E9
325 (−35)	−0.5736	55	37	60	+0.8660	239	EF
330 (−30)	−0.5000	64	40	65	+0.9063	244	F4
335 (−25)	−0.4226	74	4A	70	+0.9397	248	F8
340 (−20)	−0.3420	84	54	75	+0.9659	252	FC
345 (−15)	−0.2588	95	5F	80	+0.9848	254	FE
350 (−10)	−0.1736	106	6A	85	+0.9962	255	FF
355 (−5)	−0.0872	117	75	90	+1.0000	256	100
360 (0)	0	128	80				

ated. For this reason a different approach is adopted. The values of each sample are calculated and stored in the form of a *look-up* table (see Table 2.1).

This table contains sine values for angles from −90° to +90°, and this table is scanned forwards then in reverse for each cycle of the waveform. Values in the table are calculated according to the formula:

$$\textbf{Value} = (\textbf{sin}\ \chi \times \textbf{128}) + \textbf{128}$$

A flowchart for suitable software is shown in Figure 2.15.

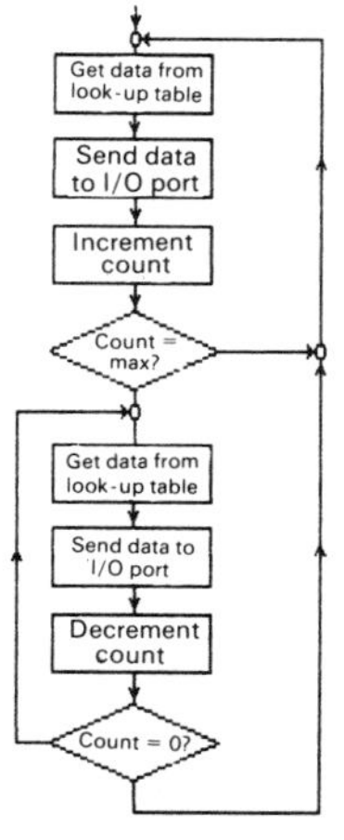

Figure 2.15

(a) 6502 sine waveshape

```
0000                    ;********************************
0000                    ; Sine waveform generator for 6502
0000                    ; with DAC0800 connected to 6530/32
0000                    ; PIA.  Output frequency approx.
0000                    ; 400 Hz (MPU clock 1 MHz)
0000                    ;********************************
0000                    ;
0000           PAD      =       $1700           ;port A data reg
0000           PADD     =       PAD+1           ;port A direction reg
0000           OUTPUT   =       $FF             ;output mode
0000           NEXT     =       0               ;up/down incr. const
0000                    ;
0200                   *=       $0200
0200                    ;
0200                    ;configure port A of 6530/32 PIA
0200                    ;
0200 A9 FF              LDA     #OUTPUT         ;configure port A
0202 8D 01 17           STA     PADD            ;as output port  0202
0202                    ;generate first part (-90deg to +90deg)
0202                    ;
0205 A0 22              LDY     #34             ;sine table counter
0207 A2 00              LDX     #0              ;table index reg
0209 86 00              STX     NEXT            ;set next for up scan
020B 18        SCAN     SEC                     ;time delay adjusts
020C A9 05              LDA     #5              ;frequency
020E E9 01     DLY      SBC     #1              ;
0210 D0 FC              BNE     DLY             ;
0212 B5 01              LDA     TABLE,X         ;get sine from table
0214 8D 00 17           STA     PAD             ;and send to port
0217 8A                 TXA                     ;adjust X to incr.
0218 18                 CLC                     ;or decr. to point
0219 65 00              ADC     NEXT            ;to next angle
021B AA                 TAX                     ;next angle
021C 88                 DEY                     ;reduce count by one
021D D0 EC              BNE     SCAN            ;to DAC
021D                    ;
021D                    ;generate second part (+90deg to -90deg)
021D                    ;
021F A0 22              LDY     #34             ;reset sample count
0221 A9 FF              LDA     #$FF            ;decrement index
0223 85 00              STA     NEXT            ;
0225 30 E4              BMI     SCAN            ;trace next half cycle
```

```
0225                    ;
0225                    ;look-up table of sine samples
0225                    ;
0001                    *= 1                         ;table in page zero
0001                    ;
0001 00        TABLE    .BYTE    0,1,4,8,12,17,23,29,37  ;-90 degree
0002 01
0003 04
0004 08
0005 0C
0006 11
0007 17
0008 1D
0009 25
000A 2E                 .BYTE    46,55,64,74,85,95,106   ;
000B 37
000C 40
000D 4A
000E 55
000F 5F
0010 6A
0011 76                 .BYTE    118,128,138,150,161,171 ;
0012 80
0013 8A
0014 96
0015 A1
0016 AB
0017 B6                 .BYTE    182,192,201,210,219,227 ;
0018 C0
0019 C9
001A D2
001B DB
001C E3
001D E9                 .BYTE    233,239,244,248,252,255 ;+90 degree
001E EF
001F F4
0020 F8
0021 FC
0022 FF
0023 FF                 .BYTE    255
```

(b) Z80 sine waveshape

```
                        ;*********************************
                        ; Sine waveform generator for Z80
                        ; with DAC0800 connected to PIO
                        ; Output frequency approx. 400Hz
                        ; (MPU clock 1.79MHz)
                        ;*********************************
                        ;
0081 =                  PBD     EQU     81H     ;port B data reg
0083 =                  PBC     EQU     PBD+2   ;port B control reg
000F =                  OUTPUT  EQU     0FH     ;PIO mode 0
                        ;
1800                    ORG     1800H
                        ;
                        ;configure port B of Z80 PIO
                        ;
1800 3E 0F              LD      A,OUTPUT        ;configure port B
1802 D3 83              OUT     (PBC),A         ;as output port
1804 0E 81              LD      C,PBD           ;C=port pointer
                        ;
                        ;generate first part (-90deg to +90deg)
                        ;
1806 21 1B 18           LD      HL,TABLE        ;sine table pointer
1809 06 22      CYCLE:  LD      B,34            ;number of samples
180B E3         FIRST:  EX      (SP),HL         ;time delay adjusts
180C E3                 EX      (SP),HL         ;frequency
180D ED A3              OUTI                    ;transfer forward scan
180F 20 FA              JR      NZ,FIRST        ;to DAC
                        ;
                        ;generate second part (+90deg to -90deg)
                        ;
1811 06 22              LD      B,34            ;reset sample count
1813 E3         SECOND: EX      (SP),HL         ;delay
1814 E3                 EX      (SP),HL
1815 ED AB              OUTD                    ;transfer reverse scan
1817 20 FA              JR      NZ,SECOND       ;to DAC
                        ;
                        ;repeat cycle
                        ;
1819 18 EE              JR      CYCLE           ;next cycle
                        ;
                        ;look-up table of sine samples
                        ;
```

```
181B 00010408 TABLE:  DEFB    0,1,4,8,12,17,23,29,37  ;-90 degree
1824 2E37404A         DEFB    46,55,64,74,85,95,106   ;
182B 76808A96         DEFB    118,128,138,150,161,171 ;
1831 B6C0C9D2         DEFB    182,192,201,210,219,227 ;
1837 E9EFF4F8         DEFB    233,239,244,248,252,255 ;+90 degree
183D FF               DEFB    255
```

(c) 6800 sine waveshape

```
0000                        ;***********************************
0000                        ; Sine waveform generator for 6800/02
0000                        ; with DAC0800 connected to 6820/21
0000                        ; PIA.  Output frequency approx.
0000                        ; 400 Hz (MPU clock 1 MHz)
0000                        ;***********************************
0000                        ;
0000            DRA     EQU     $8004           ;port A data reg
0000            DDRA    EQU     DRA             ;port A direction reg
0000            CRA     EQU     DRA+1           ;port A control reg
0000            OUTPUT  EQU     $FF             ;output control word
0000                        ;
0200                    ORG     $0200
0200                        ;
0200                        ;configure Port A of 6820/21 PIA
0200                        ;
0200 4F                 CLRA                    ;reset bit 2 of CRA
0201 B7 80 05           STAA    CRA             ;to select DDRA
0204 86 FF              LDAA    #OUTPUT         ;port A all outputs
0206 B7 80 04           STAA    DDRA            ;
0209 86 04              LDAA    #4              ;set bit 2 of CRA
020B B7 80 05           STAA    CRA             ;to select DRA
020E                        ;
020E                        ;generate first part (-90deg to +90deg)
020E                        ;
020E C6 22      CYCLE   LDAB    #34             ;sine table counter
0210 CE 02 25           LDX     #TABLE          ;table index reg
0213 A6 00      FIRST   LDAA    0,X             ;get sine from table
0215 B7 80 04           STAA    DRA             ;and send to port
020C 86 05              LDAA    #5              ;delay loop to
020E 4A         DLY1    DECA                    ;adjust frequency
0210 26 FD              BNE     DLY1            ;
0212 08                 INX                     ;next angle
0213 5A                 DECB                    ;end of table?
0214 26 F2              BNE     FIRST           ;
```

```
0216                  ;
0216                  ;generate second part (+90deg to -90deg)
0216                  ;
0216 C6 22            LDAB   #34              ;reset sample count
0218 A6 00    SECOND  LDAA   0,X              ;and output table in
021A B7 80 04         STAA   DRA              ;reverse
021D 86 05            LDAA   #5               ;adjust frequency
021F 4A       DLY2    DECA                    ;
0220 26 FD            BNE    DLY2
0222 09               DEX                     ;back through table
0223 5A               DECB                    ;
0223 26 F2            BNE    SECOND           ;
0225 30 E4            BRA    CYCLE            ;trace next half cycle
0225                  ;
0225                  ;look-up table of sine samples
0225                  ;
0225 00       TABLE   FCB   0,1,4,8,12,17,23,29,37  ;-90 degree
0226 01
0227 04
0228 08
0229 0C
022A 11
022B 17
022C 1D
022D 25
022E 2E               FCB   46,55,64,74,85,95,106   ;
022F 37
0230 40
0231 4A
0232 55
0233 5F
0234 6A
0235 76               FCB   118,128,138,150,161,171 ;
0236 80
0237 8A
0238 96
0239 A1
023A AB
023B B6               FCB   182,192,201,210,219,227 ;
023C C0
023D C9
023E D2
023F DB
0240 E3
```

```
0241 E9          FCB    233,239,244,248,252,255 ;+90 degree
0242 EF
0243 F4
0244 F8
0245 FC
0246 FF
183D FF          FCB    255
```

2 Panel meter control

In certain systems it may be necessary to interface a moving coil panel meter (or similar instrument) to the outputs of a microcomputer. In such cases the digital output signals must first be converted into analogue form and buffered so that they are compatible with the meter. A circuit of the type shown in Figure 2.16 may be used for this purpose.

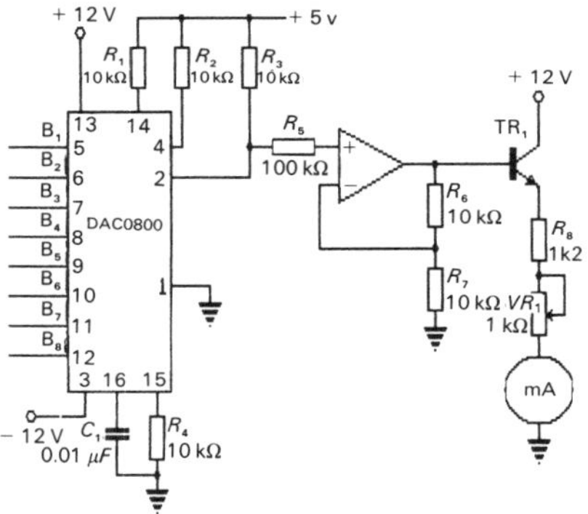

Figure 2.16

The software required for such an application is likely to be relatively simple, generally consisting of sending a data byte to the appropriate output port. In some cases it may be necessary to *scale* the output signal to adjust the full-scale reading. This process is covered in detail in Chapter 3.

3 Motor control

Many systems may be controlled by adjusting the current flow through certain parts of the system. This is often accomplished when using a microprocessor by employing pulse width modulation of a digital signal, i.e., on–off or start–stop control to maintain average current values. This form of control may be used in systems where there is sufficient inertia to sustain operation during periods when the current is interrupted. For example, the common heater/thermostat arrangement is of this type. In most cases, however, better performance may be obtained by using *continuous control* in which current flows continuously, but its magnitude is varied. This form of control requires an analogue signal to set the current level. A control system for a small DC motor is used as an example of continuous control, demonstrating how it may be used to control acceleration and deceleration of the motor. A circuit suitable for interfacing a small DC motor is shown in Figure 2.17.

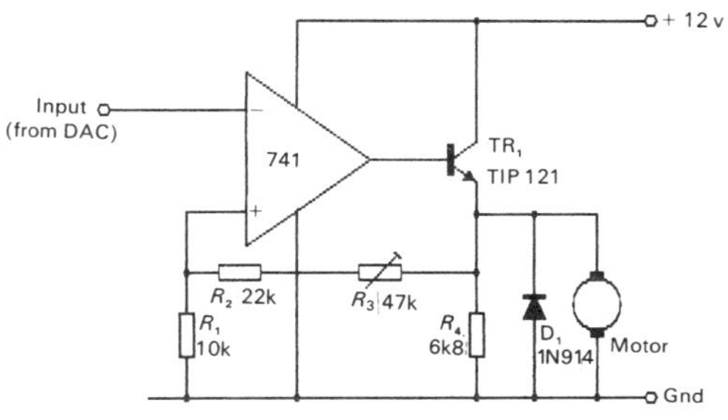

Figure 2.17

Routines which provide variable acceleration and deceleration rates for this motor are as follows:

(a) 6502

```
0000                   ;**********************************
0000                   ; Motor speed control --- provides
0000                   ; constant acceleration up to max.
0000                   ; speed.
0000                   ; Final speed attained after approx.
0000                   ; 5 seconds (assuming 1 MHz clock)
0000                   ; Port address $1700 (already
0000                   ; configured)
0000                   ;**********************************
0000                   ;
0000            PORT   =       $1700
0200                  *=       $0200
0200                   ;
0200 A9 00             LDA     #0              ; motor initially
0202 8D 00 17 ACCEL    STA     PORT            ; stationary
0205                   ;
0205                   ; step time delay (20 ms per step)
0205                   ;
```

```
0205 A0 10               LDY     #16              ; 16 x 1,28 ms
0207 A2 00               LDX     #0               ; 1,28 ms loop
0209 CA         DLY      DEX                      ; 255,254,253 ...
020A D0 FD               BNE     DLY
020C 88                  DEY                      ; 9,8,7 .........
020D D0 FA               BNE     DLY
020D                     ;
020D                     ; incremental speed increase
020D                     ;
020F EE 00 17            INC     PORT             ; increase speed
0212 D0 EE               BNE     ACCEL
0214 60                  RTS
```

(b) Z80

```
                         ;**********************************
                         ; Motor speed control --- provides
                         ; constant acceleration up to max,
                         ; speed,
                         ; Final speed attained after approx,
                         ; 5 seconds (assuming 2 MHz clock)
                         ; Port address 81H (already
                         ; configured)
                         ;**********************************
                         ;
0081 =          PORT     EQU     81H
1800                     ORG     1800H
                         ;
1800 3E00                LD      A,0              ; motor initially
1802 D381       ACCEL:   OUT     (PORT),A         ; stationary
                         ;
                         ; step time delay (20 ms per step)
                         ;
1804 160A                LD      D,10             ; 10 x 2 ms
1806 1E00                LD      E,0              ; 2 ms loop
1808 1D         DLY:     DEC     E                ; 255,254,253 ...
1809 20FD                JR      NZ,DLY
180B 15                  DEC     D                ; 9,8,7 .........
180C 20FA                JR      NZ,DLY
                         ;
                         ; incremental speed increase
                         ;
180E 3C                  INC     A                ; increase speed
180F 20F1                JR      NZ,ACCEL
1811 C9                  RET
```

(c) 6800

```
0000                    ;**********************************
0000                    ; Motor speed control --- provides
0000                    ; constant acceleration up to max.
0000                    ; speed.
0000                    ; Final speed attained after approx.
0000                    ; 5 seconds (assuming 1 MHz clock)
0000                    ; Port address $8004 (already
0000                    ; configured)
0000                    ;**********************************
0000                    ;
0000          PORT      EQU    $8004
0200                    ORG    $0200
0200                    ;
0200 4F                 CLRA                  ; motor initially
0202 B7 80 04 ACCEL     STAA   PORT           ; stationary
0204                    ;
0204                    ; step time delay (20 ms per step)
0204                    ;
0204 86 10              LDAA   #13            ; 13 x 1.536 ms
0206 C6 00              LDAB   #0             ; 1.536 ms loop
0208 5A       DLY       DECB                  ; 255,254,253 ...
0209 26 FD              BNE    DLY
020B 4A                 DECA                  ; 9,8,7 .........
020C 26 FA              BNE    DLY
020D                    ;
020D                    ; incremental speed increase
020D                    ;
020D 7C 80 04           INC    PORT           ; increase speed
0210 26 EE              BNE    ACCEL
0212 39                 RTS
```

Problems

1 (a) Describe the principle of operation of a digital to analogue converter (DAC).
(b) Explain why an *R*-2*R* network may be preferred to a binary weighted resistor network in a DAC.

2 Define the following DAC characteristics:
(a) Resolution.
(b) Monotonicity.
(c) Offset error.
(d) Gain error.

3 With the aid of a diagram, show how a DAC of the type shown in Figure 2.18 may be interfaced to:
(a) An 8-bit I/O port.
(b) An 8-bit MPU data bus.

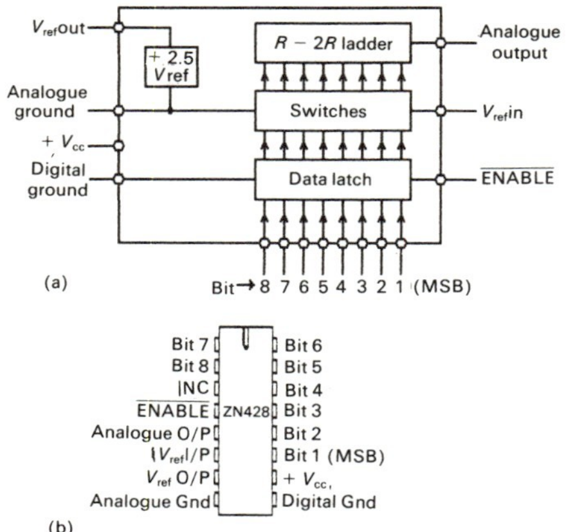

Figure 2.18

4 A 6502 based microcomputer with a 6530/32 PIA located at address \$1700 has an 8-bit DAC connected to its output port. Write a 6502 assembly language program to enable a triangular waveshape to be generated at the output of the DAC.

5 A Z80 based microcomputer with a Z80 PIO located at address 81H has an 8-bit DAC connected to its output port. Write a Z80 assembly language program to enable a triangular waveshape to be generated at the output of the DAC.

6 A 6800/02 based microcomputer with a 6821 PIA located at address \$8004 has an 8-bit DAC connected to its output port. Write a 6800 assembly language program to enable a triangular waveshape to be generated at the output of the DAC.

7 Explain how the speed of a small DC motor may be controlled by:
(a) Digital (pulse width modulation) control.
(b) Analogue control.

8 A 6502 based microcomputer with a 6530/32 PIA is used to control the speed of a small DC motor. Two switches are connected to b_0 and b_1 of port A (address \$1700), and the motor circuit may be connected to b_0 of port B (address \$1702) for pulse width control, or to the output of a DAC connected to b_0–b_7 of port B for analogue control, as shown in Figure 2.19.

D to A conversion

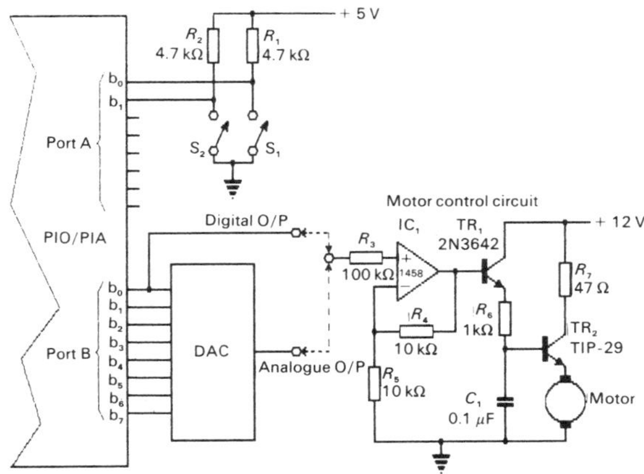

Figure 2.19

The speed of the motor depends upon the switch settings as follows:

S_1	S_0	*Speed*
Off	Off	Stop
Off	On	1/3 maximum
On	Off	2/3 maximum
On	On	Full speed

Write programs using 6502 assembly language to provide:
(a) Pulse width modulation control.
(b) Analogue control.

9 A Z80 based microcomputer with a Z80 PIO is substituted for the 6502 microcomputer in Problem 8. Port A is located at I/O address 80H and port B at 81H. Write programs in Z80 assembly language to control the motor as specified in Problem 8.

10 A 6800/02 based microcomputer with a 6821 PIA is substituted for the 6502 microcomputer in Problem 8. Port A is located at I/O address $8004 and port B at $8006. Write programs in 6800 assembly language to control the motor as specified in Problem 8.

Chapter 3

A to D conversion

Types of analogue to digital converter

An analogue to digital converter (ADC) is a device which converts an analogue signal at its input into an equivalent multibit digital output signal. The ideal transfer is expressed as:

$$V_{fs}(B_1/2 + B_2/4 + B_3/8 + \ldots Bn/2n) = V_{in} \pm \tfrac{1}{2}LSB$$

The transfer characteristic of an ideal ADC is shown in Figure 3.1, which for simplicity is restricted to three bit digital output.

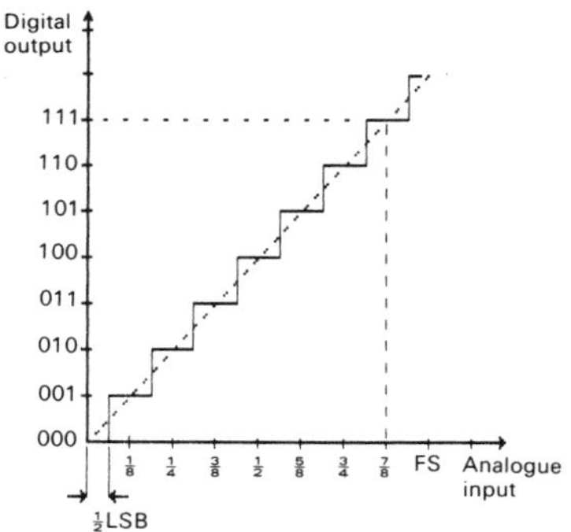

Figure 3.1

Using such an ADC, eight different digital outputs are available, 000 to 111 (0 to 7) which correspond to eight different analogue input voltage levels. In a practical situation, the analogue input seldom jumps from one value to the next but may vary continuously between 0 and full scale. Therefore each digital output code represents a range of analogue input voltages, equivalent to that required to cause a change in output of one LSB. Zero of an ADC is usually adjusted so that changes in output code occur $\pm \frac{1}{2}$ LSB either side of the actual analogue input corresponding to that code. For example, the output code 010 represents an analogue input of $1/4V_{fs}$, but the change from 001 to 010 occurs at $3/16\ V_{fs}$ and the change from 010 to 011 occurs at $5/16\ V_{fs}$.

Various methods of performing analogue to digital conversion exist, and descriptions of the most common methods are included in this chapter.

Binary counter ADC

Also known as a 'ramp' type of converter, this type of ADC consists of a binary counter, DAC and voltage comparator arranged as shown in Figure 3.2(a).

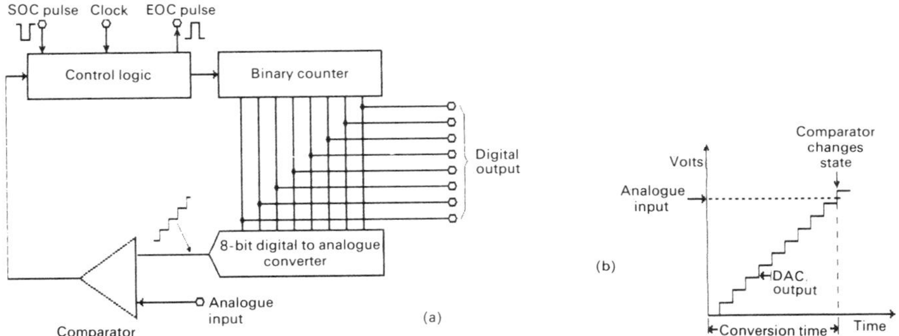

Figure 3.2

The counter is first reset to zero by a *start of conversion* (SOC) signal, and is then clocked so that its output increments in pure binary fashion which causes the DAC to generate a steadily rising (staircase) output voltage. The DAC output and the analogue input signal are both connected to the inputs of a voltage comparator circuit. If the analogue input voltage is greater than the DAC output voltage, the comparator output is logical 1 (high). This is the condition which prevails at the start of the count sequence. As the count progresses, the DAC output rises in staircase manner until its output voltage is equal to the analogue input voltage (see Figure 3.2(b)). At this point, the comparator output suddenly changes to a logical 0 (low) which causes the control logic circuit to terminate the counting sequence and latches the current count. An *end of conversion* (EOC) pulse is also generated. The residual count in the binary counter therefore represents the digital equivalent of the analogue input voltage.

Tracking converter

As its name implies, a tracking converter follows or *tracks* the analogue input. Its operation is similar to the ramp type of ADC except that it uses an up–down counter and a *window* comparator as shown in Figure 3.3.

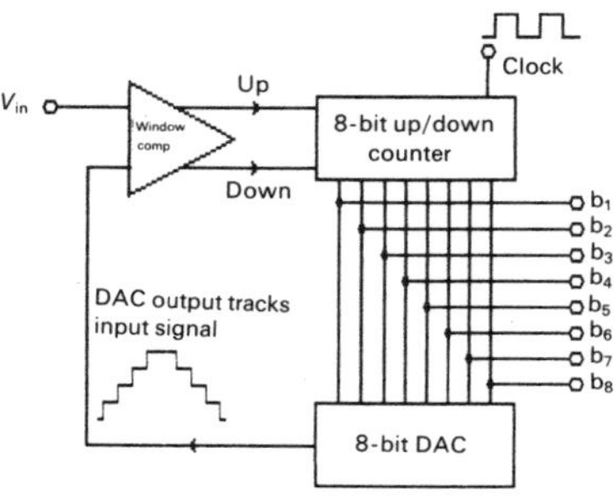

Figure 3.3

When the DAC output is less than the analogue input, the comparator instructs the counter to count up so that the DAC output increases. If the DAC output is greater than the analogue input, the comparator instructs the counter to count down so that the DAC output decreases. When the DAC output is equal to the analogue input $\pm\frac{1}{2}$ LSB, the input is within the window of the comparator and the counter is stopped. The main advantage of this type of ADC is that once an initial conversion has been performed starting from zero, subsequent conversions require only sufficient clock pulses to increase or decrease the DAC output to match the analogue input. This results in the tracking converter being faster than the ramp type.

Successive approximation

The counter types of ADC described suffer from the fact that they are relatively slow in operation, and that the conversion time varies according to the analogue input voltage. The conversion time may be greatly reduced and made more consistent by using a conversion method known as *successive approximation*. This method involves setting each bit of the input to the DAC, in turn, starting with the most significant bit. After setting each bit its effect is noted at the output from the voltage comparator, and if setting a particular bit results in the DAC output exceeding the analogue input voltage the bit is reset again. This process is repeated for each bit in the register, therefore, for an 8-bit register only eight 'trial' outputs are required for any input voltage. This process is shown in Figure 3.4(a) and (b).

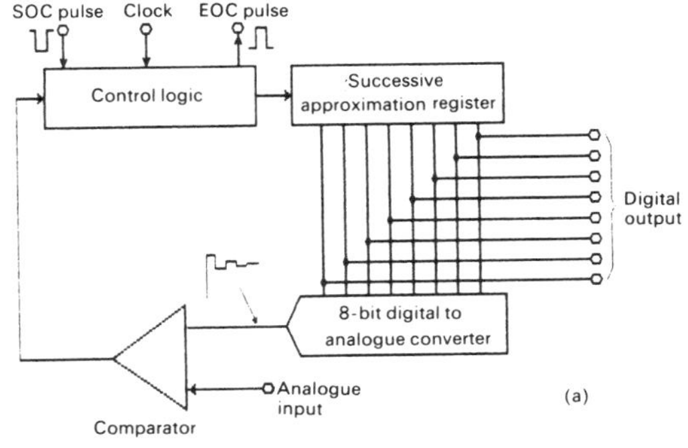

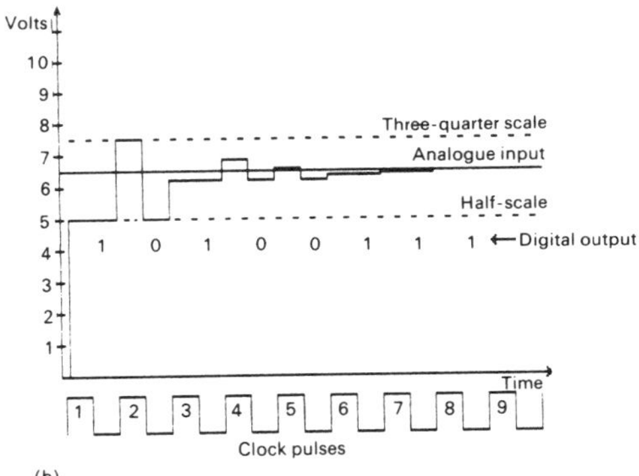

Figure 3.4

Parallel (flash) converter

In this type of ADC a resistor network is used to generate a number of different reference potentials, one for each bit of the converter. These potentials are applied to the reference inputs of an equivalent number of comparator circuits, as shown in Figure 3.5.

The analogue input signal is applied to the second input of each comparator and is thus compared simultaneously with each of the reference potentials. All comparator outputs change logic state if their reference potential exceeds their analogue input while the outputs of the remainder do not change state. The comparator outputs are then encoded into whatever form of digital coding is required. Since the only delays in the conversion process are those introduced by a single comparator plus encoding logic, this type of converter is very fast in operation, typically 10–20 MHz, which make them suitable for digital TV systems, digital storage oscilloscopes and signal ana-

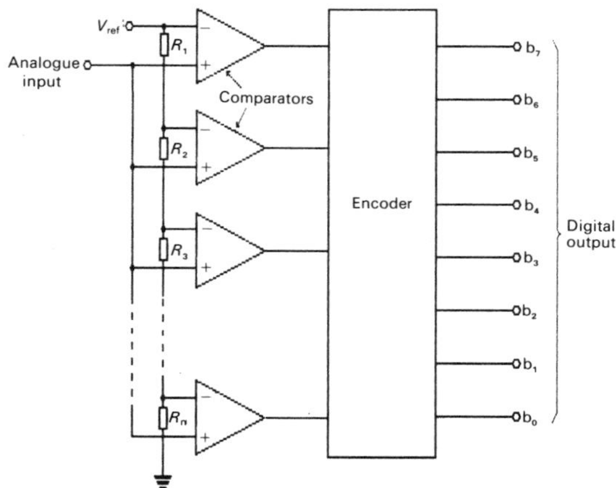

Figure 3.5

lysis. Owing to the large number of comparator circuits, however, this type of ADC tends to be rather expensive.

ADC characteristics

A large number of monolithic ADCs are available from various manufacturers. When selecting an ADC for a particular application, reference should be made to the manufacturer's data sheets to determine its suitability. The following parameters and definitions may need to be considered.

Quantizing error

In a DAC, for each input code, there is a fixed analogue output level, but for an ADC this is not the case. For each digital output level from an ADC there exists a range of analogue inputs equivalent to 1 LSB. Therefore it is not possible to determine the exact analogue input from its digital output code, there being the possibility of a quantizing error of $\pm \frac{1}{2}$ LSB. All ADCs therefore introduce a quantizing error whose magnitude depends upon the number of output bits of the ADC.

Missing codes

If the DAC used in an ADC is non-monotonic, then certain output codes cannot be generated. For example, consider the situation shown in Figure 3.6(a) which shows non-monotonicity on input code 101_2 (5).

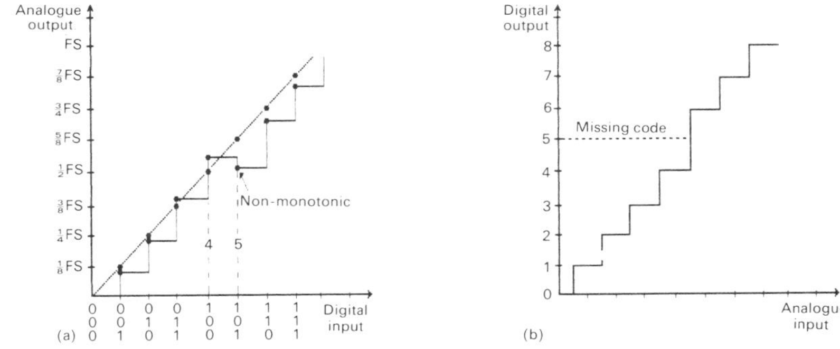

Figure 3.6

If the analogue input is lower than the output generated by a DAC input code of 100_2 (4), then the counter stops before the code for 101_2 is reached. If the analogue input is greater than the DAC output for 100_2 (4) then it must also be greater than the output for 101_2 (5), therefore the output code for 101_2 (5) is never generated and is known as a *missing code.* ADC characteristics with a missing code are shown in Figure 3.6(b).

Zero transition

An ADC is usually adjusted so that changes from one output code to the next occur $\pm \frac{1}{2}$ LSB either side of the actual analogue input corresponding to each code, i.e., the transition from 0 to 1 is offset by $\frac{1}{2}$ LSB. The DAC used in an ADC circuit does not normally have such an offset, therefore the transition from 0 to 1 occurs at 1 LSB plus errors due to DAC zero error and comparator offset. The total of these is referred to as the *zero transition.*

Gain error

Similar to the gain error for a DAC, the gain error is the difference in slope between a line drawn from actual zero to full scale and a line drawn through the ideal transition points.

Linearity

The linearity error of an ADC is the deviation of the actual characteristic from the ideal characteristic. It is specified as a percentage of full scale or a fraction of an LSB, and if less than $\pm \frac{1}{2}$ LSB, ensures that there are no missing codes.

Differential linearity

The differential linearity is a measure of the difference between an actual analogue increment required for a change from one output code to the next and the ideal size, $V_{fs}/2^n$. If the differential linearity is specified as $+\frac{1}{2}$ LSB, the step size from one state to the next may vary from half to one and a half times the ideal 1 LSB step.

Resolution

The resolution of an ADC is defined as the number of output bits it possesses. This determines the number of discrete output steps available but does not indicate the accuracy of an ADC.

Conversion time

The time taken for an ADC to complete the process of converting an analogue input into an equivalent digital output is known as the *conversion time*. For a successive approximation ADC, this time is constant and depends upon the number of bits and the clocking frequency. For a counter/comparator type of ADC, however, the conversion time varies according to the magnitude of the analogue input voltage, since this determines the number of clock pulses required before EOC (end of conversion) is achieved. Generally the conversion time is quoted for a full scale conversion and for 8-bit resolution is expressed as:

$$\textbf{Conversion time} = \frac{\textbf{256}}{\textbf{clock frequency (Hz)}}\ \textbf{s}$$

Interfacing an ADC to a microcomputer

Counter types of ADC are available in IC form, for example the Ferranti ZN425. This device contains an *R*-2*R* DAC and an 8-bit binary counter, organized so that it may be externally connected for either DAC or ADC applications. A block diagram of this device is shown in Figure 3.7(a).

A ZN435 is also available which contains an internal clock, the frequency of which is determined by choice of external *R* and *C*. The ZN425 may be connected to the I/O ports of a microcomputer, or may be directly interfaced to the data bus using D-type latches (see Figure 3.8(a) and (b)).

The MPU (microprocessor unit) clock may be used to operate the internal binary counter, provided that it is suitably divided, since the maximum clock-

A to D conversion

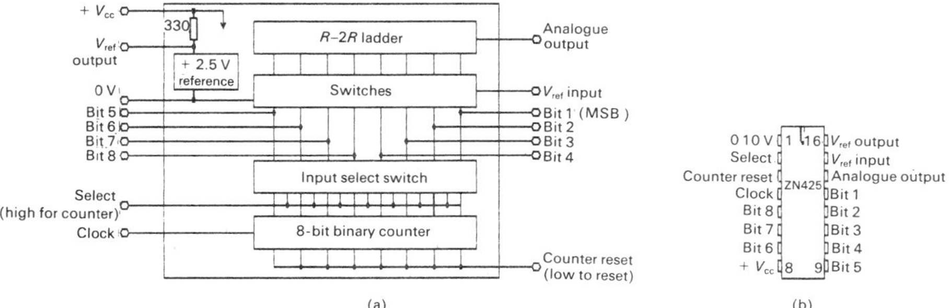

Figure 3.7

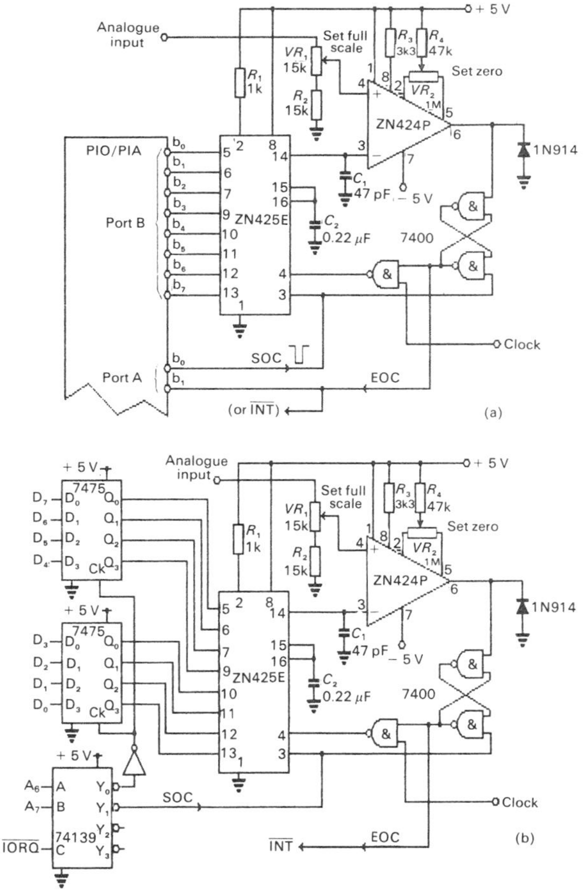

Figure 3.8

ing frequency for the ZN425 is 300 kHz. Conversion is initiated by the MPU generating a *start of conversion* (SOC) pulse which is achieved by toggling b_0 of port A in Figure 3.8(a), and by simply addressing the ADC in Figure 3.8(b). This causes the internal binary counter to be reset to zero, and the clock inhibiting flip-flop (7400) to be reset so that clock pulses are applied to pin 4 of the ZN425. The binary counter therefore increments at a rate determined by its clock input, which results in a staircase output being generated on pin 14 (DAC output). When the DAC output is equal to the analogue input voltage, the logic output on the ZN424 comparator output (pin 6) changes state. This causes the flip-flop to be set which inhibits further clocking of the counter and generates an *end of conversion* (EOC) signal. In both cases it is possible to poll the EOC signal, but since this ties up the MPU for the duration of the conversion it may be better to use the EOC signal to cause an interrupt. Software routines for operating these circuits as follows:

(a) 6502

```
0000                    ;*********************************
0000                    ; 6502 subroutine to perform A to D
0000                    ; conversion using a ZN425 ADC
0000                    ; with internal counter driven
0000                    ; from system clock
0000                    ; Assumes PIA already configured.
0000                    ;*******************************
0000                    ;
0000             PAD    =       $1700           ;port A data reg
0000             PBD    =       PAD+2           ;port B data reg
0000                    ;
0200                   *=       $0200
0200                    ;
0200                    ;generate SOC pulse on bit 0 of port A
0200                    ;
0200 AD 00 17 CONV      LDA     PAD             ;active low SOC, leave other
0203 29 FE              AND     #%11111110      ;bits unaltered to avoid
0205 8D 00 17           STA     PAD             ;conflicts
0208 A2 05              LDX     #5              ;15us minimum SOC pulse width
020A CA          PDEL   DEX                     ;(actual approx. 27us at 1MHz)
020B D0 FD              BNE     PDEL            ;exit routine with SOC left
020D EE 00 17           INC     PAD             ;inactive for next call
0210                    ;
0210                    ;wait for active EOC signal
0210                    ;
0210 AD 00 17 READ      LDA     PAD             ;poll for EOC active (low)
0213 29 02              AND     #%00000010
```

```
0215 D0 F9          BNE     READ            ;wait for start of EOC
0217                ;
0217                ;read digital equivalent of analogue input
0217                ;
0217 AD 02 17       LDA     PBD             ;return with digital value
021A 60             RTS                     ;in Acc
```

(b) Z80

```
                    ;********************************
                    ; Z80 subroutine to perform A to D
                    ; conversion using a ZN425 ADC
                    ; with internal counter driven
                    ; from system clock
                    ; Assumes PIO already configured.
                    ;********************************
                    ;
0080 =        PAD   EQU     80H             ;port A data reg
0081 =        PBD   EQU     PAD+1           ;port B data reg
                    ;
1880                ORG     1880H
                    ;
                    ;generate SOC pulse on bit 0 of port A
                    ;
1880 DB80     CONV: IN      A,(PAD)         ;active low SOC, leave other
1882 CB87           RES     0,A             ;bits unaltered to avoid
1884 D380           OUT     (PAD),A         ;conflicts
1886 E3             EX      (SP),HL         ;15us minimum SOC pulse width
1887 E3             EX      (SP),HL         ;(actual approx. 28us at 2MHz)
1888 CBC7           SET     0,A             ;exit routine with SOC left
188A D380           OUT     (PAD),A         ;inactive for next call
                    ;
                    ;wait for active EOC signal
                    ;
188C DB80     READ: IN      A,(PAD)         ;poll for EOC active (low)
188E CB4F           BIT     1,A
1890 20FA           JR      NZ,READ         ;wait for start of EOC
                    ;
                    ;read digital equivalent of analogue input
                    ;
1892 DB81           IN      A,(PBD)         ;return with digital value
1894 C9             RET                     ;in Acc
```

(c) 6800

```
0000                    ;**********************************
0000                    ; 6800/02 subroutine to perform
0000                    ; A to D conversion using a ZN425
0000                    ; ADC with internal counter driven
0000                    ; from system clock
0000                    ; Assumes PIA already configured.
0000                    ;*********************************
0000                    ;
0000             DRA    EQU     $8004          ;port A data reg
0000             DRB    EQU     DRA+2          ;port B data reg
0000                    ;
0200                    ORG     $0200
0200                    ;
0200                    ;generate SOC pulse on bit 0 of port A
0200                    ;
0200 B6 80 04    CONV   LDAA    DRA            ;active low SOC, leave other
0203 84 FE              ANDA    #%11111110     ;bits unaltered to avoid
0205 B7 80 04           STAA    DRA            ;conflicts
0208 85 05              LDAA    #5             ;15us minimum SOC pulse width
020A 4A          PDEL   DECA                   ;(actual approx. 32us at 614kHz)
020B 26 FD              BNE     PDEL           ;exit routine with SOC left
020D 7C 80 04           INC     PAD            ;inactive for next call
0210                    ;
0210                    ;wait for active EOC signal
0210                    ;
0210 B6 80 04    READ   LDAA    DRA            ;poll for EOC active (low)
0213 84 02              ANDA    #%00000010
0215 26 F9              BNE     READ           ;wait for start of EOC
0217                    ;
0217                    ;read digital equivalent of analogue input
0217                    ;
0217 B6 80 06           LDAA    DRB            ;return with digital value
021A 39                 RTS                    ;in Acc A
```

Software conversion

In applications which allow the MPU to be wholly engaged in the conversion process, a counter may be maintained within the MPU by using one of its internal registers for this purpose. This allows the hardware to be simplified, and a circuit similar to that shown in Figure 3.9(a) may be used.

A flowchart for the software is shown in Figure 3.9(b). The contents of a

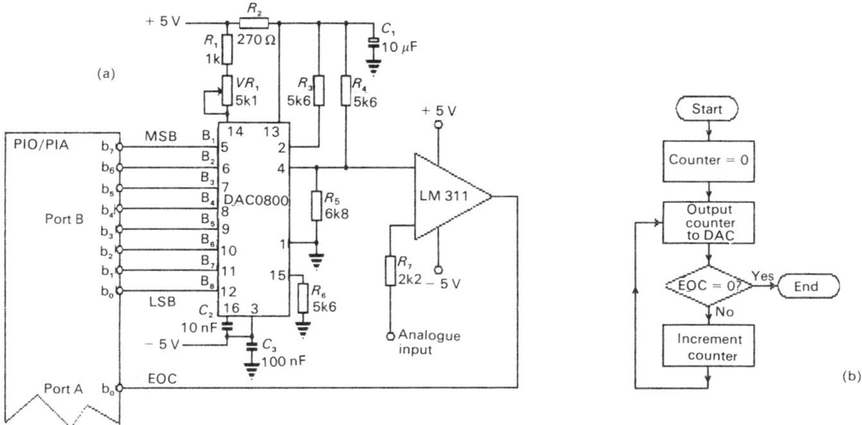

Figure 3.9

register within the MPU are incremented from zero, and the resulting binary count is sent out via the I/O port to the DAC. The comparator output (EOC) is tested at each stage of the count sequence, and the count is terminated when a logical 0 is detected. Suitable program listings are as follows:

(a) 6502

```
0000                  ;**********************************
0000                  ; Analogue to digital conversion
0000                  ; subroutine for 6502 system using
0000                  ; software counter/comparator method
0000                  ; ADC connected to Port B
0000                  ; EOC to Port A b0
0000                  ; Assumes PIA already configured.
0000                  ;**********************************
0000                  ;
0000           PAD    =     $1700
0000           PBD    =     PAD+2
0000                  ;
0200                 *=     $0200
0200                  ;
0200 A2 00     ADCON  LDX   #0          ;X = ramp counter
0202 8E 02 17  CONV   STX   PBD         ;zero ramp counter (SOC)
0205 AD 00 17         LDA   PAD         ;read comparator
0208 4A               LSR   A           ;shift b0 into C flag
0209 90 03            BCC   EXIT        ;exit if b0 set
020B E8               INX               ;inc ramp count
020C B0 F4            BCS   CONV        ;and try again
020E 60        EXIT   RTS
```

(b) Z80

```
                        ;**********************************
                        ; Analogue to digital conversion
                        ; subroutine for Z80 system using
                        ; software counter/comparator method
                        ; ADC connected to Port B
                        ; EOC to Port A b0
                        ; Assumes PIO already configured
                        ;**********************************
                        ;
0080 =                  PAD     EQU     80H
0081 =                  PBD     EQU     PAD+1
                        ;
1800                    ORG     1800H
                        ;
1800 0E81     ADCON:    LD      C,PBD           ;C = port pointer
1802 0600               LD      B,0             ;zero ramp counter (SOC)
1804 ED41     CONV:     OUT     (C),B           ;generate ramp
1806 DB80               IN      A,(PAD)         ;read comparator
1808 CB47               BIT     0,A             ;test comparator output
180A C8                 RET     Z               ;end of conversion (EOC)
180B 04                 INC     B               ;ramp up one step
180C 18F6               JR      CONV            ;and continue
```

(c) 6800

```
0000                    ;*********************************
0000                    ; Analogue to digital conversion
0000                    ; subroutine for 6800/02 system
0000                    ; using software counter/comparator
0000                    ; method.  ADC connected to Port B
0000                    ; EOC to Port A b0
0000                    ;*********************************
0000                    ;
0000          DRA       EQU     $8004
0000          DRB       EQU     PAD+2
0000                    ;
0200                    ORG     $0200
0200                    ;
0200 5F       ADCON     CLRB                    ;Acc B = ramp counter
0201 F7 80 05 CONV      STAB    PBD             ;zero ramp counter (SOC)
0204 B6 80 04           LDAA    PAD             ;read comparator
0207 44                 LSRA                    ;shift b0 into C flag
0208 24 03              BCC     EXIT            ;exit if b0 set
020A 5C                 INCB                    ;inc ramp count
020B 20 F4              BRA     CONV            ;and try again
020D 39       EXIT      RTS
```

Successive approximation software

The hardware requirements for successive approximation depend upon whether the successive approximation register (SAR) is controlled by hardware or by software. If a successive approximation integrated ADC (IC) is selected, this may be interfaced to a microcomputer in a similar manner to that used for the counter type ADC in Figure 3.8(a) and (b), using identical software. Software sucessive approximation may be used with the hardware shown in Figure 3.9 using the following routines:

(a) 6502

```
0000                  ;********************************
0000                  ; Analogue to digital conversion
0000                  ; subroutine for 6502  system using
0000                  ; successive approximation method
0000                  ; ADC connected to Port B
0000                  ; EOC to Port A b0
0000                  ; Assumes PIA already configured.
0000                  ;********************************
0000                  ;
0000           PAD    =      $1700
0000           PBD    =      PAD+2
0000           SAR    =      0
0000                  ;
0200                 *=      $0200
0200                  ;
0200 A9 80     ADCON  LDA    #%10000000     ;SAR mask initial
0202 85 00            STA    SAR            ;value
0204 05 00     CONV   ORA    SAR            ;set SAR bit
0206 8D 02 17         STA    PBD            ;and try
0209 AD 00 17         LDA    PAD            ;read comparator
020C 4A               LSR    A              ;test comparator output
020D B0 02            BCS    SHIFT          ;too big?
020F 45 00            EOR    SAR            ;reset bit
0211 46 00     SHIFT  LSR    SAR            ;shift SAR mask 1 bit
0213 90 EF            BCC    CONV           ;test next bit
0215 60               RTS
```

(b) Z80

```
                         ;**********************************
                         ; Analogue to digital conversion
                         ; subroutine for Z80 system using
                         ; successive approximation method
                         ; ADC connected to Port B
                         ; EOC to Port A b0
                         ; Assumes PIO already configured
                         ;**********************************
                         ;
0080 =                   PAD     EQU     80H
0081 =                   PBD     EQU     PAD+1
                         ;
1800                     ORG     1800H
                         ;
1800 0E 80       ADCON:  LD      C,PAD           ;C = port pointer
1802 06 80               LD      B,10000000B     ;B = SAR mask
1804 AF                  XOR     A               ;A = SAR
1805 B0          CONV:   OR      B               ;set SAR bit
1806 D3 81               OUT     (PBD),A         ;and try
1808 ED 50               IN      D,(C)           ;read comparator
180A CB 42               BIT     0,D             ;test comparator output
180C 20 01               JR      NZ,SHIFT        ;too big?
180E A8                  XOR     B               ;reset bit
180F CB 38       SHIFT:  SRL     B               ;shift SAR mask 1 bit
1811 30 F2               JR      NC,CONV         ;test next bit
1813 C9                  RET
```

(c) 6800

```
0000                     ;**********************************
0000                     ; Analogue to digital conversion
0000                     ; subroutine for 6800/02  system
0000                     ; using successive approximation
0000                     ; method.  ADC connected to Port B
0000                     ; EOC to Port A b0
0000                     ; Assumes PIA already configured.
0000                     ;**********************************
0000                     ;
0000            DRA      EQU     $8004
0000            DRB      EQU     DRA+2
0000            SAR      EQU     0
0000                     ;
```

A to D conversion

```
0200                    ORG    $0200
0200                    ;
0200 86 80     ADCON    LDAA   #%10000000     ;SAR mask initial
0202 97 00              STAA   SAR            ;value
0204 9A 00     CONV     ORAA   SAR            ;set SAR bit
0206 B7 80 06           STAA   PBD            ;and try
0209 B6 80 04           LDAA   PAD            ;read comparator
020C 44                 LSRA                  ;test comparator output
020D 25 02              BCS    SHIFT          ;too big?
020F 98 00              EORA   SAR            ;reset bit
0211 74 00 00  SHIFT    LSR    SAR            ;shift SAR mask 1 bit
0214 24 EE              BCC    CONV           ;test next bit
0216 39                 RTS
```

Voltage measurements

A microcomputer with an ADC connected to its input port may be used to carry out DC voltage measurements. The value measured may be displayed as a digital read-out using ordinary seven-segment devices, or alternatively as an analogue reading on a moving coil panel meter. The latter method requires the microcomputer to have a DAC connected to its output port. Both forms of measuring system are shown in Figure 3.10(a) and (b).

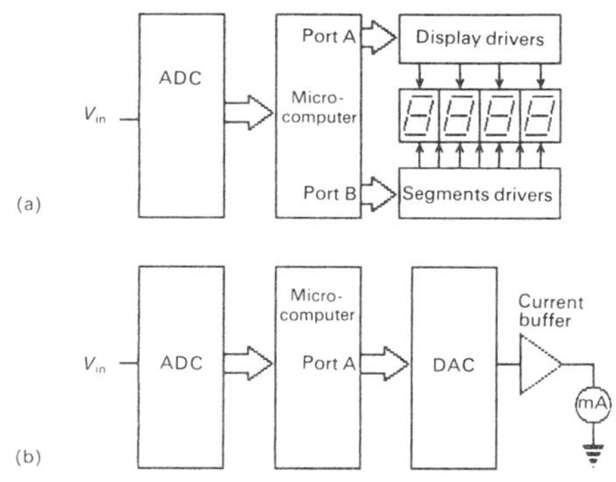

Figure 3.10

Scaling

The range of voltage readings which can be handled by the measuring system shown in Figure 3.10 depends upon the characteristics of the ADC used. Typical ADCs as described earlier in this chapter make use of a DAC circuit with an analogue scale factor of $1-2^{-n}$, which means that the full scale output is almost equal to V_{ref} with increments of $V_{ref}/256$ for an 8-bit converter. In practice, voltage readings with different parameters may have to be made, and in these cases *scaling* must take place in the following manner:

1 For full scale readings much larger than V_{ref}, some form of attenuation is necessary.
2 For full scale readings lower than V_{ref} it may appear that no action is required, however this is not the case, since an effective reduction in resolution would result owing to the higher order bits being unused. In this case some form of amplification is required.

The object of scaling, therefore, is to ensure that for all input signal ranges, maximum information is obtained from the ADC. A signal conditioning stage (op-amp) is therefore included, and its gain is adjusted so that full scale input voltage for each range delivers full scale input to the ADC. A simple scaling circuit is shown in Figure 3.11.

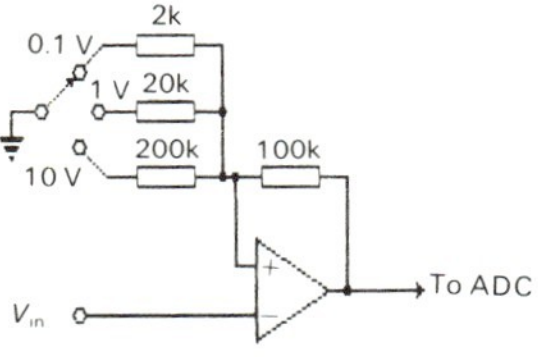

Figure 3.11

Having ensured that the ADC gives maximum resolution by scaling of the input signal, further scaling may be required after processing so that the output gives a true indication of the quantity being measured. For example, if the 8-bit digital output from an ADC, is converted into equivalent segment codes by an MPU and transferred directly to its display port, readings in the range 0 to FF_{16} are obtained (or 0 to 255_{10} if binary to BCD correction is included). Such readings are unsuitable for the majority of applications and must be adjusted by scaling. Similarly, some form of scaling may be required where analogue indicating devices are used.

Scaling algorithm

Essentially, for a finite number of output bits, scaling consists of multiplying all output values by a fixed fractional constant. For example, to convert readings in the range 0 to 255_{10} into display values 0 to 99_{10}, a scaling factor of 99/255 or 0.388 is required. A simple method of achieving such a scale factor involves shifting data to the right, and selecting appropriate combinations to

Table 3.1

Shift by	*Scale*
1	0.5
2	0.25
3	0.125
4	0.0625
5	0.03125
6	0.015625
7	0.0078125

give the closest figure. Scaling factors obtained by shifting are shown in Table 3.1.

A scale factor of approximately 0.388 (0.39) may be obtained as follows:

$$\textbf{Scaled data} = (\textbf{data} \times \textbf{0.25}) + (\textbf{data} \times \textbf{0.125}) + (\textbf{data} \times \textbf{0.015625})$$

A flowchart showing how a scaling factor of 0.39 may be obtained is shown in Figure 3.12.

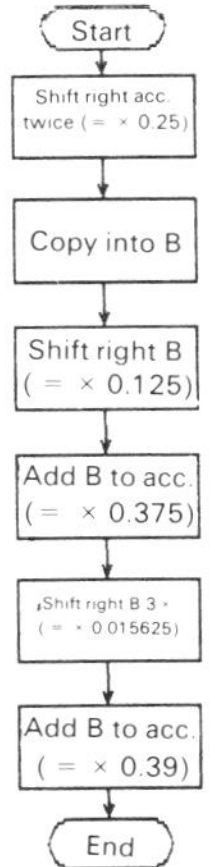

Figure 3.12

Software routines which enable readings from the ADC to be displayed in digital form in the range 00 to 99 are as follows:

(a) 6502

```
0000                      ;******************************
0000                      ; Scaling routine for 6502 MPU
0000                      ; Uses 16-bit precision
0000                      ; Entry: A = basic reading
0000                      ; Exit:  scaled reading in 0000
0000                      ; Scale factor approx. 0.39
0000                      ;******************************
0000                      ;
0000            SUMH      =       0        ; = running total
0000            SUML      =       1
0000            SREGH     =       2        ; = 16-bit shift
0000            SREGL     =       3        ; register
0200                     *=       $0200
0200                      ;
0200 85 02      SCALE     STA     SREGH    ; save basic reading
0202 A9 00                LDA     #0       ; in shift register
0204 85 03                STA     SREGL    ;
0206 85 00                STA     SUMH     ; clear summing
0208 85 01                STA     SUML     ; register
020A A2 02                LDX     #2       ; = x 0.25
020C 20 16 02             JSR     SHIFT
020F A2 01                LDX     #1       ; = x 0.125
0211 20 16 02             JSR     SHIFT
0214 A2 03                LDX     #3       ; = x 0.015625
0216 46 02      SHIFT     LSR     SREGH    ; 16 bit shift
0218 66 03                ROR     SREGL    ; subroutine
021A CA                   DEX              ; count number of
021B D0 F9                BNE     SHIFT    ; shifts
021D 18                   CLC              ; perform 16-bit
021E A5 01                LDA     SUML     ; addition
0220 65 03                ADC     SREGL
0222 85 01                STA     SUML
0224 A5 00                LDA     SUMH
0226 65 02                ADC     SREGH
0228 85 00                STA     SUMH
022A 60                   RTS
```

(b) Z80

```
                        ;****************************
                        ; Scaling routine for Z80 MPU
                        ; Uses 16-bit precision
                        ; Entry: A = basic reading
                        ; Exit:  H = scaled reading
                        ; Scale factor approx. 0.39
                        ;****************************
                        ;
1800                    ORG     1800H
                        ;
1800 210000   SCALE:    LD      HL,0     ; HL = summing register
1803 5D                 LD      E,L      ; DE = shift register
1804 57                 LD      D,A      ;
1805 0602               LD      B,2      ; = x 0.25
1807 CD1118             CALL    SHIFT
180A 0601               LD      B,1      ; = x 0.125
180C CD1118             CALL    SHIFT
180F 0603               LD      B,3      ; = x 0.015625
1811 CB3A     SHIFT:    SRL     D        ; 16 bit shift
1813 CB1B               RR      E        ; subroutine
1815 10FA               DJNZ    SHIFT
1817 19                 ADD     HL,DE    ; running total
1818 C9                 RET
```

(c) 6800

```
0000                    ;*******************************
0000                    ; Scaling routine for 6800/02 MPU
0000                    ; Uses 16-bit precision
0000                    ; Entry: Acc A = basic reading
0000                    ; Exit:  scaled reading in 0000
0000                    ; Scale factor approx. 0.39
0000                    ;*******************************
0000                    ;
0000          SUMH      EQU     0        ; = running total
0000          SUML      EQU     1
0000          SREGH     EQU     2        ; = 16-bit shift
0000          SREGL     EQU     3        ; register
0200                    ORG     $0200
0200                    ;
0200 97 02    SCALE     STAA    SREGH    ; save basic reading
```

```
0202 4F                 CLRA              ; in shift register
0203 97 03              STAA    SREGL     ;
0205 97 00              STAA    SUMH      ; clear summing
0207 97 01              STAA    SUML      ; register
0209 C6 02              LDAB    #2        ; = x 0,25
020B 8D 06              BSR     SHIFT
020D C6 01              LDAB    #1        ; = x 0,125
020F 8D 02              BSR     SHIFT
0211 C6 03              LDAB    #3        ; = x 0,015625
0213 74 00 02 SHIFT     LSR     SREGH     ; 16 bit shift
0216 76 00 03           ROR     SREGL     ; subroutine
0219 5A                 DECB              ; count number of
021A 26 F7              BNE     SHIFT     ; shifts
021C 96 01              LDAA    SUML      ;
021E 98 03              ADDA    SREGL     ; 16-bit
0220 97 01              STAA    SUML      ; addition
0222 96 00              LDAA    SUMH
0224 99 02              ADCA    SREGH
0226 97 00              STAA    SUMH
0228 39                 RTS
```

Problems

1 (a) With the aid of diagrams, explain the difference between analogue and digital signals.
  (b) Give an example of one sensor which provides an analogue signal, and one sensor which produces a digital signal.

2 (a) Describe the principle of operation of the following types of ADC:
    (i) Binary counter.
    (ii) Successive approximation.
  (b) State the main advantage of the successive approximation method compared to the binary counter method.

3 Define the following analogue to digital (ADC) characteristics:
  (a) Quantizing error.
  (b) Missing codes.
  (c) Zero transition error.
  (d) Conversion time.

4 An ADC uses SOC and EOC handshake signals.
   (a) Describe the function of each of these signals.
   (b) Describe two methods for:
      (i) Generating SOC signals.
      (ii) Using EOC signals.

5 A potentiometer is used to sense angular rotation of a shaft.
   (a) With the aid of a diagram, show how the potentiometer may be interfaced to a microcomputer.
   (b) For the system illustrated in (a), write an assembly language subroutine which provides an output value proportional to the angle of rotation of the shaft.

6 (a) Explain why a scaling routine may be necessary when using an ADC.
   (b) Write an appropriate scaling routine for problem 5 such that the subroutine delivers an output value in degrees of rotation.

Chapter 4

Data transfer techniques

In order that a microcomputer may interact with external devices and thus form part of a control system, some means of getting data into and out of it must be provided. The previous two chapters dealt with the problem of converting analogue signals into digital form and vice-versa. However, this is only a part of the interface problem, and for data transfers to effectively take place between systems and subsystems, other factors must be considered. These include:

1 *Timing:* For effective transfers, data must be present in the correct place at the exact time expected. Since a microcomputer and its peripheral devices often operate asynchronously, timing controls may be necessary in order to synchronize data transfers.

2 *Electrical:* A microcomputer generally operates at TTL (transistor transistor logic) voltage and current levels, i.e., 0 V and + 5 V with 1.6 mA current sink capability. Changes in voltage and current levels may be required, and when controlling mains operated equipment, electrical isolation must be considered.

3 *I/O lines:* For a given application, the number of I/O lines required may exceed that which is available with a given microcomputer. A reduction in the number of lines may be achieved by the use of *multiplexing* techniques.

4 *Serial data:* Transfers of information between a microcomputer and its peripheral devices (or a second microcomputer) often take place using a *bit serial* form of data. It is therefore necessary to convert between parallel and bit serial form.

5 *Bus structure:* The construction of microcomputer controlled equipment is simplified if some form of bus standard is adopted so that electrical compatibility is assured and that all control signals necessary are available.

Synchronization of data transfers

Most peripheral devices do not operate at the same speed as a microcomputer, and they seldom share a common clocking signal. Attempts at transferring data between a microcomputer and its peripheral devices under these conditions, i.e., *asynchronous transfers*, would inevitably result in lost or duplicated data. Data could be lost owing to being transferred at too fast a rate by a microprocessor, such that new data is supplied before the peripheral device has had time to accept the previous data. Data could also be duplicated owing to being transferred at too slow a rate so that repetitive reading of the same data byte occurs due to the much faster response of a microcomputer or its peripherals. Asynchronous data transfers are therefore unacceptable unless appropriate buffering techniques are employed.

These difficulties indicate that in order to transfer data in satisfactory manner, i.e., *synchronously*, a system of common timing is required between a microcomputer and its peripheral devices. Several different techniques are available for controlling the transfer of data, and these include the following:

1 Polling.
2 Handshaking.
3 Interrupts.
4 Buffering.
5 Direct memory access (DMA).

Polling

Polling is a software technique which involves a microcomputer interrogating each peripheral device, in turn, to determine whether it is ready for

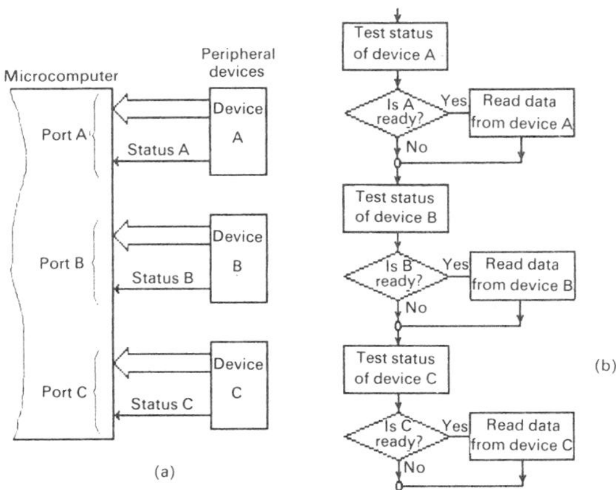

Figure 4.1

transfer of data or some other action by the microprocessor. This technique is illustrated in Figure 4.1(a) and (b).

A special control line called a *status line* is used to indicate that a peripheral device is ready for the transfer of data. The logic level on this line indicates the current status of the peripheral. An example showing the operation of a status line is illustrated in Figure. 4.2.

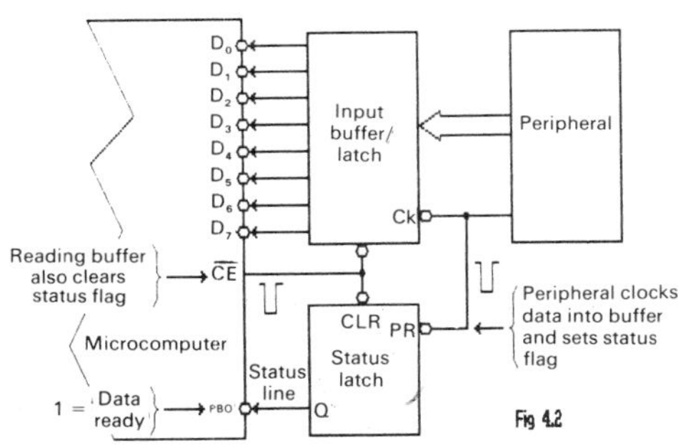

Figure 4.2

Handshaking

Handshaking takes the form of two-way communication between a microprocessor and its peripheral for the correct timing of data transfers. Each data transfer channel is provided with two handshake lines. An active level on one handshake line is used to indicate *new data available*, while an active level on the second handshake line indicates *data received – send more data*. Therefore a microprocessor and its peripheral remain constantly in synchronism by informing each other of their current condition in relation to the transfer. A typical arrangement for the Z80 PIO is shown in Figure 4.3(a) and (b).

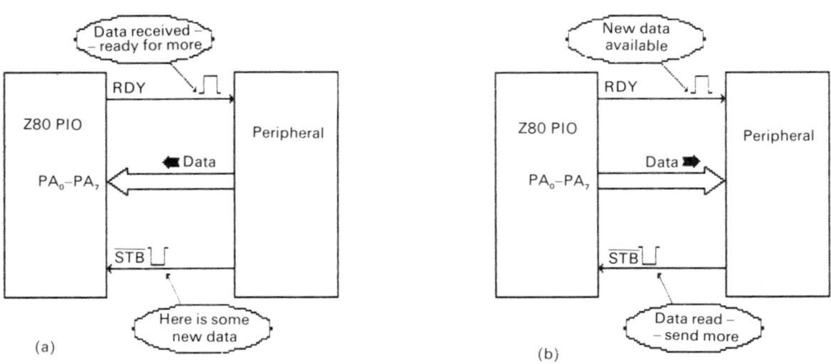

Figure 4.3

The sequence of events for transfers of data between a microcomputer and its peripheral devices is as follows:

1 ***Peripheral to MPU:***

(a) When the peripheral device is ready to transfer data to the microcomputer, it generates a signal to pull the PIO $\overline{\text{STB}}$ (strobe) input low. This informs the PIO that new data is available on the peripheral bus.
(b) Data is transferred from the peripheral bus into the PIO input register.
(c) In response, the PIO generates a low on its RDY (ready) output to indicate to the peripheral device that its input register is full, and that no further data can be accepted at present.
(d) Once the microprocessor reads the contents of the PIO input register, the RDY output becomes high again to indicate that more data can be accepted, and (a) to (d) may be repeated.

2 ***MPU to peripheral:***

(a) The microprocessor transfers new data to the PIO output register and sets RDY high to indicate this fact to the peripheral.
(b) When the peripheral is ready to accept more data, it reads the peripheral bus.
(c) The peripheral pulls the PIO $\overline{\text{STB}}$ input low to indicate that it has accepted the data.
(d) Once the microprocessor detects a low level on the PIO $\overline{\text{STB}}$ input, it transfers more data to the PIO output register, and (a) to (d) may be repeated.

Interrupts

Interrupts are hardware initiated. Each peripheral device is connected to an interrupt request pin ($\overline{\text{INT}}$ or $\overline{\text{IRQ}}$) on the microprocessor, and indicates that it is ready for transfer of data by changing the logic state of this input. This action causes a break in the main program, followed by execution of an interrupt service routine (ISR) which effects the actual data transfer. After completion of the ISR, a return to the main program occurs which then continues as though it had never been interrupted. Thus synchronization of data transfers is accomplished by ensuring that no data can be transferred until an interrupt request is received and acknowledged by the microprocessor, and that further interrupts are ignored until completion of each ISR. This process is illustrated in Figure 4.4.

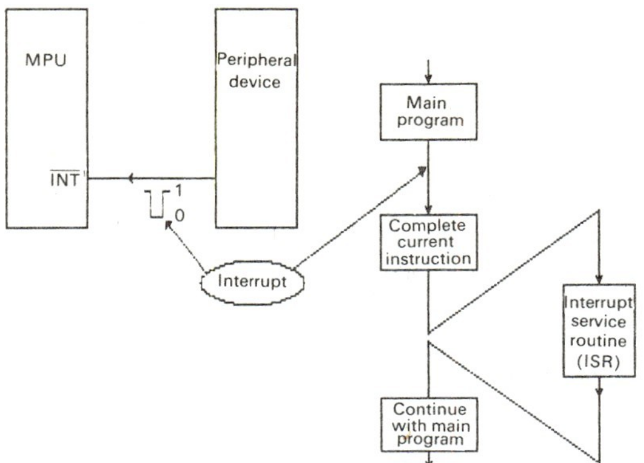

Figure 4.4

Buffer memory

A buffer memory may be used in conjunction with slow peripheral devices when other methods may slow down the operation of a microprocessor, e.g. when transferring data between a microcomputer and a printer. In such cases, data is transferred into the buffer memory at a rate determined by the microprocessor, and is transferred out of the memory at a rate determined by the peripheral. The buffer memory fills and empties to compensate for differences between the two transfer rates. The size of the buffer memory and the difference in transfer rates determine the capabilities of such an arrangement, and it is usual to employ some form of handshake line to avoid loss of data if the buffer becomes full (see Figure 4.5).

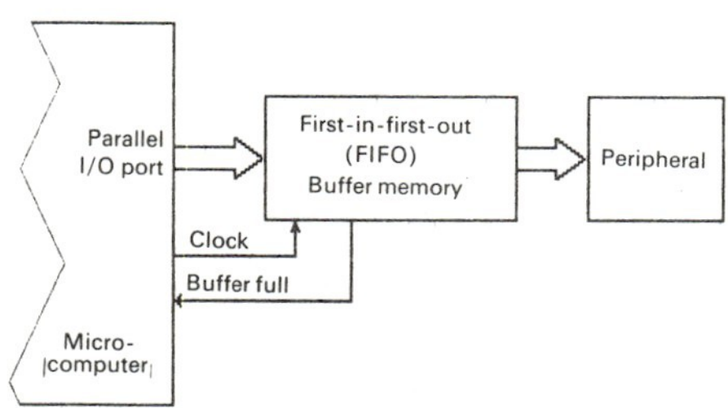

Figure 4.5

Direct memory access

Certain peripheral devices, e.g. hard disk drives, transfer data at a rate far higher than that which can be accepted by a microprocessor. For example, if a microprocessor reads data in from a port using LOAD or IN instructions, then even simple transfer programs would restrict the data transfer rate, as shown by the following program modules:

6502

```
                          Cycles
      LDX    #$FF           2
TRANS LDA    BUFF,X         4        Total = 2+255*(4+4+2+3)+(4+4+2+2)+6
      STA    PORT           4              = 3335 clock cycles
      DEX                   2              = 3,335 ms (1 MHz clock)
      BPL    TRANS        3/2                --------
      RTS                   6
```

Z80

```
                        'T' States
      LD     C,PORT         7
      LD     B,0            7       Total = 7+7+10+255*21+16+10
      LD     HL,BUFF       10             = 5405 T states
      OTIR              21/16             = 2,7025 ms (2 MHz clock)
      RET                  10               ---------
```

6800

```
                        Cycles
      LDX    #$100          3
TRANS LDAA   BUFF,X         5       Total = 3+256*(5+5+4+4)+5
      STAA   PORT           5             = 4616 clock cycles
      DEX                   4             = 4,616 ms (1 MHz clock)
      BNE    TRANS          4               --------
      RTS                   5
```

Direct memory access (DMA) may be used to allow much higher transfer rates. When DMA is used, the microprocessor is put into a 'hold' state, is isolated from its address and data buses, and a DMA control circuit (DMA controller) takes over the buses for the duration of the transfer. The DMA controller generates all necessary address and control signals, and transfers data directly to memory via the system data bus. DMA transfers may involve single bytes of data using *cycle stealing* techniques which involve identifying those cycles when the buses are unused by the microprocessor. Where the transfer of large amounts of data is involved, however, *burst* transfers are more likely to be employed in which operation of the microprocessor is suspended while a block of data is transferred (see Figure 4.6).

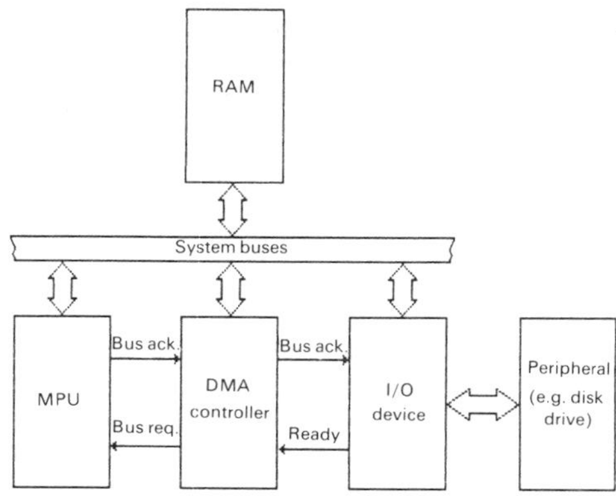

Figure 4.6

Electrical buffering

Most dedicated I/O devices are TTL compatible and their outputs are capable of driving one TTL load only. Basically this means that the outputs of these devices operate at the following voltage levels:

1 Logical 0: 0 V to +0.4 V.
2 Logical 1: 2.4 V to + 5 V.

The current *sourcing* capability is very low (tens of microamperes only), but the *sinking* capability is of the order of 1.6 mA. These figures indicate that few peripheral devices can be directly interfaced without the aid of some form of electrical buffering. For most circuits, this generally consists of some form of current amplification with perhaps changes in voltage levels and may be achieved by a variety of different means. Typical examples are as follows:

1 Bipolar transistor

The circuit for interfacing a resistive load to a PIO output line is shown in Figure 4.7.

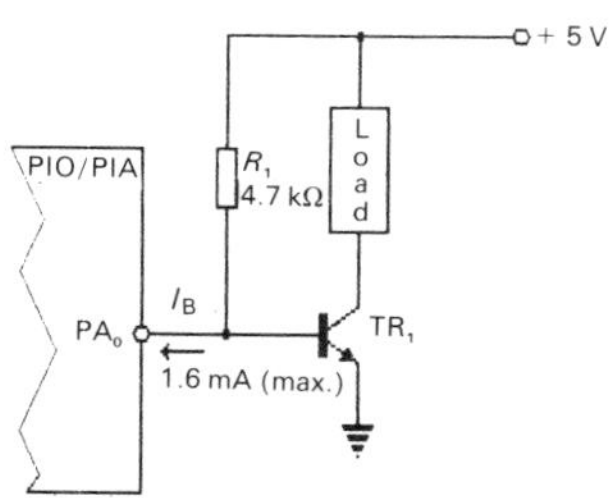

Figure 4.7

A simple transistor switching circuit is used to supply the 100 mA demanded by the load. When the PIO output is at logical 0, all of the current through R_1 flows into the PIO, and this must be kept below 1.6 mA, therefore the base current I_B cannot exceed this value.

In this application, using a transistor with a minimum h_{FE} of 100 and a load current of 100 mA, requires a minimum base current of 1 mA. This is within the limit specified, therefore:

$$R_1 = \frac{5\,\text{V}}{1\,\text{mA}} = 5\,\text{k}\Omega$$

In practice a preferred value of 4.7 kΩ could be used which would ensure that TR_1 saturates without exceeding the maximum allowable figure of 1.6 mA.

2 TTL logic inverter

For relatively low current loads a TTL inverter may be employed as an interface circuit. Typically an ordinary TTL output can drive up to 10 unit loads (10 × 1.6 mA), or 30 unit loads for 'open-collector' devices. This is sufficient current for interfacing light-emitting diodes (LEDs) to an output port. A typical circuit is shown in Figure 4.8(a).

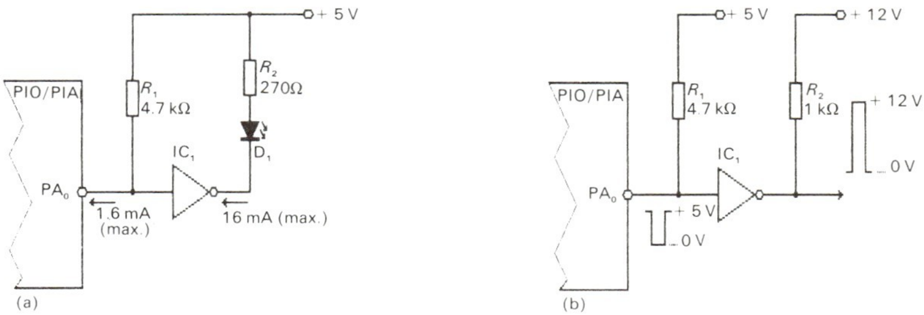

Figure 4.8

In this circuit, the LED is illuminated by a logical 1 at the port output. This causes a logical 0 at the output of the inverter which sinks current through the LED from the + 5 V supply. R_1 limits the current through the LED to a safe value (approximately 10 mA). Open-collector devices have the advantage that supplies up to 30 V may be used for the load, thus enabling changes in voltage level to be achieved, as shown in Figure 4.8(b).

3 Darlington driver

It was stated in example 1 that the maximum base current that could be used when driving a bipolar transistor from an output port was 1.6 mA. When relatively large load currents, e.g. 0.5 to 1 A are required, then much higher transistor gains are required to compensate for the limited base current. Typically an h_{FE} in excess of 1000 is required, and this is normally obtainable only by using a *Darlington* configuration (Darlington pair), as shown in Figure 4.9.

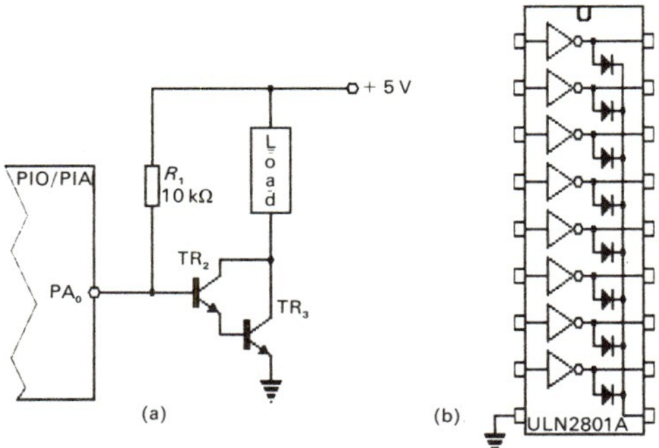

Figure 4.9

IC packages which contain up to eight Darlington driver stages are available, as shown in Figure 4.9(b).

4 VMOS FET driver stage

An alternative to using Darlington drivers, VMOS FETs are capable of switching currents of up to 2 A. These are voltage controlled devices with an extremely high input impedance and therefore connection to an output port is a relatively simple matter, as shown in Figure 4.10.

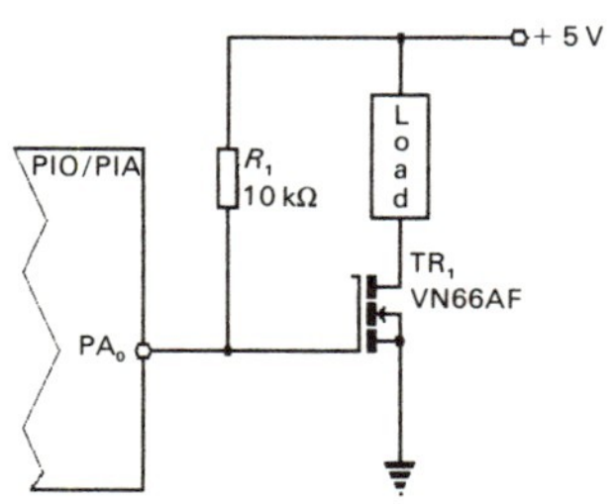

Figure 4.10

5 Inductive loads

The load interfaced to a microcomputer output port may be of an inductive nature, e.g. solenoids, relay coils, and this introduces the additional problem of high potential 'back'-emfs being generated when current is switched. This problem must not be ignored, otherwise damage will occur to semiconductor devices used in the interface circuit. A common method of dealing with this problem is to connect a diode across the device so that energy stored in the inductor may be safely dissipated (see Figure 4.11). In certain IC devices, e.g. Darlington drivers, a diode is often included for protection purposes.

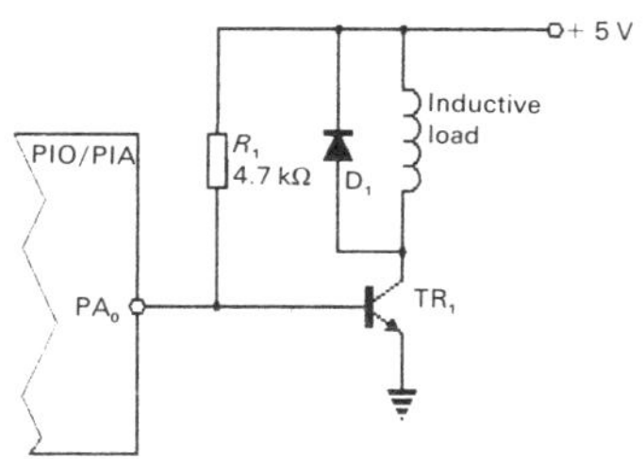

Figure 4.11

6 Switch debouncing

When a mechanical switch is operated its contacts do not make cleanly, but bounce for a period of 10–20 ms before finally coming to rest. A microcomputer operates at such high speed relative to this time period that it interprets switch bounce as a succession of individual switch closures. A method of preventing a microcomputer from responding to switch bounce is therefore necessary, and this is known as *switch debouncing*. There are two ways of dealing with this problem:

(a) Hardware switch debouncing in which an *R*-S bistable is employed as shown in Figure 4.12(a).

When S_1 is operated so that it moves to position A, the *R*-S flip-flop output falls to logical 0 and cannot return to logical 1 until S_1 is once again moved to position B. Moving S_1 to position A causes it to bounce several times against this contact, but with insufficient movement to contact B again. The reverse situation applies when S_1 moves from A back to B and the flip-flop output changes to logical 1. Therefore the output changes cleanly from one logic state to the other, as shown in Figure 4.12(a).

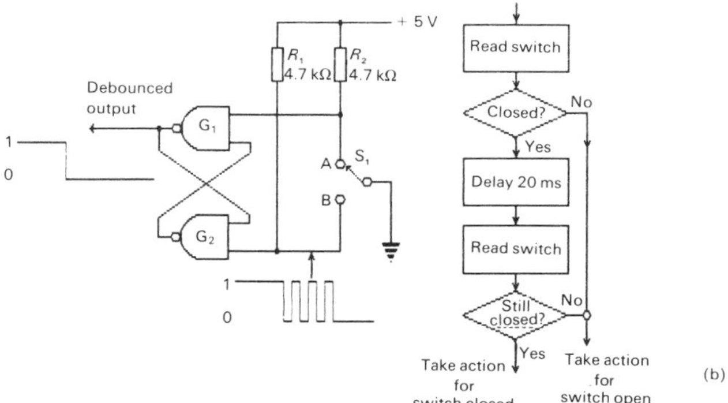

Figure 4.12

(b) Software switch debouncing, as shown in Figure 4.12(b). When switch closure is detected by the software, a time delay of approximately 20 ms is introduced to allow time for the switch contacts to settle, i.e., bouncing to cease. The switch is then read again, and the steady state value is passed on to the microcomputer.

Serial/parallel and parallel/serial conversion

Within a microcomputer system, data is often manipulated eight bits at a time. It may therefore be considered logical to transfer data from a microcomputer to its peripheral devices (or even another microcomputer) in a similar manner. Such a method requires eight data paths between source and destination, and is called *parallel data transfer*.

It is not always possible, or may present practical difficulties to provide enough data paths for parallel data transfers. For example, data transfers over long distances may require use of the public telephone system and could create problems if eight simultaneous data paths were required. In such circumstances, data may be transferred along a single data path, one bit after another, and this is called *serial data transfer*. Inevitably this is a slower method of data transfer.

The differences between parallel and serial data transfers are shown in Figure 4.13.

It is necessary to convert parallel data into serial form for transmission along the data path, and upon reception at the receiving end, it is necessary to convert the incoming serial data back into parallel form. In order to implement such a system, parallel to serial and serial to parallel code conversion facilities are required. This topic is covered in greater detail in Chapter 6.

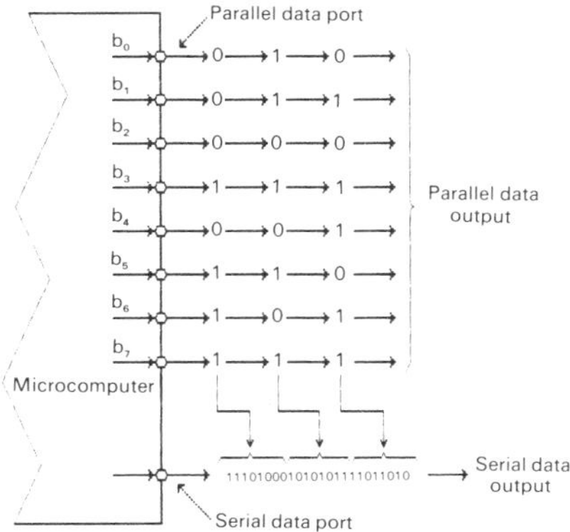

Figure 4.13

Multiplexing

The number of I/O lines available on a microcomputer is limited, often confined to two 8-bit ports. Sometimes this is insufficient and it becomes necessary to operate a system such that two or more peripherals share the same I/O lines. This is really no different to several different devices all sharing a common data bus within the microcomputer, and is a technique known as 'multiplexing'. Obviously it is not possible for two peripheral devices to simultaneously use an I/O line, therefore each is allocated a particular time slot, i.e., *time division multiplexing.*

A simple multiplexed system is shown in Figure 4.14.

This arrangement has the advantage that for a fixed number of port I/O lines, the number of actual peripheral lines available is almost double that available without the use of multiplexing. The reason why exactly twice as

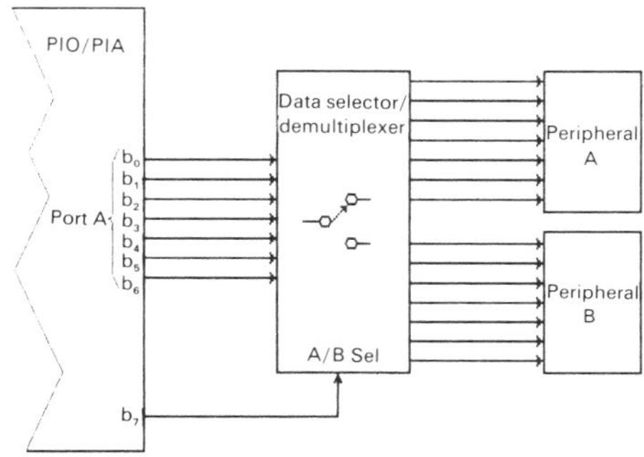

Figure 4.14

many peripheral I/O lines are not available lies in the fact that one line must be used to act as a peripheral select signal. When using this circuit, peripheral A is selected if the MSB of the data byte sent to the I/O port is at logical 0, otherwise it is sent to peripheral B. The main disadvantage of this system is that the maximum rate at which data may be transferred is halved due to the time sharing arrangement.

Multiplexed displays

One common application for multiplexing in a microprocessor based system is that of display multiplexing. Often four seven-segment devices are used on a display panel, and since each device needs eight control signals (nine if the 'point' is included), without multiplexing a total of thirty-two I/O lines would be required. Typical circuits for display multiplexing are shown in Figure 4.15(a) and (b).

The circuit shown in Figure 4.15(a) allows the user to control all segments independently, thus enabling the creation of a limited number of alphabetic as well as all numeric characters. Signals generated on b_0–b_3 of port B switch on each display, in turn for a duration of 0.5 to 1 ms. Simultaneously, the segment codes required for each selected device are sent to port A. Thus the devices display the required characters one after another in time sequence, but if the process is repeated rapidly, to the human eye all characters appear as though displayed simultaneously.

Where a single 8-bit port must be used for such a display, further savings may be made by using a hardware decoder for the displays (see Figure 4.15(b)). This does have the disadvantage that characters displayed are limited to those provided by the decoder.

Multiplexed inputs

A microprocessor system may be required to monitor and store the signals obtained from a number of different sensors. Such an application is known as a *data acquisition system*, or *data logger* and it may be implemented as shown in Figure 4.16.

Up to eight sensors may be connected to the system, and each sensor requires signal processing and analogue to digital converter stages. A digital multiplexer is used, and output signals from port B are applied to its A, B and C inputs to select the required signal source. The converted data may then be read in via port A and stored in memory. The software is generally organized so that the sensors are scanned in sequence and all received data is stored for further digital processing.

One disadvantage of the system depicted in Figure 4.16 concerns the large

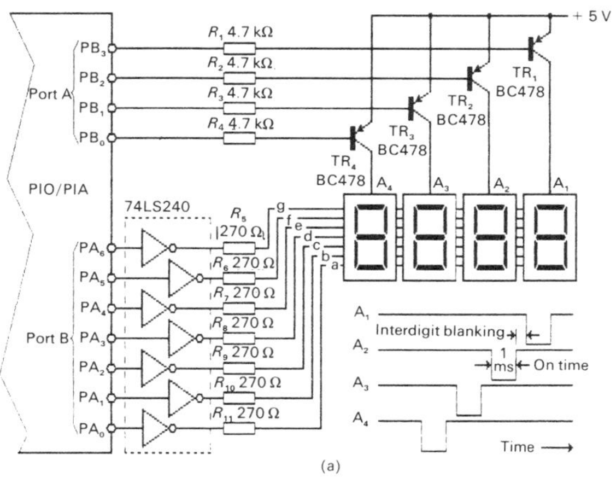

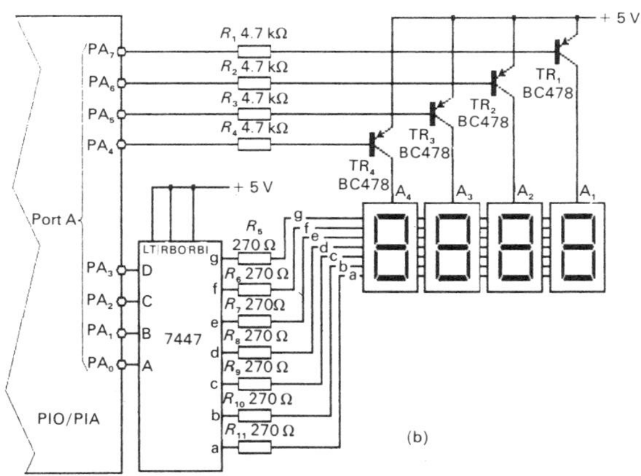

Figure 4.15

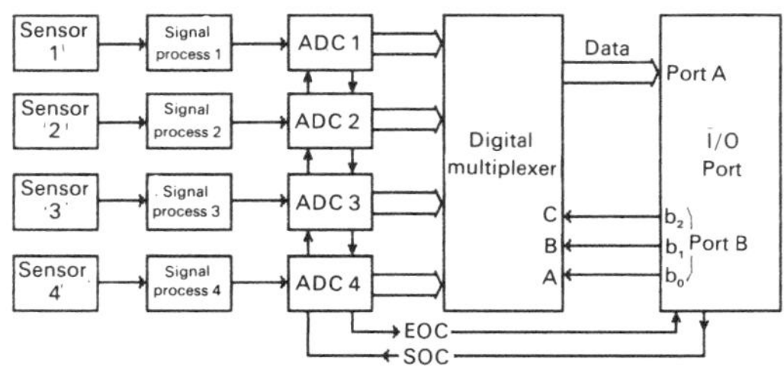

Figure 4.16

number of ADC circuits required. An alternative approach makes use of an analogue multiplexer as shown in Figure 4.17(a).

In this case, multiplexing takes place prior to signals being converted into digital form and therefore requires only one ADC circuit. Each sensor requires only a signal conditioning stage so that all input signals are compatible with the analogue multiplexer inputs. ADC circuits are available which contain an analogue multiplexer and are known as *data acquisition* chips (see Figure 4.17(b) and (c)).

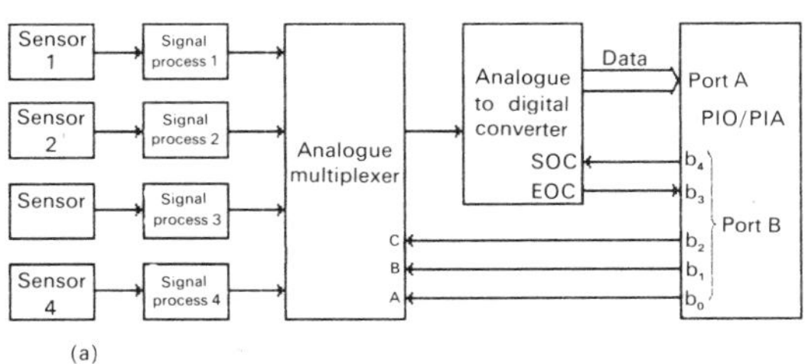

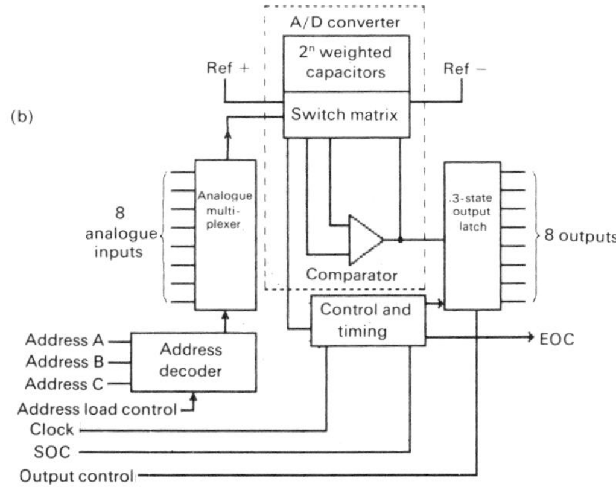

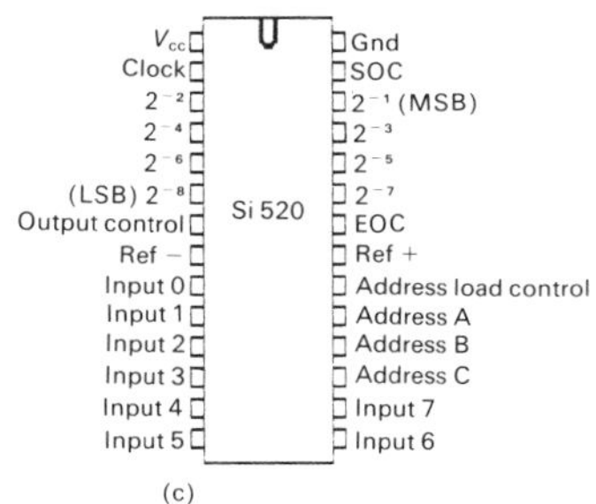

Figure 4.17

Standard buses

The construction of a microprocessor based system usually involves interconnecting various systems or subsystems. A major problem which may be encountered concerns the multiplicity of different connectors, control signals, operating speeds and logic levels which make each interconnection a somewhat tedious process. This problem may be simplified if standards can be specified for buses to which all manufacturers adhere. A bus standard therefore specifies the type of connector to be used, and defines the signals available and their position on the connector. Systems and subsystems constructed for a given bus standard may be freely interconnected. This is of course an ideal situation, and in reality several different bus standards have evolved, both for use within a microcomputer and for connection of peripherals to a microcomputer. Parallel buses only are considered in this chapter, since bit-serial buses are dealt with in Chapter 6. Typical parallel buses are:

1 STD microcomputer bus.
2 IEEE-488 system bus.

STD (standard) bus

Originally conceived by Mostek and Pro-log, this bus was designed to provide a cost-effective modular approach for 8-bit controller types of system. The STD bus was designed to be totally independent of system components, therefore implementations may be found based around a range of different MPUs such as the 8085, Z80, 6502, 6800 and even 16-bit MPUs which use an 8-bit data bus structure such as the 8088. The STD bus consists of 56 conductors which are grouped as follows:

1 6 power lines
2 8 bi-directional data lines
3 16 address lines
4 22 control lines
5 4 auxiliary power lines

A 56-way connector (two rows of 28) is specified on which the lines are logically grouped as shown in Table 4.1.

All STD cards have standard dimensions of 6.5 in × 4.5 in and use a dual 28-pin edge connector, which may be plugged into any slot of an STD 'motherboard'. Thus the construction of a system may be achieved by simply selecting appropriate STD boards from the wide range available and interconnecting via this standard bus.

Table 4.1

	Component side			Circuit side		
	Pin	*Mnemonic*	*Description*	*Pin*	*Mnemonic*	*Description*
Logic power bus	1	+ 5 V	+ 5 V DC	2	+ 5 V	+ 5 V DC
	3	GND	Signal ground	4	GND	Signal ground
	5	– 5 V	– 5 V DC	6	– 5 V	– 5 V DC
Data bus	7	D3	Data bus low	8	D7	Data bus high
	9	D2	Data bus low	10	D6	Data bus high
	11	D1	Data bus low	12	D5	Data bus high
	13	D0	Data bus low	14	D4	Data bus high
Address bus	15	A7	Address bus low	16	A15	Address bus high
	17	A6	Address bus low	18	A14	Address bus high
	19	A5	Address bus low	20	A13	Address bus high
	21	A4	Address bus low	22	A12	Address bus high
	23	A3	Address bus low	24	A11	Address bus high
	25	A2	Address bus low	26	A10	Address bus high
	27	A1	Address bus low	28	A9	Address bus high
	29	A0	Address bus low	30	A8	Address bus high
Control bus	31	WR	Memory or I/O write	32	RD	Memory or I/O read
	33	IORQ	I/O address sel.	34	MEMRQ	Memory address sel.
	35	IOEXP	I/O expansion	36	MEMEX	Memory expanson
	37	REFRESH	Refresh timing	38	MCSYNC	CPU M cycle sync.
	39	STATUS 1	CPU status	40	STATUS 0	CPU status
	41	BUSAK	Bus acknowledge	42	BUSRQ	Bus request
	43	INTAK	Interrupt acknowledge	44	INTRQ	Interrupt request
	45	WAITRQ	Wait request	46	NMIRQ	Non-maskable interrupt
	47	SYSRESET	System reset	48	PBRESET	Push-button reset
	49	CLOCK	Clock from CPU	50	CNTRL	Auxiliary timing
	51	PCO	Priority chain out	52	PCI	Priority chain in
Power bus	53	AUX GND	Auxiliary ground	54	AUX GND	Auxiliary ground
	55	AUX + V	Auxiliary positive (+ 12 V)	56	AUX – V	Auxiliary negative (– 12 V)

IEEE-488 bus

The IEEE-488 bus (also known as GPIB – general purpose interface bus) is a parallel bus which was first defined by the American Institute of Electrical and Electronic Engineers (IEEE) in 1975, primarily for connecting measuring instruments to a microcomputer.

Using an IEEE-488 bus, up to fifteen devices may be interconnected, with communication taking place at speeds of up to 1 Mbit/s over a maximum distance of 20 metres. The actual bus consists of twenty-four lines of which sixteen are TTL compatible signal lines and eight are ground return lines. Eight of the signal lines are bidirectional data transfer lines, three are handshake lines and the remaining five are for general control purposes. Each of the fifteen devices falls into at least one of the following catagories:

1 *Talker:* This is a device which puts data on to the bus, for example, a measuring instrument putting its reading out on to the bus is classified as a 'talker'.
2 *Listener:* This is a device which accepts data from the bus, for example a measuring instrument accepting setting up instructions from the bus is referred to as a 'listener'.
3 *Controller:* This is a device that controls communication activity on the bus.

A given device may behave as a combination of these categories. For example, a measuring instrument may behave as a 'listener' so that it can accept setting up instructions such as range setting, and also act as a 'talker' so that it can transfer its reading on to the bus. A typical bus structure is shown in Figure 4.18.

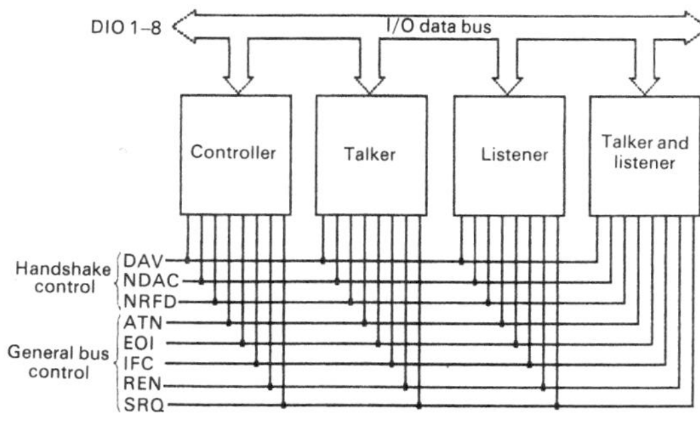

Figure 4.18

IEEE-488 control lines

The following five active low control lines are used to manage the bus:

1 *IFC* (interface clear) which resets all devices to a known state and may therefore be used as a general reset line.

2 *ATN* (attention) which alerts all devices on the bus that the data lines DIO 1–8 contain a 7-bit command or 7-bit address. This initiates a transfer of data to or from the addressed device.
3 *SRQ* (service request) which enables any device to signal the controller that it needs attention.
4 *REN* (remote enable) which selects remote control operation of any device. Devices may be operated locally from the front panel until 'locked out' by this line.
5 *EOI* (end or identify) which is used to either signify the end of a message sequence from a 'talker' device, or if made active (after SRQ) by a controller, requests that the device identify itself by transferring its own discrete address on to the bus (each device is assigned a unique address, normally selected by a set of small switches at the rear of the device).

IEEE-488 handshake lines

The following three handshake lines are available for controlling the transfer of data:

1 *DAV* (data valid) which is set low by a 'talker' to indicate that the information that it has transferred to the bus is valid and ready for reading.
2 *NRFD* (not ready for data) which is connected to each 'listener' and is held low by any device which is not yet ready for data transfer.
3 *NDAC* (not data accepted) which is used by 'listeners' to indicate that a data byte has been accepted and may be removed from the bus.

The timing of data transfers is shown in Figure 4.19.

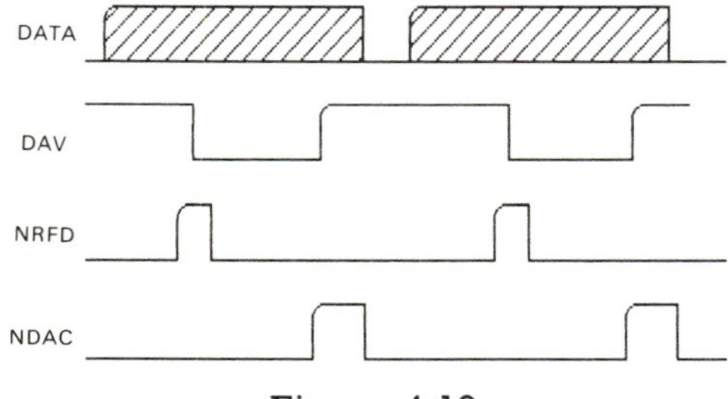

Figure 4.19

The typical handshake sequence between a 'talker (and a number of 'listening' devices consists of the following steps:

1 The 'talker' indicates that DIO 1–8 carries valid data by pulling DAV low.
2 The fastest 'listener' pulls NRFD low to indicate that it is busy, and data transfer continues until the slowest 'listener' signals that it has accepted the data by setting NDAC high.

3 The 'talker' responds to NDAC by removing the data from the bus and setting DAV high again.
4 The 'listeners' respond to this by resetting NDAC, thus indicating that they are ready for the transfer of a further byte of data.

Electrical isolation

Microprocessor based systems are often interfaced to mains operated equipment or other high voltage systems. Direct connection between a microcomputer and equipment of this nature is to be avoided for two reasons:

1 *Equipment damage:* microcomputer components are designed to operate at low DC potentials and would therefore be damaged by the application of high potentials, particularly where the common lines for the signal are at different potentials.
2 *Operator safety:* due to fault conditions or other reasons, an operator could come into contact with mains or other high potentials with possibly lethal results.

For these reasons it is essential to electrically isolate a microcomputer from its peripherals with devices which typically provide 2–3000 V isolation. One commonly used isolating device is the *opto-isolator* or *photocoupler*.

Opto-isolator

An opto-isolator operates on the principle of coupling wanted signals by means of a beam of light (often infra-red). Since light is not a conductor of electricity, this provides suitable isolation between input and output. Although is it possible to construct an opto-isolator from discrete components, normally IC packages are used which contain an LED and a photosensitive device placed in close proximity to one another, as shown in Figure 4.20.

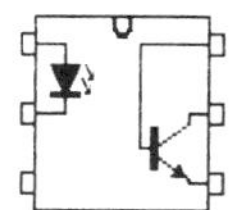

Figure 4.20

An input signal source controls the magnitude of current flowing through the LED, and hence controls its light output (just on or off in digital systems). A phototransistor acts as a light sensor such that its conduction increases as the level of light intensity falling upon it increases.

Operating conditions

Full operating conditions may be established by referring to manufacturers' data sheets, but the design of a simple opto-isolator interface circuit may be studied by referring to the circuit and data shown in Figure 4.21.

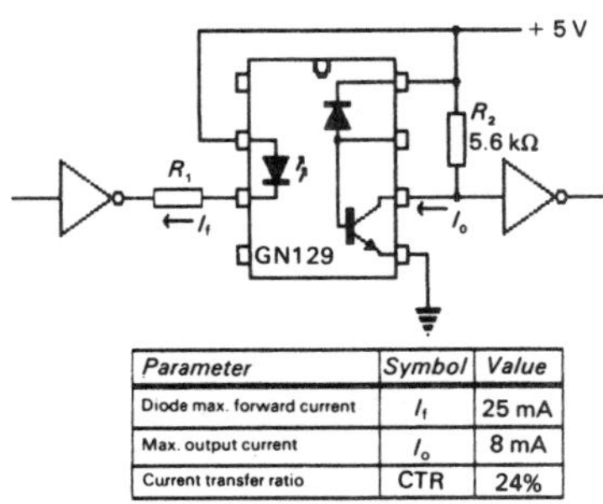

Parameter	Symbol	Value
Diode max. forward current	I_f	25 mA
Max. output current	I_o	8 mA
Current transfer ratio	CTR	24%

Figure 4.21

Collector current (I_o):

$$\begin{aligned} \text{TTL load current} &= 1.6\,\text{mA (1 UL)} \\ \text{Pull-up load current} &= 5\,\text{V}/5.6\,\text{k}\Omega \\ &= 0.89\ \text{mA} \\ \text{Therefore } I_o &= (1.6 + 0.89)\ \text{mA} \\ &= \mathbf{2.49\ mA}\ \text{(8 mA maximum)} \end{aligned}$$

Diode forward current (I_f):

$$\begin{aligned} \text{Current transfer ratio, CTR} &= 24\% \\ I_F &= 2.49/0.24 \\ &= \mathbf{10.375\ mA}\ \text{(25 mA maximum)} \end{aligned}$$

Value of R_1:

$$\begin{aligned} R_1 &= 5\ \text{V}/10.46\ \text{mA} \\ &= \mathbf{482\ \Omega}\ (470\ \Omega) \end{aligned}$$

Opto-isolator applications

A typical application for opto-isolators is in interfacing a microcomputer to its peripherals as shown in Figure 4.22.

Opto-isolators are also available with built-in Schmitt triggers for pulse shaping, Darlington pairs for high gain, and optically isolated triacs and SCRs to form solid state relays for control of mains equipment. Examples of these devices are shown in Figure 4.23(a) to (c).

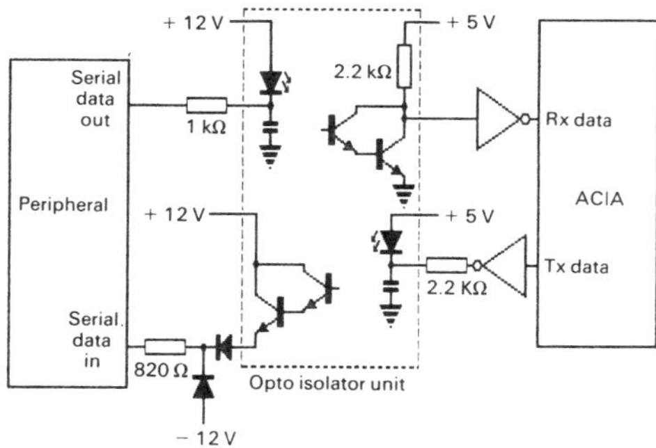

Figure 4.22

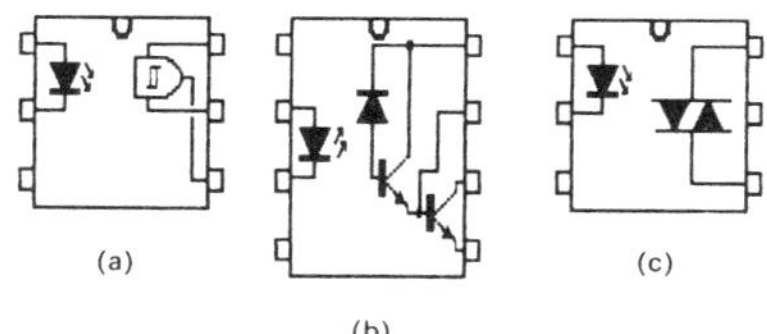

Figure 4.23

Problems

1 (a) Explain why peripheral devices cannot usually be connected directly to the I/O lines of a microcomputer.
  (b) List the main factors which must be considered when interfacing a peripheral device to the PIA/PIO of a microcomputer.

2 (a) Explain why the timing of data transfers between a microcomputer and its peripheral devices is important.
  (b) Describe two methods used to synchronize data transfers between a microcomputer and its peripherals.

3 Explain why interrupts may be preferred to polling techniques as a means of controlling data transfers.

4 (a) Explain the meaning of the term 'handshaking'.
  (b) With the aid of a diagram, show how handshaking may be implemented between a microcomputer and its peripheral and describe the sequence of events which occur.

5 (a) With the aid of a diagram, explain how data transfers between a microcomputer and its peripheral devices take place when using DMA (direct memory access) techniques.

(b) Explain why it is necessary to use DMA for data transfers between a hard disk drive and a microcomputer.

6 (a) Explain why electrical buffering may be required between the I/O port of a microcomputer and a peripheral device.
(b) Draw a diagram to show the interfacing circuit required when interfacing a 12 V relay to the I/O port of a microcomputer.

7 (a) Explain the difference between parallel and serial data transfers.
(b) State one advantage and one disadvantage of using serial data.

8 (a) State why multiplexing techniques may be required when connecting peripherals to a microcomputer.
(b) With the aid of a diagram, show how multiplexing techniques may be used to connect two 6-bit peripheral devices to an 8-bit I/O port.
(c) Explain how software may be used to control the interface shown in (b) so that the correct data may be transferred to each peripheral.

9 State the advantages of using standard buses:
(a) Within a microcomputer.
(b) For peripheral devices.

10 (a) Describe the principle of operation of an 'opto-isolator' device.
(b) With the aid of a diagram, show how a 240 V 1 kW load may be interfaced to the I/O port of a microcomputer.

Chapter 5

Parallel I/O controllers

Need for I/O controllers

It is possible to construct peripheral controller circuits from ordinary TTL devices, and for very simple interfacing problems this may be the preferred solution. Many peripheral devices are, however, very complex in nature, e.g. disk drives, printers or VDUs, and therefore require correspondingly complex controller circuits.

In such cases it is advantageous to use dedicated very large scale integration (VLSI) controller devices which are often included in the *family* of devices associated with a particular MPU. The advantages of using such devices are as follows:

1 They may be directly connected to the address, data and control buses of the MPU concerned without the need for additional logic circuits.
2 They offer sophisticated operation which would not be practical to implement with discrete TTL circuits.
3 Software control is often provided for selecting modes of operation.
4 Sophisticated handshake facilities may be provided.

This chapter considers both discrete TTL and dedicated solutions to the problem of controlling peripherals.

Simple parallel I/O ports

Simple TTL input port

An input port may be constructed by using a tristate buffer device plus associated decoder and control circuits as shown in Figure 5.1(a) and (b).

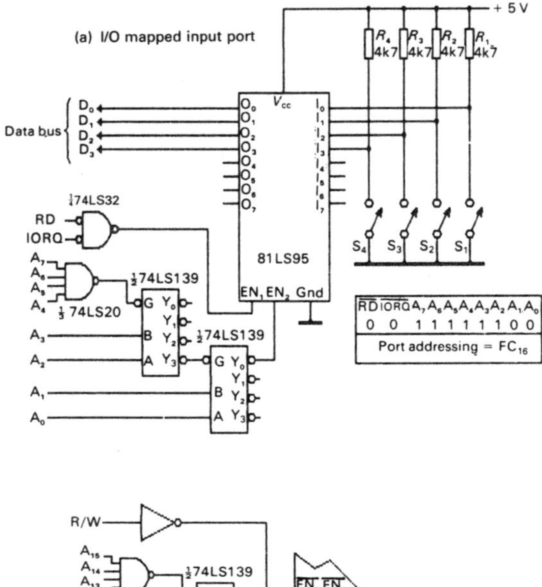

$\overline{RD}$	$\overline{IORQ}$	A_7	A_6	A_5	A_4	A_3	A_2	A_1	A_0
0	0	1	1	1	1	1	1	0	0

Port addressing = FC_{16}

(a) I/O mapped input port

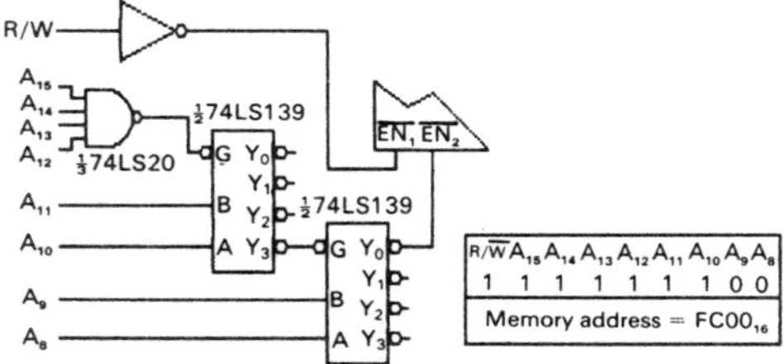

R/$\overline{W}$	A_{15}	A_{14}	A_{13}	A_{12}	A_{11}	A_{10}	A_9	A_8
1	1	1	1	1	1	1	0	0

Memory address = $FC00_{16}$

(b) Memory mapped input port

Figure 5.1

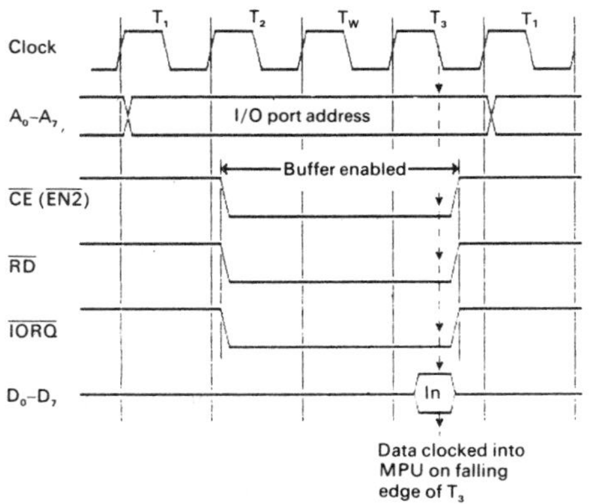

Figure 5.2

An 81LS95 tristate buffer device may be used to transfer switch data on to a microcomputer data bus during a memory read cycle (or Z80 input cycle). The address decoder output and inverted R/$\overline{\text{W}}$ signal (or Z80 $\overline{\text{RD}}$ signal) are used as enabling inputs to the tristate buffer. Only when both inputs are at logical 0 will the buffer be enabled. Resistors R_1 to R_4 are used as pull-ups to ensure that the buffer inputs are maintained at logical 1 when the switches are in the open condition. When the switches are closed, a logical 0 is applied to each input of the buffer. The data from these switches is applied directly to the data bus each time that the buffer is enabled, as shown in Figure 5.2.

A block of data may be read in from the input port shown in Figure 5.1 by means of the following programs. Note that without any form of handshake it is necessary to use bit 7 as a strobe input (active high) which must be polled by each of the routines.

(a) 6502

```
                          ;*********************************
                          ; 6502 subroutine to read in an
                          ; ASCII data block from 81LS95
                          ; input port, using b7 as a
                          ; 'data ready' strobe
                          ;*********************************
                          ;
0000            PORT   =        $FC00          ;input port addr
0000            SIZE   =        256            ;size of data block
                          ;
0200                   *=       $0200
                          ;
                          ;initialise registers for data transfer
                          ;
0200 A0 00             LDY      #SIZE          ;Y=data byte counter
0202 A2 00             LDX      #0             ;buffer index = 0
                          ;
                          ;perform data transfer from input port
                          ;
0204 2C 00 FC STBL     BIT      PORT           ;test b7 of input port
0207 10 FB             BPL      STBL           ;wait for active strobe
0209 2C 00 FC STBH     BIT      PORT           ;look for end of strobe
020C 30 FB             BMI      STBH           ;pulse
020E AD 00 FC          LDA      PORT           ;read input port
0211 9D 19 02          STA      BUFF,X         ;store data in buff
0214 E8                INX                     ;move buff pointer
0215 88                DEY                     ;decrement counter and
0216 D0 EC             BNE      STBL           ;check for end of block
0218 60                RTS
                          ;
0219            BUFF  * =       *+256          ;space for buffer
```

(b) Z80

```
                          ;*********************************
                          ; Z80 subroutine to read in an
                          ; ASCII data block from 81LS95
                          ; input port, using b7 as a
                          ; 'data ready' strobe
                          ;*********************************
                          ;
00FC =        PORT        EQU     0FCH           ;input port addr
0100 =        SIZE        EQU     256            ;size of data block
                          ;
0100                      ORG     0100H
                          ;
                          ;initialise registers for data transfer
                          ;
0100 0E00                 LD      C,SIZE         ;C=data byte counter
0102 211701               LD      HL,BUFF        ;buffer pointer
                          ;
                          ;perform data transfer from input port
                          ;
0105 DBFC     STBL:       IN      A,(PORT)       ;read input port
0107 CB7F                 BIT     7,A            ;check for data
0109 28FA                 JR      Z,STBL         ;strobe low
010B DBFC     STBH:       IN      A,(PORT)       ;wait until
010D CB7F                 BIT     7,A            ;end of strobe
010F 20FA                 JR      NZ,STBH        ;pulse
0111 77                   LD      (HL),A         ;store data in buff
0112 23                   INC     HL             ;move buff pointer
0113 0D                   DEC     C              ;decrement counter and
0114 20EF                 JR      NZ,STBL        ;check for end of block
0116 C9                   RET
                          ;
0117          BUFF:       DEFS    256            ;space for buffer
```

(c) 6800

```
                        ;********************************
                        ; 6800 subroutine to read in an
                        ; ASCII data block from 81LS95
                        ; input port, using b7 as a
                        ; 'data ready' strobe
                        ;********************************
                        ;
0000            PORT    EQU     $FC00           ;input port addr
0000            SIZE    EQU     256             ;size of data block
                        ;
0200                    ORG     $0200
                        ;
                        ;initialise registers for data transfer
                        ;
0200 C6 00              LDAB    #SIZE           ;Y=data byte counter
0202 CE 02 19           LDX     #BUFF              ;buffer index = 0
                        ;
                        ;perform data transfer from input port
                        ;
0205 7D 00 FC STBL      TST     PORT            ;test b7 of input port
0208 2A FB              BPL     STBL            ;wait for active strobe
020A 7D 00 FC STBH      TST     PORT            ;look for end of strobe
020D 2B FB              BMI     STBH            ;pulse
020F B6 00 FC           LDAA    PORT            ;read input port
0212 A7 00              STAA    0,X             ;store data in buff
0214 08                 INX                     ;move buff pointer
0215 5A                 DECB                    ;decrement counter and
0216 26 ED              BNE     STBL            ;check for end of block
0218 39                 RTS
                        ;
0219                    RMB     256             ;space for buffer
```

Simple TTL output port

An output port may be constructed by using data latches plus associated decoder and control circuits as shown in Figure 5.3(a) and (b).

A 7475 quadruple TTL latch may be used to capture information from a microcomputer data bus during a memory write cycle (or Z80 output cycle). The address decoder output is gated with the R/$\overline{W}$ signal (or Z80 $\overline{WR}$ signal), and is used to generate a positive pulse which clocks data into the 7475

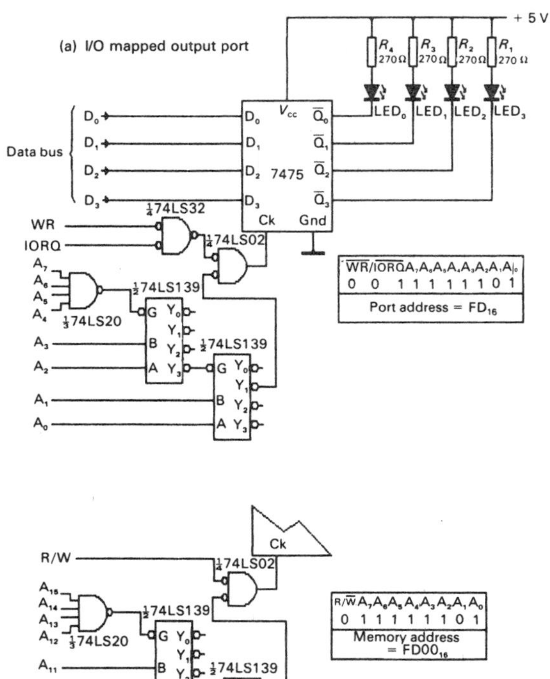

Figure 5.3

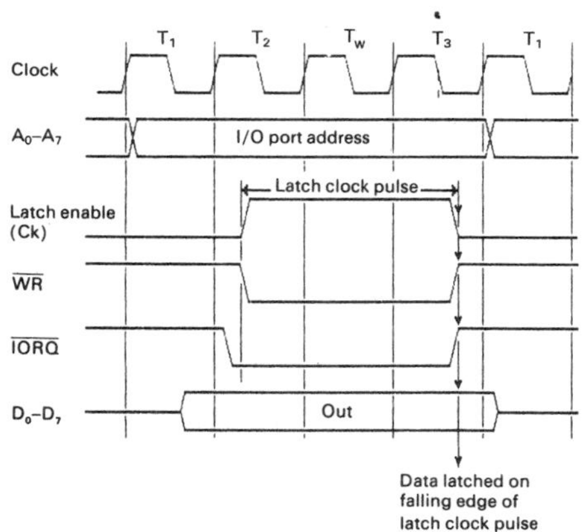

Figure 5.4

latches from the data bus. Data is latched in the 7475 on the falling edge of the pulse, as shown in Figure 5.4.

Each TTL output (16 mA maximum) of the 7475 is capable of sinking the current for one LED, and the $\overline{Q}$ outputs are used in this particular application so that a logical 1 may be sent to the port to illuminate an LED.

A block of data may be transferred from memory to the output port shown in Figure 5.3 by means of the following programs. Note that without any form of handshake it is necessary to include a time delay in each of the output routines in order to slow down the transfer rate.

(a) 6502

```
                           ;*********************************
                           ; 6502 subroutine to write an ASCII
                           ; data block from memory to a 7475
                           ; outpu  port, using a time delay
                           ; to control transfer rate
                           ;*********************************
                           ;
0000            PORT       =       $FD00        ;output port addr
0000            SIZE       =       256          ;size of data block
0000            TDEL       =       256          ;time delay constant
                           ;
0200                      *=       $0200
                           ;
                           ;initialise registers for transfer
                           ;
0200 A0 00                 LDY     #SIZE        ;Y=data byte counter
0202 A2 00                 LDX     #0           ;buffer pointer
                           ;
                           ;perform data transfer
                           ;
0204 BD 21 02 TRANS        LDA     BUFF,X       ;get byte from buffer
0207 E8                    INX                  ;increment pointer
0208 8D 00 FD              STA     PORT         ;send byte to port
020B 20 12 02              JSR     DELAY        ;slow down transfer rate
020E 88                    DEY                  ;decrement counter and
020F D0 F3                 BNE     TRANS        ;check for end of block
0211 60                    RET
                           ;
                           ;time delay subroutine
                           ;
0212 A9 00      DELAY      LDA     #TDEL        ;control time delay
0214 85 00                 STA     COUNT1       ;initialise delay
0216 85 01                 STA     COUNT2       ;counters in page zero
```

```
0218 C6 01     DLY      DEC     COUNT2            ;inner loop
021A D0 FC              BNE     DLY               ;256,255,254 ....
021C C6 00              DEC     COUNT1            ;outer loop
021E D0 F8              BNE     DLY               ;256,255,254 ....
0220 60                 RTS
                        ;
0221           BUFF     * =     *+256             ;space for buffer
```

(b) Z80

```
                        ;*********************************
                        ; Subroutine to write an ASCII
                        ; data block from memory to a 7475
                        ; output port, using a time delay
                        ; to control transfer rate
                        ;*********************************
                        ;
00FD =          PORT    EQU     0FDH            ;output port addr
0100 =          SIZE    EQU     256             ;size of data block
0200 =          TDEL    EQU     512             ;time delay constant
                        ;
0100                    ORG     0100H
                        ;
                        ;initialise registers for transfer
                        ;
0100 0E00               LD      C,SIZE          ;C=data byte counter
0102 211E01             LD      HL,BUFF         ;buffer pointer
                        ;
                        ;perform data transfer
                        ;
0105 7E         TRANS:  LD      A,(HL)          ;get byte from buffer
0106 23                 INC     HL              ;increment pointer
0107 D3FD               OUT     (PORT),A        ;send byte to port
0109 CD1001             CALL    DELAY           ;slow down transfer rate
010C 0D                 DEC     C               ;decrement counter and
010D 20F6               JR      NZ,TRANS        ;check for end of block
010F C9                 RET
                        ;
                        ;time delay subroutine
                        ;
0110 110002     DELAY:  LD      DE,TDEL         ;control time delay
0113 0600               LD      B,0             ;B=inner loop count
0115 05         DLY:    DEC     B               ;0,255,254,253 .......
```

```
0116 20FD              JR     NZ,DLY          ;count down to zero
0118 1B                DEC    DE              ;512,511,510 .......
0119 7A                LD     A,D             ;set Z flag if DE=0
011A B3                OR     E               ;else keep on looping
011B 20F8              JR     NZ,DLY          ;
011D C9                RET
                       ;
011E           BUFF:   DEFS   256             ;space for buffer
```

(c) 6800

```
                      ;**********************************
                      ; 6800 subroutine to write an ASCII
                      ; data block from memory to a 7475
                      ; output port, using a time delay
                      ; to control transfer rate
                      ;**********************************
                      ;
0000          PORT    EQU    $FD00          ;output port addr
0000          SIZE    EQU    256            ;size of data block
0000          TDEL    EQU    256            ;time delay constant
                      ;
0200                  ORG    $0200
                      ;
                      ;initialise registers for transfer
                      ;
0200 C6 00            LDAB   #SIZE          ;Y=data byte counter
0202 CE 02 22         LDX    #BUFF          ;buffer pointer
                      ;
                      ;perform data transfer
                      ;
0205 A6 00    TRANS   LDAA   0,X            ;get byte from buffer
0207 08               INX                   ;increment pointer
0208 B7 FD 00         STAA   PORT           ;send byte to port
020B 8D 04            BSR    DELAY          ;slow down transfer rate
020D 5A               DECB                  ;decrement counter and
020E D0 F5            BNE    TRANS          ;check for end of block
0210 39               RET
                      ;
                      ;time delay subroutine
                      ;
0211 86 00    DELAY   LDAA   #TDEL          ;control time delay
0213 97 00            STA    COUNT1         ;initialise delay
```

```
0215 97 01              STA    COUNT2         ;counters in page zero
0217 7A 00 01 DLY       DEC    COUNT2         ;inner loop
021A 26 FB              BNE    DLY            ;256,255,254 ....
021C 7A 00 00           DEC    COUNT1         ;outer loop
021F 26 F6              BNE    DLY            ;256,255,254 ....
0221 39                 RTS
                        ;
0222            BUFF    RMB    256            ;space for buffer
```

Simple I/O port device

A number of devices are available which contain latches and buffers and are specifically designed for constructing I/O ports. One such device is the 8212 I/O port, and the logic block diagram of this device is shown in Figure 5.5(a) and (b).

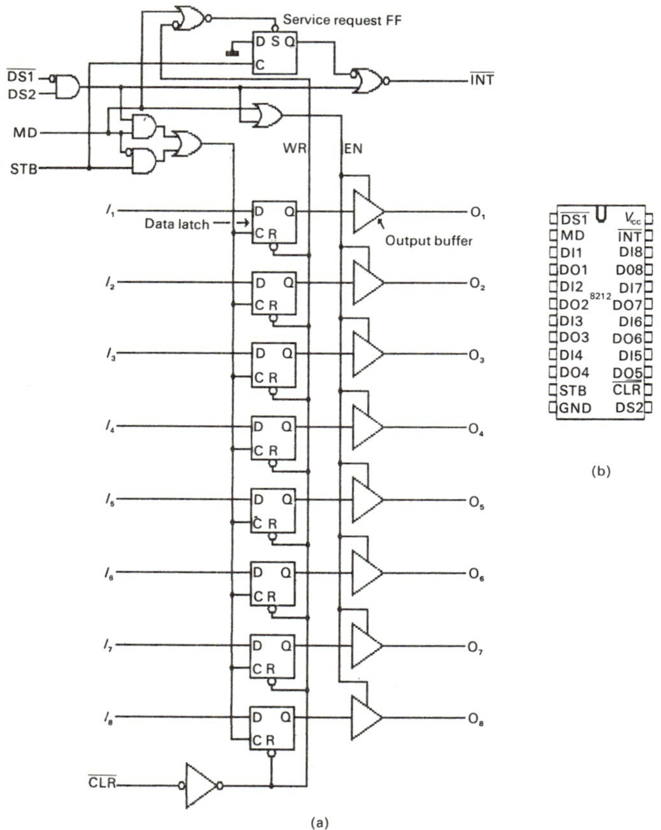

Figure 5.5

The operation of this device is controlled by its MD (mode) input.

When used as an input port, the MD input of an 8212 must be connected to a logical 0 level, as shown in Figure 5.6.

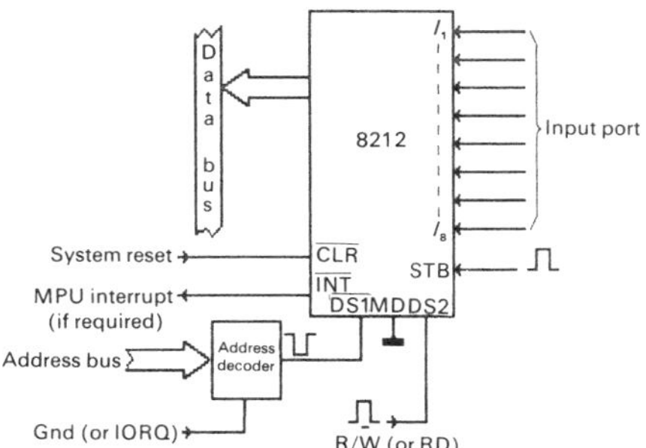

Figure 5.6

Data is read from the peripheral device and transferred into the data latches on the falling edge of a positive STB (strobe) pulse which is usually generated by the peripheral itself. When an MPU wishes to read the peripheral data, it enables the output buffers by generating the necessary device select signals and applying these to $\overline{DS_1}$ and DS_2. The 8212 responds by transferring the contents of its data latches on to the data bus. The $\overline{INT}$ output of an 8212 may be used to interrupt an MPU, and this output becomes active low in response to a STB pulse.

When used as an output port, the MD input of an 8212 must be connected to a logical 1 level, as shown in Figure 5.7.

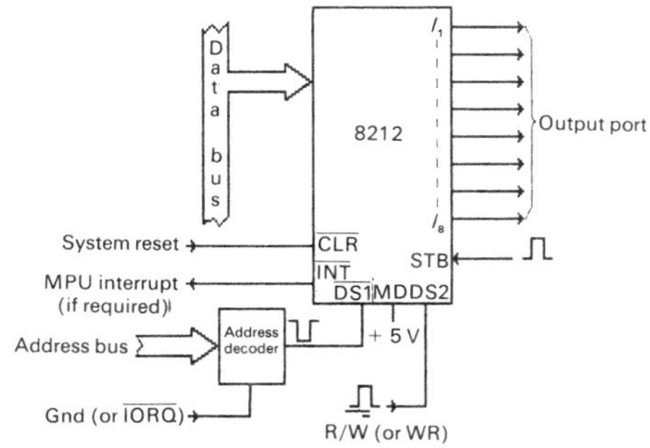

Figure 5.7

A logical 1 on the MD input permanently enables the output buffers and allows data to be transferred from the data latches to the peripheral device. When an MPU wishes to transfer new data to the peripheral, it transfers information from the data bus into the data latches by generating appropriate signals and applying these to $\overline{DS_1}$ and DS_2. These input signals act as a clock signal for the data latches. If desired, the STB (strobe) input may be used by the peripheral device to indicate to the MPU that it has received the data. It does this by generating an active $\overline{INT}$ (interrupt) output which causes the MPU to be interrupted and thus initiate the transfer of further data to the output port.

Programs of the type given for the simple input and output ports are also suitable for this type of device.

Hardware/software for general purpose interfaces

Special programmable I/O devices are available which permit various different input and output options to be selected by means of appropriate software.

These are known as *peripheral interface adapters* (PIA) or *parallel input/output* (PIO) devices. The internal construction of each I/O device varies considerably according to the particular facilities offered, but devices may include the following sections:

1 A data input register.
2 A data output register.
3 A data direction register.
4 A control register.
5 A status flag register.

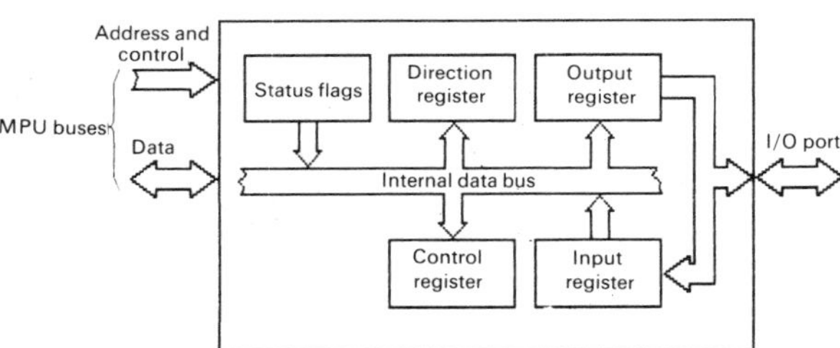

Figure 5.8

A block diagram of an I/O device which uses these components is shown in Figure 5.8. By assigning a unique address, or by other means, each of these components within an I/O device may be treated as an individual entity. The function of each of these blocks may be summarized as follows:

Data input register

A data input register is used to store peripheral generated data until the MPU is ready to read this data. This arrangement allows the peripheral to supply data asynchronously, i.e., the peripheral device does not need to be synchronized to the MPU clock. The peripheral device may determine when data is transferred to the input register by means of an $\overline{\text{STB}}$ (strobe) input if this is available (see Figure 5.9).

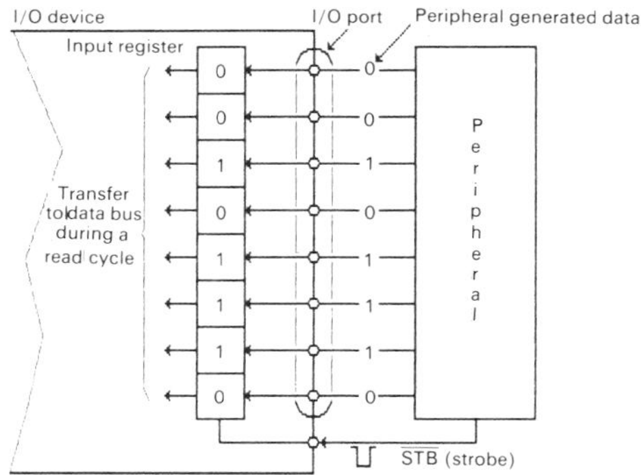

Figure 5.9

Data output register

A data output register is used to store MPU generated output data until the peripheral device is ready to accept the data. This arrangement allows the MPU to continue with other tasks without having to wait until the peripheral is ready to accept the data. An RDY (ready) signal may be available to indicate to the peripheral that new data is available (see Figure 5.10).

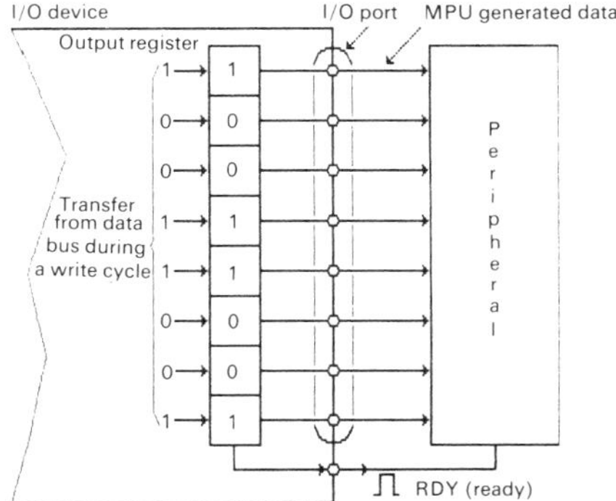

Figure 5.10

Data direction register

Theoretically it should be possible to connect the outputs from the output register in parallel with the inputs to the input register so that the port may be used to transfer data in either direction. Such an arrangement could, however, give rise to problems owing to signals from a peripheral being interfered with by conflicting signals from the output register. This problem is resolved by only enabling selected bits in the output register, thus freeing the remaining bits to be used as inputs. A data direction register is used to store the enabling bit pattern for the output register. This arrangement is shown in Figure 5.11.

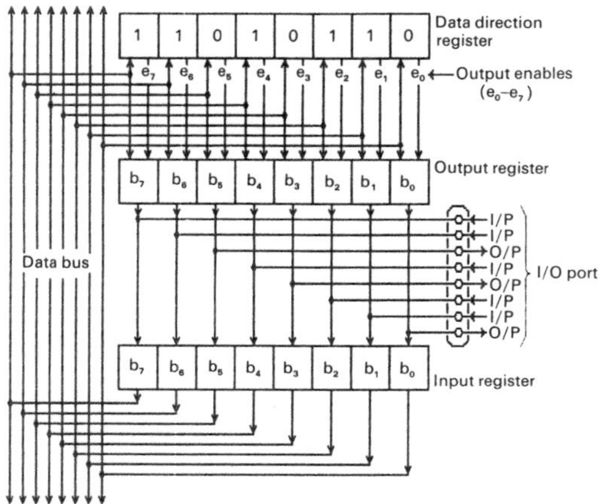

Figure 5.11

All bits in the input register are permanently enabled, thus it can be seen that when an MPU reads an I/O port, the data received consists of output data where bits have been defined as outputs, and peripheral input data in the remaining bits.

Control register

A control register is used to store information specifying programmable options within an I/O device which determine the manner in which it operates. For example, this register may determine which register is allocated to a certain address, whether interrupts are implemented, nature of handshaking etc.

Status flags

Status flags are bistables within an I/O device which provide information concerning the state of data transfers. For example, when an MPU writes new data to an output port, a flag associated with that port may be set and used to prevent the MPU from sending further information until it has been cleared. When a peripheral device reads this port, its status flag is automatically cleared thus allowing further data to be sent.

Ports

Each group of conductors fom an I/O device are terminated with a conductor to which a peripheral device may be attached. This is known as an I/O *port*, and an I/O device may possess more than one port (typically two or three). A number of two-state switching devices may be connected to an I/O port as shown in Figure 5.12.

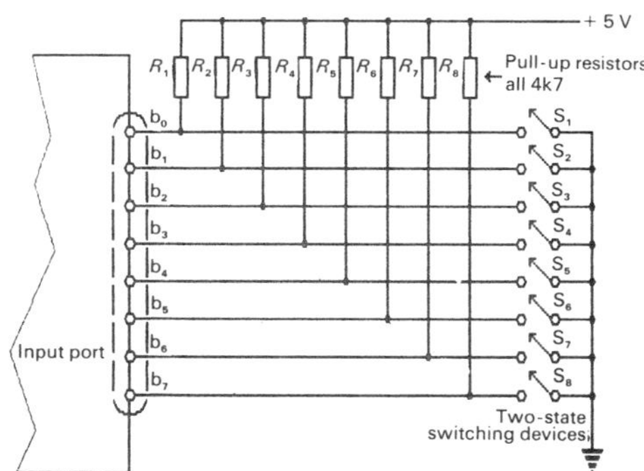

Figure 5.12

If the PIA is *memory mapped* (i.e., assigned addresses within the memory address space), the two-state devices may be interrogated by using an appropriate LOAD instruction. If the PIA is not memory mapped, but is assigned to separate I/O address space, as is possible with the Z80 MPU, the two-state devices may be interrogated by means of an appropriate IN (input) instruction.

A number of two-state indicator devices may be connected to an I/O port as shown in Figure 5.13.

If the PIA is memory mapped, the indicators may be controlled by means of appropriate STORE instructions. If the PIA is not memory mapped, an OUT (output) instruction may be used to control the indicators.

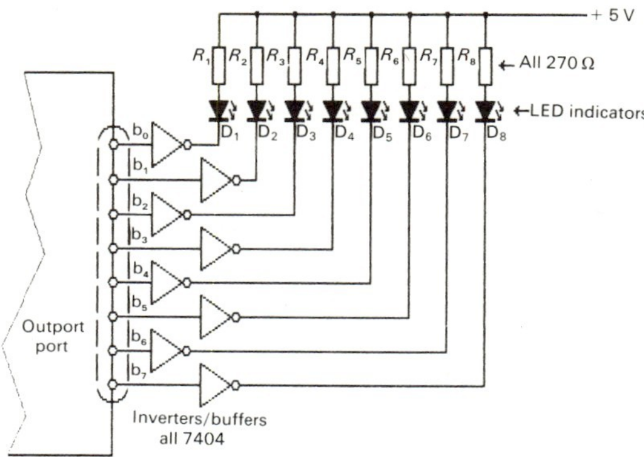

Figure 5.13

Programmable parallel I/O controllers

Each manufacturer includes at least one type of programmable parallel I/O controller in the family of devices associated with a particular MPU. Typical examples are included in this chapter.

6530 RRIOT

The 6530 device contains 1K bytes of mask programmed ROM, 64 bytes of RAM, two 8-bit I/O ports and an interval timer (hence the term RRIOT). The internal organization of the 6530 is shown in Figure 5.14.

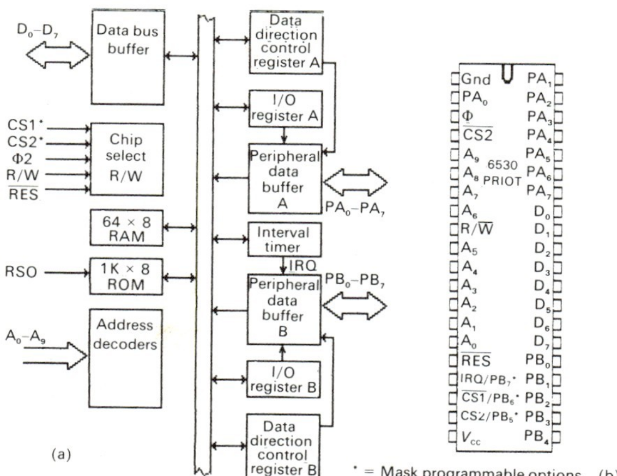

Figure 5.14

It can be seen that this device, when combined with a 6502 MPU contains all of the essential elements to form a complete microcomputer (see Figure 5.15).

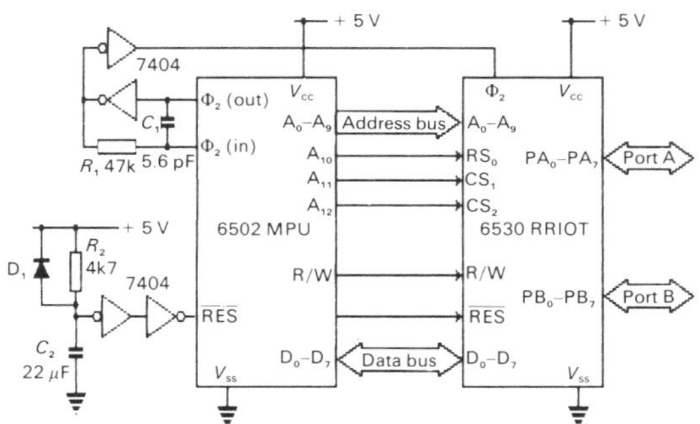

Figure 5.15

The main disadvantage of this arrangement lies in the fact that the 6530 uses a mask programmed ROM whose contents are fixed during manufacture and are therefore only suitable for use in high volume applications. One way of overcoming this problem is to use a 6532 device which is logically similar to the 6530, but which does not contain ROM (this device is known as a RIOT, and contains 128 bytes of RAM). The read-only requirements of a microcomputer may be provided by an EPROM (e.g., 2516), thus increasing the chip count by one for a complete microcomputer.

I/O facilities

The 6530 has 16 pins available for interfacing parallel peripheral devices. Each pin may be programmed to act as either an input or an output. The 16 pins are divided into two 8-bit ports, PA_0–PA_7 and PB_0–PB_7. When an I/O line is defined as an input, its corresponding buffer in the I/O register is disabled and the MPU reads the peripheral input pin directly. When an I/O line is defined as an output, the corresponding bit in the I/O register is enabled and the MPU stores data in this bit.

The I/O pins are all TTL compatible and, in addition, PA_0 and PB_0 are capable of sourcing 3 mA at 1.5 V, thus making them suitable for Darlington drive. PB7 may be used as an interrupt pin from the internal timer, and this line has no internal pull-up resistor, thus permitting several 6530 devices to be 'wired-ORed' to the 6502 $\overline{IRQ}$ pin. PB5 or PB6 may be used for chip select purposes and thus be unavailable to the user as I/O lines.

Direction control registers

Each of the data I/O lines of port A or port B may be configured as an input line or an output line. The contents of data direction registers A and B determine how each of the I/O lines of their respective ports are defined. A logical 0 in a particular bit position in a data direction register defines the corresponding port bit as an input, while a logical 1 defines it as an output. For example, in order to configure a 6530 as indicated in Table 5.1, the contents of each data direction register must be shown as in Figure 5.16.

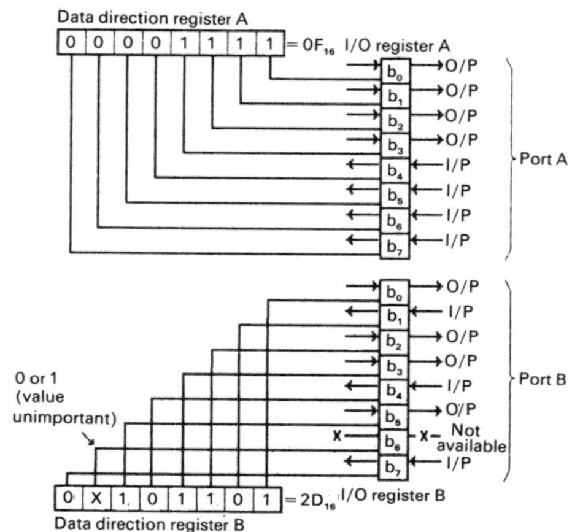

Figure 5.16

Table 5.1

Port	*Bit no.*	*Direction*
	0	Output
	1	Output
	2	Output
A	3	Output
	4	Input
	5	Input
	6	Input
	7	Input
	0	Output
	1	Input
	2	Output
B	3	Output
	4	Input
	5	Output
	6	X ←
	7	Input

The following 6502 assembly language program may be used to configure the ports according to Table 5.1:

```
A9 0F        LDA  %00001111  ;direction def A
8D 01 17     STA  PADD       ;config port A
A9 2D        LDA  %00101101  ;direction def B
8D 03 17     STA  PBDD       ;config port B
```

Timer

A 6530 contains an interval timer which may be used as an integral part of the interface between a 6502 MPU and its peripheral device. The interval timer contains the following three basic sections:

1 A preliminary divide down register.
2 A programmable 8-bit register.
3 Interrupt logic.

These sections are organized as shown in Figure 5.17.

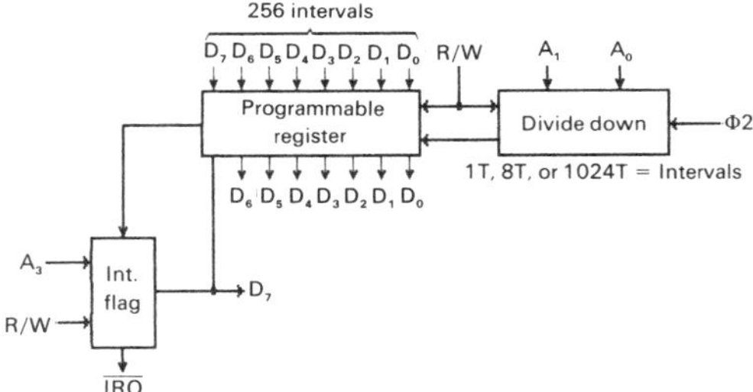

Figure 5.17

The interval times allows the user to specify a preset count of up to 256_{10} and a clock divide rate of 1, 8, 64 or 1024 by writing to a particular memory location. As soon as the write occurs, counting at the specified rate begins. The timer counts down by one for every 1, 8, 64, or 1024 clock cycles, according to the divide ratio selected. The current count may be read at any time and, at the user's option, the timer may be programmed to generate an interrupt when a count of zero is passed. Once the timer has passed zero, the divide rate is automatically set to 1, and the counter continues to count down at the clock rate, starting at a count of FF_{16}. This allows the user to determine how many clock cycles have passed since a count of zero.

Loading the timer

The divide rate and the interrupt enable/disable options are selected by decoding the least significant address bits A_0, A_1 and A_3. The starting count for the timer is determined by the value written to a specified address. The addresses used in Figure 5.17 and the options available are shown in Table 5.2.

Table 5.2

Address	*Divide ratio*	*Interrupt capabiluty*	*Maximum time interval*
1704	1	Disabled	255 μs
1705	8	Disabled	2 ms
1706	64	Disabled	16 ms
1707	1024	Disabled	260 ms
170C	1	Enabled	255 μs
170D	8	Enabled	2 ms
170E	64	Enabled	16 ms
170F	1024	Enabled	260 ms

After timing has started, the timer status may be determined by reading address 1707_{16}. If the counter has passed the count of zero, bit 7 of this location is set to a logical 1, otherwise bit 7 (and all other bits at this address) is at a logical 0. This allows a program to monitor location 1707_{16} and determine when the timer has timed out. If the timer has not counted past zero, reading location 1706_{16} provides the current timer count and disables the interrupt option. Reading location $170E_{16}$ provides the current timer count and enables the interrupt option, thus the interrupt option may be changed during the count down period. Once the timer has passed zero, reading locations 1706_{16} or $170E_{16}$ restores the divide ratio to its previously programmed value, disables or enables the interrupt option and leaves the timer with its current count. The timer never stops counting, and continues to count down at the clock frequency unless new information is written to it.

Use of the timer for generating a square wave

As part of an interfacing problem, it may be necessary to generate a square wave output from the PIA. The following two 6502 assembly language examples show how a 5 kHz square wave may be generated on bit 0 of port A of a 6502 microcomputer which operates with a 1 MHz clock. The first example uses polling to determine when the timer has timed out, but the second example generates an interrupt upon time out.

Example 1

A flowchart for this example is shown in Figure 5.18.

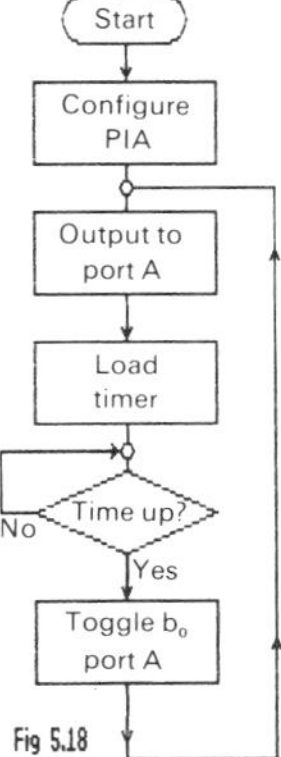

Figure 5.18

```
                               ;*****************************
                               ;5 kHz square wave generator
                               ;6530 timer with polled status
                               ;*****************************
                               ;
0000               PAD         =$1700
0000               PADD        =$1701
0000               TIME        =$1704
0200                          *=$0200
0200                           ;
0200   A9 01                   LDA    #1           ;configure PIA
0202   8D 01 17                STA    PADD         ;b0 port A output
0205   49 01       SQWV        EOR    #1           ;toggle b0
0207   8D 00 17                STA    PAD          ;of port A
020A   A2 64                   LDX    #$64         ;X=clock periods
020C   8E 04 17                STX    TIME         ;load timer
020F   2C 07 17    POLL        BIT    TIME+3       ;test status
0212   10 FB                   BPL    POLL         ;time up?
0214   30 EF                   BMI    SQWV         ;next half-cycle
```

Example 2

If the timer interrupt is selected, bit 7 of port B goes to a logical 0 each time that the counter passes zero, therefore this bit should be connected to $\overline{\text{IRQ}}$ or $\overline{\text{NMI}}$ on the 6502 MPU in order to create an interrupt driven system. This arrangement is shown in Figure 5.19.

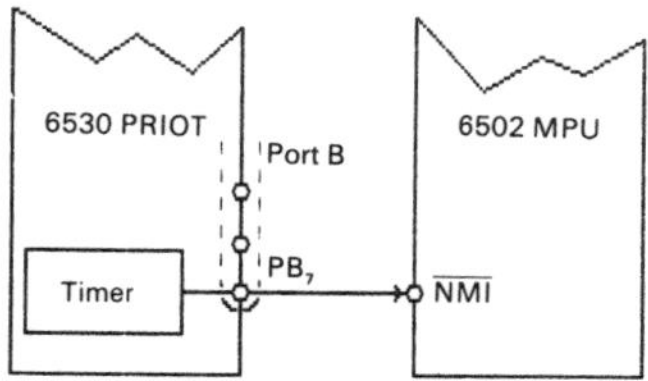

Figure 5.19

An interrupt service routine is used which contains a routine to toggle b_0 of port A and reload the timer. This means that once the timing process has been initiated in the main program, the MPU is free to run any desired program, since the timer automatically requests the appropriate I/O operation as and when required. A 6502 assembly language program to implement this system is as follows:

```
                         ;******************************
                         ;5 kHz square wave generator
                         ;6530 timer with interrupts
                         ;******************************
                         ;
0000            PAD      =$1700
0000            PADD     =$1701
0000            TIME     =$170C
0000            NMIV     =$FFFA
0200                    *=$0200
0200                     ;
0200  A9 50              LDA   #$50      ;low byte of interrupt
0202  8D FA FF           STA   NMIV      ;routine address
0205  A9 02              LDA   #2        ;high byte of interrupt
0207  8D FB FF           STA   NMIV+1    ;routine address
020A  A9 01              LDA   #1        ;config b0 of port A
020C  8D 01 17           STA   PADD      ;as an output
020F  A2 64              LDX   #$64      ;X=clock periods
0211  8E 0C 17           STX   TIME      ;load timer
....  .. .. ..
....  .. .. ..
....  .. .. ..                          ;user's program

                         ;interrupt service routine
                         ;toggle b0 of port A when
                         ;timer count reaches zero
                         ;
```

```
0250                *=$0250
0250                ;
0250  49 01         EOR  #1         ;toggle b0
0252  8D 00 17      STA  PAD        ;of port A
0255  8E 0C 17      STX  TIME       ;reload timer
0258  40            RTI             ;back to user prog
```

Note: Bit 7 of port B must be configured as an input. This will normally be the case after reset, but if in doubt, port B should be configured during the initial program sequence.

6522 VIA

The 6522 VIA is a general purpose interface device which contains all of the major elements required to perform parallel data transfers, timing, and to a limited extent, serial transfers. A block diagram of this device is shown in Figure 5.20.

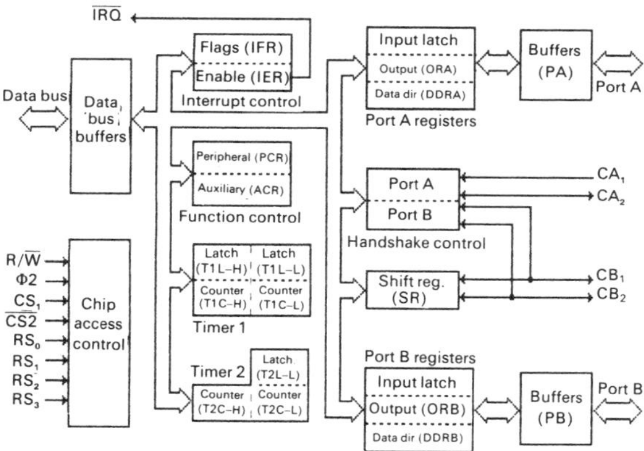

Figure 5.20

The 6522 VIA offers the following facilities:

1 An I/O section which consists of two 8-bit bidirectional ports, A and B, each with handshaking facilities. Associated with each port is an input register, an output register and a data direction register. Port A may be used without handshake facilities. Each port is configured by loading its data direction register in a similar manner to that already described for the 6530 device (see page 110).

2 Two interval timers which may be used as either inputs or outputs. When

used as an input, a timer may be used to measure the duration or count the number of pulses applied to port B bit 6 (timer 2 only). When used as an output, each timer may generate a single pulse of programmable duration (*one-shot* mode), and timer 1 may also generate a continuous train of pulses of programmable duration (*free-running* mode).

3 A shift register which may be used to perform serial data transfers into or out of CB_2 pin under the control of an internal modulo-8 counter. Shift pulses may be generated by either timer 2, the system clock (02), or by externally generated pulses applied to CB_1. The various shift register operating modes are determined by the contents of an *auxiliary control register* (ACR).

4 A set of control registers which enable the 6522 VIA to operate under a wide variety of conditions, all under software control, to provide the flexibility required when interfacing different peripherals to a microcomputer system.

The memory assignment of the programmable elements of a 6522 VIA are shown in Table 5.3.

Peripheral control register

The contents of the peripheral control register (PCR) determine the operation of the control lines CA_1/CA_2 and CB_1/CB_2 associated with I/O ports A and B. Each bit in the PCR relates to one of the control lines as indicated in Figure 5.21.

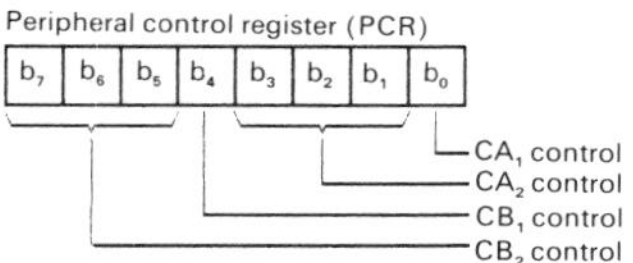

Figure 5.21

The control lines CA_1/CA_2 and CB_1/CB_2 enable the timing of data transfers between a microcomputer and its peripheral devices to be controlled by means of interrupts or by full handshaking. The contents of the PCR determine whether these control lines act simply as interrupt lines or as handshake lines, and also allow the active edge of the control signals to be defined. Full details of the use of the PCR are shown in Table 5.4.

A 6522 VIA may be interfaced to a 6502 MPU as shown in Figure 5.22.

Table 5.3

ADDRESS	FUNCTION		
A000	Output Data Register B (ORB)		
A001	Output Data Register A (ORA) : controls handshake		
A002	Data Direction Register B (DDRB)	0 = Input	
A003	Data Direction register A (DDRA)	1 = Output	
	TIMER	R/W = 0	R/W = 1
A004	T1	Write to T1 latch low	Read T1 counter low Reset T1 Interrupt Flag
A005	T1	Write to T1 latch high Write to T1 counter high Latch low → counter low Reset T1 Interrupt Flag	Read T1 counter high
A006	T1	Write to T1 latch low	Read T1 latch low
A007	T1	Write to T1 latch high Reset T1 Interrupt Flag	Read T1 latch high
A008	T2	Write to T2 latch low	Read T2 counter low Reset T2 Interrupt Flag
A009	T2	Write to T2 counter high Latch low → counter low Reset T2 Interrupt Flag	Read T2 counter high
A00A	Shift Register (SR)		
A00B	Auxiliary Control Register (ACR)		
A00C	Peripheral Control Register (PCR)		
A00D	Interrupt Flag Register (IFR)		
A00E	Interrupt Enable Register (IER)		
A00F	Output Data Register A (ORA) : no effect on handshake		

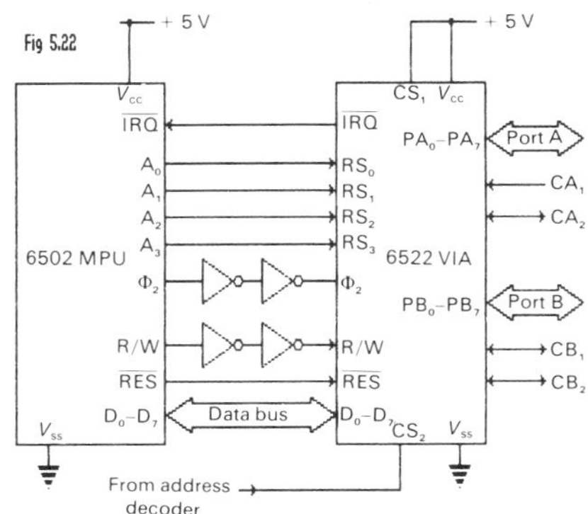

Figure 5.22

Table 5.4

CB1 CONTROL				CA1 CONTROL			
PCR4		= 0	The CB1 Interrupt Flag (IFR4) will be set by a negative transition (high to low) on the CB1 pin.	PCR0		= 0	The CB1 Interrupt Flag (IFR1) will be set by a negative transition (high to low) on the CA1 pin.
		= 1	The CB1 Interrupt Flag (IFR4) will be set by a positive transition (low to high) on the CB1 pin.			= 1	The CA1 Interrupt Flag (IFR1) will be set by a positive transition (low to high) on the CA1 pin.
CB2 CONTROL				**CA2 CONTROL**			
PCR7	PCR6	PCR5	MODE	PCR3	PCR2	PCR1	MODE
0	0	0	CB2 negative edge interrupt (IFR3/ORB clear) mode -- Set CB2 interrupt flag (IFR3) on a negative transition of the CB2 input signal. Clear IFR3 on a read or write of the ORB or by writing logic 1 into IFR3.	0	0	0	CA2 negative edge interrupt (IFR0/ORA clear) mode -- Set CA2 interrupt flag (IFR0) on a negative transition of the CA2 input signal. Clear IFR0 on a read or write of the ORA or by writing logic 1 into IFR0.
0	0	1	CB2 negative edge interrupt (IFR3 clear) mode -- set IFR3 on a negative transition of the CB2 input signal. Clear IFR3 by writing logic 1 into IFR3.	0	0	1	CA2 negative edge interrupt (IFR0 clear) mode -- set IFR0 on a negative transition of the CA2 input signal. Clear IFR0 by writing logic 1 into IFR0.
0	1	0	CB2 positive edge interrupt (IFR3/ORB clear) mode -- Set CB2 interrupt flag (IFR3) on a positive transition of the CB2 input signal. Clear IFR3 on a read or write of the ORB or by writing logic 1 into IFR3.	0	1	0	CA2 positive edge interrupt (IFR0/CRA clear) mode -- Set CA2 interrupt flag (IFR0) on a positive transition of the CA2 input signal. Clear IFR0 on a read or write of the ORA or by writing logic 1 into IFR0.
0	1	1	CB2 positive edge interrupt (IFR3 clear) mode -- Set IFR3 on a positive transition of the CB2 input signal. Clear IFR3 by writing logic 1 into IFR3.	0	1	1	CA2 positive edge interrupt (IFR0 clear) mode -- Set IFR0 on a positive transition of the CA2 input signal. Clear IFR0 by writing logic 1 into IFR0.
1	0	0	CB2 handshake output mode -- Set CB2 output low on a write of the Peripheral B Output Register. Reset CB2 high with an active transition on CB1.	1	0	0	CA2 handshake output mode -- Set CA2 output low on a write of the Peripheral A Output Register. Reset CA2 high with an active transition on CA1.
1	0	1	CB2 pulse output mode -- CB2 goes low for one cycle following read or write of the Peripheral B Output Register.	1	0	1	CA2 pulse output mode -- CA2 goes low for one cycle following read or write of the Peripheral A Output Register.
1	1	0	CB2 low output mode -- CB2 output is held low in this mode.	1	1	0	CA2 low output mode -- CA2 output is held low in this mode.
1	1	1	CB2 high output mode -- CB2 output is held high in this mode.	1	1	1	CA2 high output mode -- CA2 output is held high in this mode.

Configuring examples

1 Simple input port without control options.

```
                              ;*****************************
                              ;Simple 6522 VIA input port
                              ;without protocols
                              ;*****************************
                              ;
0000                ORA       =$A001
0000                DDRA      =$A003
0000                BUFF      =$0080
0200                         *=$0200
0200                          ;
0200  A9 00                   LDA    #0          ;configure VIA
0202  8D 03 A0                STA    DDRA        ;port A all inputs
0205  AD 01 A0                LDA    ORA         ;read port A
0208  85 80                   STA    BUFF        ;save in memory
....  .. .. ..
....  .. .. ..
```

2 Input port with an active low-to-high *data ready* strobe applied to CA_1.

```
                              ;*****************************
                              ;6522 input port with strobe
                              ;strobe is high-to-low on CA1
                              ;*****************************
                              ;
0000                ORA       =$A001
0000                DDRA      =$A003
0000                PCR       =$A00C
0000                IFR       =$A00D
0000                BUFF      =$0080
0200                         *=$0200
0200                          ;
0200  A9 00                   LDA    #0          ;configure VIA
0202  8D 03 A0                STA    DDRA        ;port A all inputs
0205  A9 01                   LDA    #1          ;define CA1 active
0207  8D 0C A0                STA    PCR         ;edge low to high
020A  AD 0D A0      FLAG      LDA    IFR         ;read CA1 int, flag
020D  29 02                   AND    #2          ;mask unwanted bits
020F  F0 F9                   BEQ    FLAG        ;wait until ready
0211  AD 01 A0                LDA    ORA         ;read port A
0214  85 80                   STA    BUFF        ;save in memory
....  .. .. ..
....  .. .. ..
```

In this example, CA_1 is connected to the peripheral device. CA_1 is programmed to accept an active low-to-high transition by storing a logical 1 in the bit 0 position of the PCR at address $A00C_{16}$. When the peripheral device is ready to send new data to port A, it activates CA_1 which causes the CA_1 interrupt flag in the interrupt flag register (IFR) to be set. The IFR is located at address $A00D_{16}$ in this example, and the CA_1 interrupt flag is bit 1 of this register. The program polls this flag, and waits until a logical 1 is detected before reading port A and transferring data into memory at address 0080_{16}.

3 Input port with full handshaking.

```
0000                    ;******************************
0000                    ;6522 input port, with full
0000                    ;handshake control of transfer
0000                    ;Data inputs not latched
0000                    ;Ready:   positive pulse on CA2
0000                    ;Strobe: low-to-high on CA1
0000                    ;******************************
0000                    ;
0000             ORA    =$A001
0000             DDRA   =$A003
0000             PCR    =$A00C
0000             IFR    =$A00D
0000             BUFF   =$0080
0200                   *=$0200
0200                    ;
0200  A9 00             LDA   #0          ;configure VIA
0202  8D 03 A0          STA   DDRA        ;port A all inputs
0205  A9 0C             LDA   #$0C        ;select CA2 low
0207  8D 0C A0          STA   PCR         ;output mode
020A  49 01             EOR   #1          ;generate MPU
020C  8D 0C A0          STA   PCR         ;ready pulse
020F  49 01             EOR   #1          ;
0211  8D 0C A0          STA   PCR         ;
0214  AD 0D A0   FLAG   LDA   IFR         ;read CA1 int flag
0217  29 02             AND   #2          ;mask unwanted bits
0219  F0 F9             BEQ   FLAG        ;wait for strobe
021B  AD 01 A0          LDA   ORA         ;read port A data
021E  85 80             STA   BUFF        ;save in memory
....  .. .. ..
....  .. .. ..
```

Note that in examples 2 and 3 the interrupt flag register is polled in each program in order to determine when the peripheral has sent a *data ready* strobe. By appropriate changes to these programs, an interrupt driven input may be implemented. This involves removing the polling sequence, inclusion of an appropriate interrupt service routine, and loading the 6522 *interrupt enable* register (IER) at address $A00E_{16}$ with 02 to enable CA_1 to generate an interrupt. Also, data may be latched on the 6522 inputs by setting bit 0 of the auxiliary control register (ACR) at address $A00B_{16}$.

8255 programmable peripheral interface

The 8255 is a programmable peripheral interface (PPI) device which may be interfaced directly to 8080/85 and Z80 MPUs. It provides a total of three 8-bit parallel I/O ports (port A, port B and port C), as shown in the block diagram (see Figure 5.23(a)).

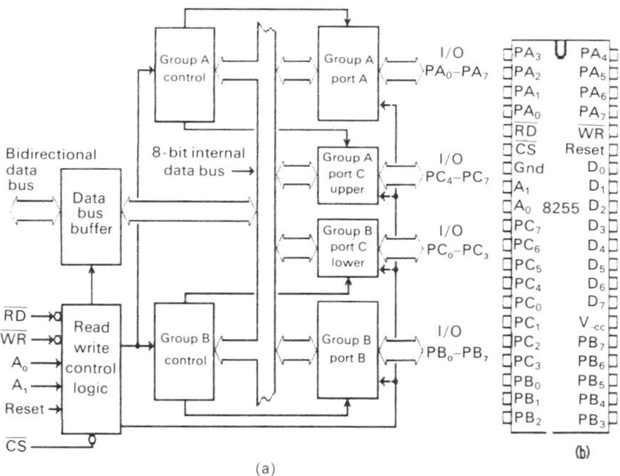

Figure 5.23

The twenty-four I/O pins may be programmed in two groups of twelve to form various combinations of 4- and 8-bit parallel ports depending upon the operating mode selected.

Operating modes

The 8255 may be operated in any of the following three modes:

1 Mode 0: basic I/O mode.
2 Mode 1: strobed I/O mode.
3 Mode 2: bidirectional I/O mode.

Mode 0: This mode provides *simple I/O* operations without handshake facilities, data being simply written to or read from each of the three I/O ports as required. Ports A and B operate as two 8-bit ports, while port C is operated as two 4-bit ports, and any port may be configured as either an input port or an output port.

Mode 1: This mode provides I/O operations with *handshake* facilities. Ports A and B may be defined as either input ports or output ports, and handshaking is provided by port C. Six bits of port C are used for handshaking and interrupt control, three bits for port A, and three bits for port B.

Table 5.5

	MODE 0		MODE 1		MODE2
	IN	OUT	IN	OUT	Group A only
PA0	IN	OUT	IN	OUT	⟷
PA1	IN	OUT	IN	OUT	⟷
PA2	IN	OUT	IN	OUT	⟷
PA3	IN	OUT	IN	OUT	⟷
PA4	IN	OUT	IN	OUT	⟷
PA5	IN	OUT	IN	OUT	⟷
PA6	IN	OUT	IN	OUT	⟷
PA7	IN	OUT	IN	OUT	⟷
PB0	IN	OUT	IN	OUT	—
PB1	IN	OUT	IN	OUT	—
PB2	IN	OUT	IN	OUT	—
PB3	IN	OUT	IN	OUT	—
PB4	IN	OUT	IN	OUT	—
PB5	IN	OUT	IN	OUT	—
PB6	IN	OUT	IN	OUT	—
PB7	IN	OUT	IN	OUT	—
PC0	IN	OUT	INTR B	INTR B	I/O
PC1	IN	OUT	IBF B	$\overline{OBF}$ B	I/O
PC2	IN	OUT	$\overline{STB}$ B	$\overline{ACK}$ B	I/O
PC3	IN	OUT	INTR A	INTR A	INTR A
PC4	IN	OUT	$\overline{STB}$ A	I/O	$\overline{STB}$ A
PC5	IN	OUT	IBF A	I/O	IBF A
PC6	IN	OUT	I/O	$\overline{ACK}$ A	$\overline{ACK}$ A
PC7	IN	OUT	I/O	$\overline{OBF}$ A	$\overline{OBF}$ A

(PB0–PB7: Mode 0 or Mode 1 only)

INTR = Interrupt
IBF = Input Buffer Full
$\overline{OBF}$ = Output Buffer Full
$\overline{STB}$ = Strobe
$\overline{ACK}$ = Acknowledge

Mode 2: This mode provides *bidirectional I/O* operations on port A only. Handshaking is provided by five bits of port C.

These modes of operation are summarized in Table 5.5.
An 8255 PPI may be interfaced to a Z80 MPU as shown in Figure 5.24.

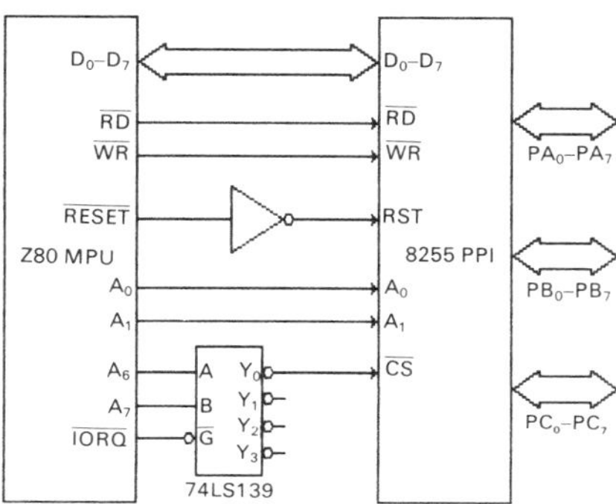

Figure 5.24

Configuring an 8255

The 8255 PPI has two port select signals (A_0 and A_1) which, in conjunction with the $\overline{RD}$ and $\overline{WR}$ inputs control selection of one of the three I/O ports or the control word register. Selection of an I/O port or the control word register is achieved by using an appropriate address in conjunction with an IN or OUT instruction (or LOAD in memory-mapped I/O systems), and the least significant two bits of the address identify the port or control register as shown in Table 5.6.

The contents of the control word register determine the mode selection and the port configuration, as shown in Figure 5.25.

Therefore, configuring an 8255 PPI involves storing an appropriate control word in this register.

Configuring example

An 8255 is to be operated in mode 0 as follows:

Port A input mode.
Port B output mode.
Port C (low) output mode.
Port C (high) input mode.

The control word required to configure the 8255 in this manner is shown in Figure 5.26.

Table 5.6

A1	A0	$\overline{RD}$	$\overline{WR}$	$\overline{CS}$	INPUT OPERATION (READ)
0	0	0	1	0	Port A → Data Bus
0	1	0	1	0	Port B → Data Bus
1	0	0	1	0	Port C → Data Bus
					OUTPUT OPERATION (WRITE)
0	0	1	0	0	Data Bus → Port A
0	1	1	0	0	Data Bus → Port B
1	0	1	0	0	Data Bus → Port C
1	1	1	0	0	Data Bus → Control
					DISABLE FUNCTION
X	X	X	X	1	Data Bus → 3-State
1	1	0	1	0	Illegal Condition

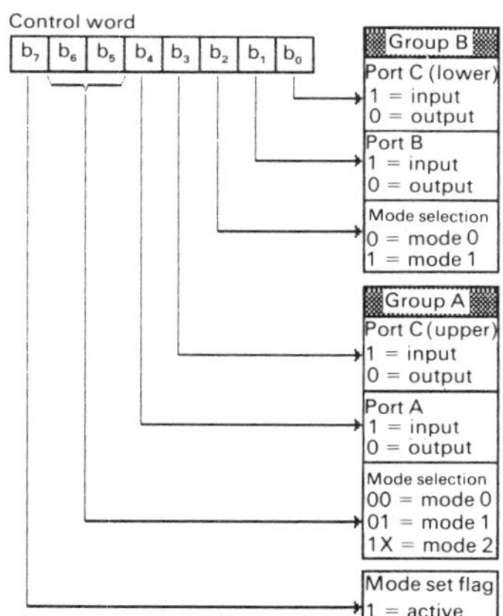

Figure 5.25

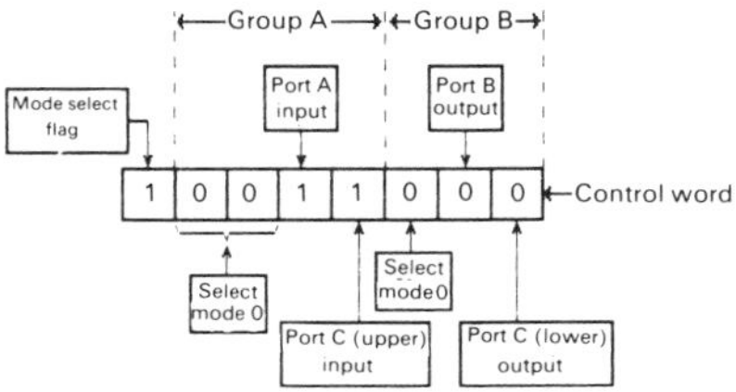

Figure 5.26

An instruction sequence similar to the following may be used to perform the actual configuring:

```
                  PPIBASE  EQU  0
                  CWORD    EQU  10011000B ;control word
                  CWREG    EQU  PPIBASE+3 ;control word reg
                           ;
                           ORG    1800H
                           ;
1800   3E 98               LD A,98H          ;
1802   D3 03               OUT (3),A         ;
```

Single bit control

For normal mode selection and configuring operations on a 8255 PPI, bit 7 of the control word register is set to a logical 1. This bit behaves as a *mode set* flag and ensures that the data sent to the control address is stored in the *mode definition register* of the PPI. If a control word with bit 7 reset to 0 is used, a different function is provided at the control address. This function enables any of the eight bits of port C to be set or reset using a single OUT instruction, as shown in Figure 5.27.

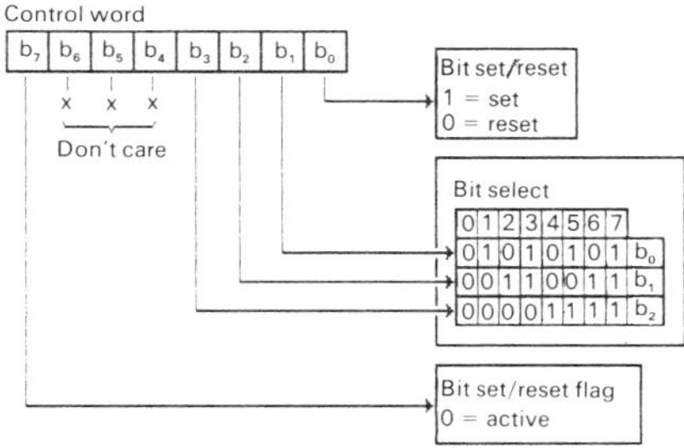

Figure 5.27

When the 8255 PPI is used in mode 1 or mode 2, control signals are provided which may be used as interrupt requests to the MPU. The interrupt request signals generated by port C may be enabled or disabled by setting or resetting the appropriate *INTE flip-flop* using the bit set/reset facility of port C.

Status word

When operating in mode 0, port C is used for peripheral data transfers. When using modes 1 or 2, however, port C generates or accepts handshaking signals

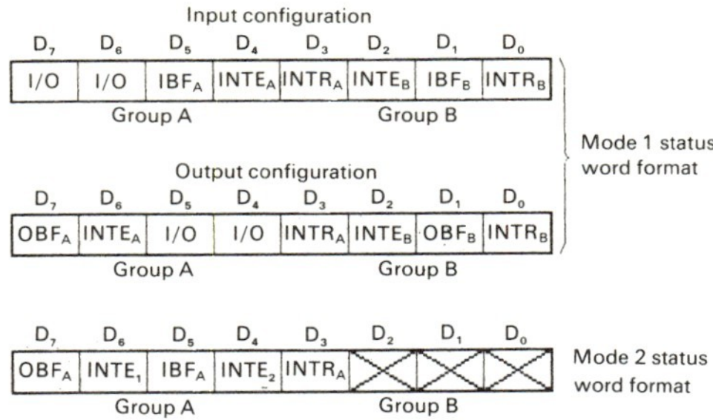

Figure 5.28

for data transfers via ports A and B. Reading port C enables the status of each peripheral to be tested. The status word format for modes 1 and 2 is shown in Figure 5.28.

Z80 PIO

The Z80 PIO is a parallel I/O device which is designed to interface directly to a Z80 MPU. It consists of two virtually identical sections, each of which provides an 8-bit parallel port which may be configured for data transfer or control applications. A block diagram of the Z80 PIO is shown in Figure 5.29(a) and (b).

Address lines A_0 and A_1 are used to select the required registers in the PIO, as shown in Table 5.7.

Table 5.7

A1	A0	$\overline{RD}$	$\overline{CS}$	$\overline{IORQ}$	INPUT OPERATION (READ)
0	0	0	0	0	Port A → Data Bus
0	1	0	0	0	Port B → Data Bus
					OUTPUT OPERATION (WRITE)
0	0	1	0	0	Data Bus → Port A
0	1	1	0	0	Data Bus → Port B
1	0	1	0	0	Data Bus → Control A
1	1	1	0	0	Data Bus → Control B
					DISABLE FUNCTION
X	1	X	1	X	Data Bus → 3-State

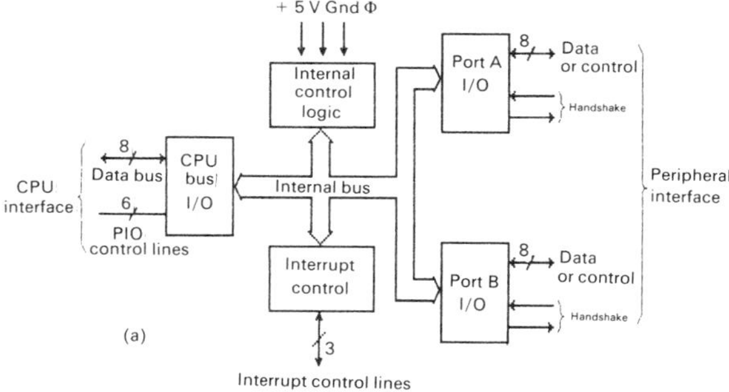
+ 5 V Gnd Φ
Internal control logic
Port A I/O
8
Data or control
Handshake
CPU interface
8
Data bus
CPU bus I/O
Internal bus
6
PIO control lines
Peripheral interface
Interrupt control
Port B I/O
8
Data or control
Handshake
(a)
3
Interrupt control lines

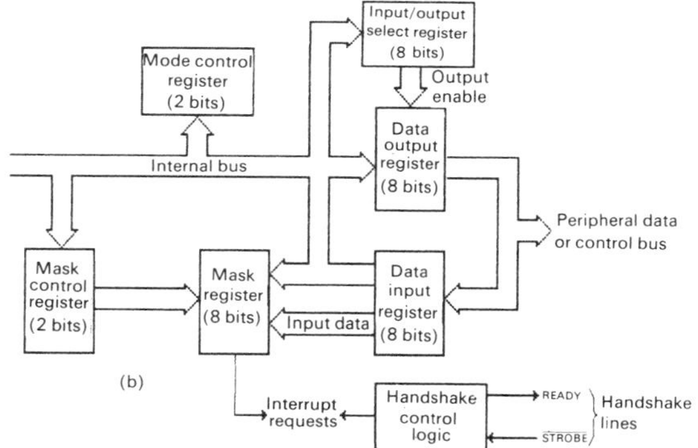
Input/output select register (8 bits)
Mode control register (2 bits)
Output enable
Data output register (8 bits)
Internal bus
Peripheral data or control bus
Mask control register (2 bits)
Mask register (8 bits)
Data input register (8 bits)
Input data
(b)
Interrupt requests
Handshake control logic
READY
STROBE
Handshake lines

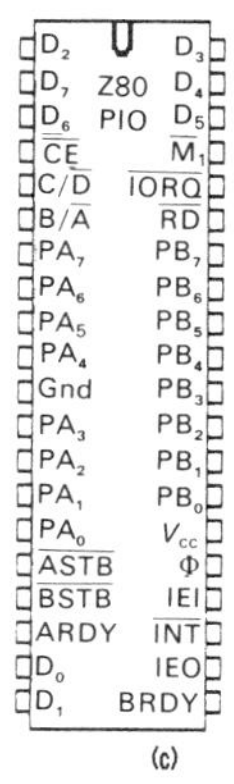
Z80 PIO
D2 D3
D7 D4
D6 D5
CE M1
C/D IORQ
B/A RD
PA7 PB7
PA6 PB6
PA5 PB5
PA4 PB4
Gnd PB3
PA3 PB2
PA2 PB1
PA1 PB0
PA0 Vcc
ASTB Φ
BSTB IEI
ARDY INT
D0 IEO
D1 BRDY
(c)

Figure 5.29

The function of each of the registers is as follows:

Mode control register

The mode control register is a 2-bit register whose contents are used to select one of the four operating modes of the Z80 PIO. These four modes are:

1 Output mode (mode 0).
2 Input mode (mode 1).
3 Bidirectional mode (mode 2).
4 Bit mode (mode 3).

The mode numbers have been chosen to have mnemonic significance, i.e., 0 = out, 1 = in, and 2 = bidirectional. Port A may operate in any of these four modes; port B may be operated in all modes except mode 2.

Input/output select register

This is an 8-bit register which is used in mode 3 only to specify which I/O lines of a port act as inputs, and which lines act as outputs. A logical 0 in a particular bit position in this register defines the corresponding I/O line as an output, and a logical 1 defines the corresponding I/O line as an input. Note the mnemonic significance of this, i.e., 0 = output, 1 = input.

Mask control register

This is a 2-bit register which is used in mode 3 only. In mode 3 (bit mode), the I/O lines may function as interrupt inputs if so programmed. One bit in the mask control register determines the active state of the interrupts for initiating an interrupt (i.e., active high or active low). The other bit determines whether the PIO requires all enabled inputs to be active to initiate an interrupt (AND condition), or if any single enabled input active may initiate an interrupt (OR condition).

Mask register

This is an 8-bit register, the contents of which determine which I/O lines in mode 3 may *not* be used to initiate interrupts, i.e., which bits are to be masked. Only those port bits whose corresponding bits in this register are at logical 0 will be monitored for generating interrupts.

A Z80 PIO may be interfaced to a Z80 MPU as shown in Figure 5.30.

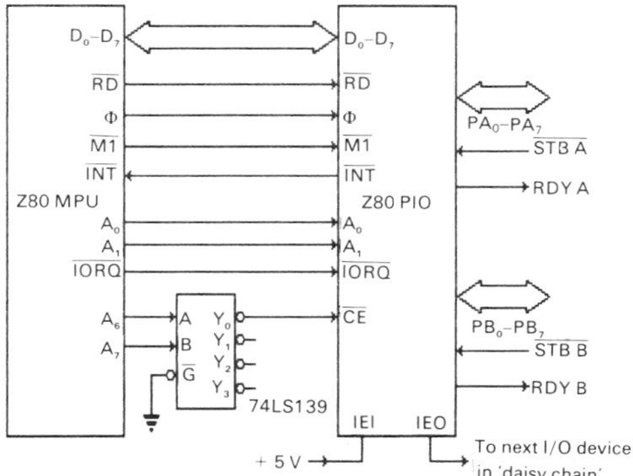

Figure 5.30

Configuring a Z80 PIO

A Z80 PIO is arranged such that all control words for a particular port are sent to the same I/O address. It is therefore necessary for the PIO to distinguish between the different control words so that they may be directed to the correct register. This is achieved by either using a specific format for the control word, or in the case of 8-bit control words, by the order in which they are sent to the PIO. The following descriptions show how each of the Z80 PIO options may be set up:

1 *Load interrupt vector*

An interrupt vector may be loaded into the PIO by writing a control word to the desired port, using the format shown in Figure 5.31. It can be seen that an interrupt vector is recognized by the fact that its least significant bit is always logical 0, i.e., a vector is an *even number*.

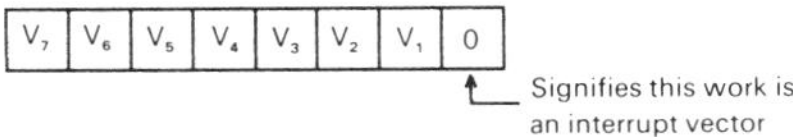

Figure 5.31

2 *Select mode*

The Z80 PIO is capable of operating in any of the following four modes:

(a) Byte output mode (mode 0).
(b) Byte input mode (mode 1).

(c) Bidirectional mode (mode 2).
(d) Bit mode (mode 3).

The mode of operation may be selected by writing a control word to the PIO with the format shown in Figure 5.32.

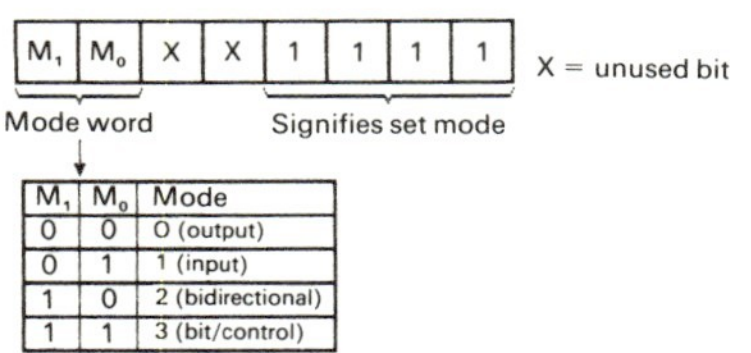

Figure 5.32

It may be seen from this diagram that bits D_0 to D_3 must be set to 1111 to signal the PIO control section that this is a *set mode* word. Bits D_4 and D_5 are ignored and may assume any value (typically both 0). If mode 3 (bit mode) is selected, the next control word written to the PIO *must* be an I/O definition word. Each bit in the I/O definition word defines its corresponding bit in the I/O port as an output if it is a logical 0, or as an input if it is a logical 1.

3 *Interrupt control word*

The interrupt control word for each port has the format shown in Figure 5.33.

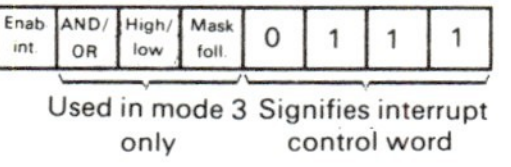

Figure 5.33

It can be seen from this diagram that bits D_0 to D_3 must be 0111 to signal the PIO control section that this is a *set interrupt control word.* Bits D_4 to D_6 are only used in mode 3 and are ignored by other modes. In mode 3, bits D_4

Table 5.8

BIT		0	1
MASK FOLLOWS	D4	No mask to follow	Next word sent to control port must be an interrupt mask
HIGH/LOW	D5	Interrupt active low	Interrupt active high
AND/OR	D6	Any unmasked input active generates an interrupt	All unmasked inputs must be active to generates an interrupt

to D_6 are used to select different forms of interrupt monitoring, as shown in Table 5.8.

If the control word sent to the PIO has its *mask follows* bit (bit D_4) set, the next control word sent to the PIO is interpreted as an interrupt mask and is transferred to the mask register. Port lines whose corresponding mask bit is 0 are monitored for generating an interrupt. The remaining lines are unmonitored and therefore cannot cause an interrupt.

Configuring examples

These simple tasks demonstrate the configuring procedure for a Z80 PIO.

Example 1: Read eight bits of data from port A (address 80H), invert the data and send it back out through port B (address 81H).

```
                        ;*******************************************
                        ; Z80 PIO with I/O addresses in the range 80H
                        ; to 83H (isolated I/O)
                        ; STB connected to logical 0 to transfer data
                        ; to Port A input register
                        ;*******************************************
                        ;
0080 =                  PAD     EQU     80H     ;PIO base address (Port A data)
0081 =                  PBD     EQU     PAD+1   ;Port B data
0082 =                  PAC     EQU     PAD+2   ;Port A control register
0083 =                  PBC     EQU     PBD+2   ;Port B control register
000F =                  OUTPUT  EQU     0FH     ;Mode 0 control word
004F =                  INPUT   EQU     4FH     ;Mode 1 control word
                        ;
1800                    ORG     1800H
                        ;
                        ;configure Z80 PIO
                        ;
1800 3E4F               LD      A,INPUT         ;configure Port A
1802 D382               OUT     (PAC),A         ;for byte input
1804 3E0F               LD      A,OUTPUT        ;configure Port B
1806 D383               OUT     (PBC),A         ;for byte output
                        ;
                        ;main program
                        ;
1808 DB80       READ:   IN      A,(PAD)         ;read Port A
180A 2F                 CPL                     ;invert data
180B D381               OUT     (PBD),A         ;and output it
180D 18F9               JR      READ            ;repeat indefinitely
```

Example 2: Read in four bits of data from port A (address 80H) bits 0 to 3, invert the data and send it back out through port A bit 4 to 7.

```
                        ;********************************************
                        ; Z80 PIO with I/O addresses in the range 80H
                        ; to 83H (isolated I/O)
                        ; Uses Mode 3, therefore STB is
                        ; inoperative
                        ;********************************************
                        ;
0080 =                  PAD     EQU     80H     ;PIO base address (Port A data)
0082 =                  PAC     EQU     PAD+2   ;Port A control register
00CF =                  MODE    EQU     0CFH    ;Mode 3 mode definition
000F =                  IODEF   EQU     0FH     ;I/O definition word
000F =                  MASK    EQU     0FH     ;invert mask
                        ;
1800                    ORG     1800H
                        ;
                        ;configure Z80 PIO
                        ;
1800 3ECF               LD      A,MODE          ;configure Port A
1802 D382               OUT     (PAC),A         ;for bit mode (3)
1804 3E0F               LD      A,IODEF         ;b0-b3 inputs
1806 D382               OUT     (PAC),A         ;b4-b7 outputs
                        ;
                        ;main program
                        ;
1808 DB80       READ:   IN      A,(PAD)         ;read Port A
180A 87                 ADD     A,A             ;shift left A four
180B 87                 ADD     A,A             ;times to move lower
180C 87                 ADD     A,A             ;nibble into upper
180D 87                 ADD     A,A             ;nibble position
180E EE0F               XOR     MASK            ;invert b4 - b7
1810 D380               OUT     (PAD),A         ;and output it
1812 18F4               JR      READ            ;repeat indefinitely
```

Example 3: A Z80 based microcomputer with a Z80 PIO is used to monitor an industrial process as shown in Figure 5.34. If an abnormal operating condition is detected, the *PWR. FAIL*, *TEMP* or *PRESS* alarm inputs to the PIO become active (high) and an interrupt is generated.

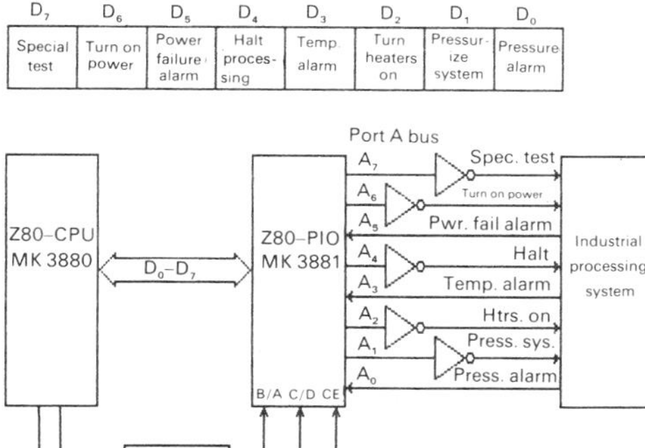

Figure 5.34

The sequence of operations required to configure a Z80 PIO for this application is shown in Figure 5.35.

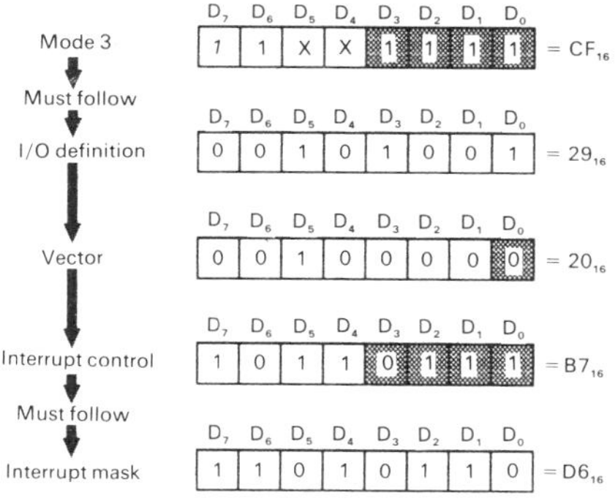

Figure 5.35

From this diagram the following configuring program may be devised:

```
                        ;*******************************************
                        ; Z80 Control Application
                        ; PIO with I/O addresses in the range 80H
                        ; to 83H (isolated I/O)
                        ; Mode 2 Interrupt with ISR Vector at 1980H
                        ; Mode 3 PIO operations, STB ignored
                        ;*******************************************
                        ;
0080 =                  PAD     EQU     80H     ;PIO base address (Port A data)
0082 =                  PAC     EQU     PAD+2   ;Port A control register
```

```
00CF =            MODE    EQU     0CFH      ;Mode 3 mode definition
0029 =            IODEF   EQU     29H       ;I/O definition word
0080 =            VECT    EQU     80H       ;PIO interrupt vector
00B7 =            INTCRL  EQU     0B7H      ;PIO interrupt control word
00D6 =            IMASK   EQU     0D6H      ;PIO interrupt mask word
                  ;
1800              ORG     1800H
                  ;
                  ;configure Z80 PIO
                  ;
1800 3ECF         LD      A,MODE            ;configure Port A
1802 D382         OUT     (PAC),A           ;for bit mode (3)
1804 3E29         LD      A,IODEF           ;b0,3,5 inputs
1806 D382         OUT     (PAC),A           ;b1,2,4,6,7 outputs
1808 3E80         LD      A,VECT            ;low byte of vector location
180A D382         OUT     (PAC),A           ;(1980H) supplied by PIO
180C 3EB7         LD      A,INTCRL          ;interrupt control word
180E D382         OUT     (PAC),A           ;
1810 3ED6         LD      A,IMASK           ;PIO interrupt control mask
1812 D382         OUT     (PAC),A
                  ;
                  ;main program
                  ;
```

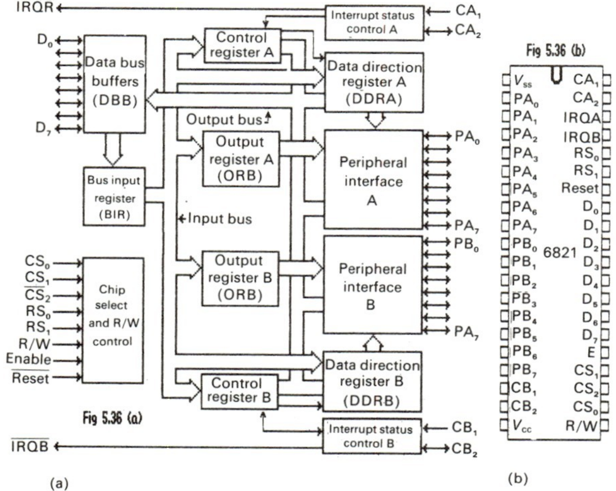

Figure 5.36

6821 PIA

The 6821 peripheral interface adapter (PIA) is designed to provide a universal parallel interface between peripheral devices and Motorola MPUs such as 6800, 6802 or 6809. It is, however, a relatively simple matter to interface to other types of MPU using this device. A 6821 PIA provides two virtually identical parallel 8-bit ports, organized as shown in Figure 5.36(a).

A 6821 PIA may be connected to a 6800/02 MPU as shown in Figure 5.37.

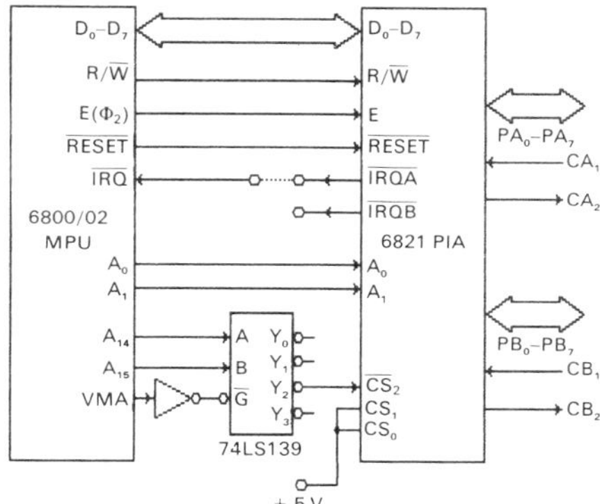

Figure 5.37

The following registers are programmer accessible.

1 *Output registers*

Each of the peripheral data lines PA_0–PA_7 may be programmed to act as either an input or an output by loading *data direction register A* with appropriate bits. The data stored in *output register A* will appear on the peripheral data lines that are programmed to be outputs. A logical 1 written into output register A causes a logical 1 to appear on the corresponding peripheral data line, while a logical 0 written into output register A causes a logical 0 to appear on the corresponding data line. During an MPU *read peripheral data* operation, the data on the peripheral lines programmed as inputs appear directly on the correponding MPU data bus lines (D_0–D_7), while the contents of the output register are read for those peripheral lines programmed as outputs.

The peripheral data lines of port B (PB_0–PB_7) may be programmed in a similar manner to those of port A. The output buffers driving these lines, however, are different and enter a high impedance state when the peripheral data line is used as an input.

2 *Data direction register*

The two *data direction registers* allow the MPU to control the direction of data transfers through each corresponding peripheral data line. A data direction register bit at logical 0 defines the corresponding peripheral data line as an input, and a data direction register bit at logical 1 defines the corresponding peripheral data line as an output.

3 *Control registers*

The two *control registers* (CRA and CRB) allow the MPU to control the operation of the four peripheral control lines CA_1, CA_2, CB_1 and CB_2. In addition, bits in the control registers enable MPU interrupts, allow the MPU to monitor the status of interrupt flags and select either peripheral interface register or data direction register (these two registers share the same address). The function of each bit in the control registers may be summarized as follows:

CA_1/CB_1 control (bits 0 and 1). These two bits in the control register determine the operation of interrupt inputs CA_1 and CB_1. The interrupt inputs may be programmed to have either positive or negative edges which cause bit 7 (IRQA1 or IRQB1) of the control register to be set (logical 1). IRQA1 and IRQB1 are *interrupt status flags* which may be polled, or optionally made to initiate an MPU interrupt request. The function of these two bits is summarized in Table 5.9.

DDRA/DDRB access (bit 2). The 6821 PIA assigns the data direction register and peripheral interface register of each port to the same address. Bit 2 of each control register determines which register is selected, such that a logical 0 in this position causes the *data direction register* to be selected, and a logical 1 causes the *peripheral interface register* to be selected. At system reset time, the control registers are cleared (loaded with 00), therefore initially the data direction registers are selected.

CA_2/CB_2 control (bits 3, 4 and 5). Bits 3, 4 and 5 of the control registers are used to control the CA_2/CB_2 peripheral control lines. These lines may function as interrupt inputs (similar to CA_1/CB_1), or as peripheral control outputs. When bit 5 of the control register is at logical 0, CA_2/CB_2 act as interrupt inputs. When bit 5 of the control register is at logical 1, CA_2/CB_2 act as peripheral control outputs. The characteristics of CA_2 and CB_2 are slightly different when used as outputs, and a summary of the available operating modes is given in Table 5.10(a), (b) and (c).

IRQA1/2 and IRQB1/2 (bits 6 and 7). These are *interrupt flag* bits which are set by active transitions on the interrupt and peripheral control lines (CA_1/CB_1 and CA_2/CB_2) when programmed as inputs. These bits cannot be dir-

Table 5.9

(a) Control word format

	7	6	5	4	3	2	1	0
CRA	IRQA1	IRQA2	CA2 Control			DDRA Access	CA1 Control	
CRB	IRQB1	IRQB2	CB2 Control			DDRB Access	CB1 Control	

(b) Control of interrupt inputs CA_1 and CB_1

CRA-1 (CRB-1)	CRA-0 (CRB-0)	Interrupt Input CA1 (CB1)	Interrupt Flag CRA-7 (CRB-7)	MPU Interrupt Request IRQA (IRQB)
0	0	↓ Active	Set high on ↓ of CA1 (CB1)	Disabled — $\overline{IRQ}$ remains high
0	1	↓ Active	Set high on ↓ of CA1 (CB1)	Goes low when the interrupt flag bit CRA-7 (CRB-7) goes high
1	0	↑ Active	Set high on ↑ of CA1 (CB1)	Disabled — $\overline{IRQ}$ remains high
1	1	↑ Active	Set high on ↑ of CA1 (CB1)	Goes low when the interrupt flag bit CRA-7 (CRB-7) goes high

Notes:

1 ↑ indicates positive transition (low to high).
2 ↓ indicates negative transition (high to low).
3 The interrupt flag bit CRA-7 is cleared by an MPU read of the A data register and CRB-7 is cleared by an MPU read of the B data register.
4 If CRA-0 (CRB-0) is low when an interrupt occurs (interrupt disabled) and is later brought high, IRQA (IRQB) occurs after CRA-0 (CRB-0) is written to a 'one'.

Table 5.10

(*a*) *Control of CA_2 and CB_2 as interrupt inputs, CRA5 (CRB5) low*

CRA-5 (CRB-5)	CRA-4 (CRB-4)	CRA-3 (CRB-3)	Interrupt Input CA2 (CB2)	Interrupt Flag CRA-6 (CRB-6)	MPU Interrupt Request $\overline{IRQA}$ ($\overline{IRQB}$)
0	0	0	↓ Active	Set high on ↓ of CA2 (CB2)	Disabled — $\overline{IRQ}$ remains high
0	0	1	↓ Active	Set high on ↓ of CA2 (CB2)	Goes low when the interrupt flag bit CRA-6 (CRB-6) goes high
0	1	0	↑ Active	Set high on ↑ of CA2 (CB2)	Disabled — $\overline{IRQ}$ remains high
0	1	1	↑ Active	Set high on ↑ of CA2 (CB2)	Goes low when the interrupt flag bit CRA-6 (CRB-6) goes high

Notes:

1 ↑ indicates positive transition (low to high).
2 ↓ indicates negative transition (high to low).
3 The interrupt flag bit CRA-6 is cleared by an MPU read of the A data register and CRB-6 is cleared by an MPU read of the B data register.
4 If CRA-3 (CRB-3) is low when an interrupt ocurs (interrupt disabled) and is later brought high, IRQA (IRQB) occurs after CRA-3 (CRB-3) is written to a 'one'.

(*b*) *Control of CB_2 as an output (CRB-5 is high)*

CRB-5	CRB-4	CRB-3	CB2 Cleared	CB2 Set
1	0	0	Low on the positive transition of the first E pulse following an MPU Write 'B' Data Register operation	High when the interrupt flag bit CRB-7 is set by an active transition of the CB1 signal
1	0	1	Low on the positive transition of the first E pulse after an MPU Write 'B' Data Register operation	High on the positive edge of the first E pulse following an E pulse which occured while the port was deselected
1	1	0	Low when CRB-3 goes low as a result of an MPU Write in Control Register 'B'	Always low as long as CRB-3 is low. Will go high on an MPU Write in Control Register 'B' that changes CRB-3 to 'one'
1	1	1	Always high as long as CRB-3 is high. Will be cleared when an MPU Write Control Register 'B' results in clearing CRB-3 to 'zero'	High when CRB-3 goes high as a result of an MPU Write into Control Register 'B'

(c) *Control of CA_2 as an output (CRA-5 is high)*

CRA-5	CRA-4	CRA-3	CA2 Cleared	CA2 Set
1	0	0	Low on negative transition of E after an MPU Read 'A' Data operation	High when the interrupt flag bit CRA-7 is set by an active transition of the CA1 signal
1	0	1	Low on negative transition of E after an MPU Read 'A' Data operation	High on the negative edge of the first 'E' pulse which occurs during a deselect
1	1	0	Low when CRA-3 goes low as a result of an MPU Write in Control Register 'A'	Always low as long as CRA-3 is low. Will go high on an MPU Write to Control Register 'A' that changes CRA-3 to 'one'
1	1	1	Always high as long as CRA-3 is high. Will be cleared on an MPU Write to Control Register 'A' that clears CRA-3 to a 'zero'	High when CRA-3 goes high as a result of an MPU Write into Control Register 'A'

ectly written to by the MPU, but may be reset indirectly by reading data from the appropriate port.

Configuring examples

The following examples show how the 6821 PIA is configured for a variety of different applications:

Example 1: Read eight bits of data from port A (address $8004), invert the data and send it back out through port B (address $8006).

```
0000                 ;***************************************
0000                 ; Routine to read in 8-bits of data from
0000                 ; 6821 PIA port A (address $8004), invert
0000                 ; the data and send back out through port
0000                 ; B (address $8006).
0000                 ;***************************************
0000                 ;
0000      DRA    EQU    $8004        ;PIA base address
0000      DDRA   EQU    DRA          ;data direction reg.
0000      CRA    EQU    DRA+1        ;control reg.
```

```
0000            DRB    EQU    DRA+2
0000            DDRB   EQU    DRB
0000            CRB    EQU    DRB+1
0100                   ORG    $0100
0100                   ;
0100 4F                CLRA               ;select DDR
0101 B7 80 05          STAA   CRA
0104 B7 80 07          STAA   CRB
0107 B7 80 04          STAA   DRA         ;port A all inputs
010A 43                COMA               ;invert A
010B B7 80 06          STAA   DRB         ;port B all outputs
010E 86 04             LDAA   #4          ;select I/O registers
0110 B7 80 05          STAA   CRA         ;A and B
0113 B7 80 07          STAA   CRB         ;bit 2 of CR = 1
0116 B6 80 04   READ   LDAA   DRA         ;read the input port
0119 43                COMA               ;invert data
011A B7 80 06          STAA   DRB         ;send out via port B
011D 20 F7             BRA    READ        ;keep repeating
```

Example 2: Read in four bits of data from port A (address \$8004) b_0 to b_8, invert the data and send it back out through port A b_4 to b_7.

```
0000                   ;****************************************
0000                   ; Routine to read in 4-bits of data from
0000                   ; 6821 PIA port A b0-3 (address $8004),
0000                   ; invert the data and send back out
0000                   ; through port A b4-7.
0000                   ;****************************************
0000                   ;
0000            DRA    EQU    $8004       ;PIA base address
0000            DDRA   EQU    DRA         ;data direction reg.
0000            CRA    EQU    DRA+1       ;control reg.
0100                   ORG    $0100
0100                   ;
0100 4F                CLRA               ;select DDR
0101 B7 80 05          STAA   CRA
0104 86 F0             LDAA   #$F0        ;I/O definition word
0106 B7 80 04          STAA   DRA         ;0-3 input, 4-7 output
```

```
0109 86 04            LDAA   #4         ;select I/O register A
010B B7 80 05         STAA   CRA        ;
010E B6 80 04   READ  LDAA   DRA        ;read port A
0111 48               ASLA              ;shift bits 4-7
0112 48               ASLA              ;into lower four
0113 48               ASLA              ;bit positions
0114 48               ASLA
0115 43               COMA              ;invert data
0116 B7 80 04         STAA   DRA        ;send back out via port A
0119 20 F7            BRA    READ       ;keep repeating
```

Example 3: Increment the binary number displayed on eight LEDs connected to port A (address \$8004) each time that a negative-going transition is applied to control input CA_1.

```
0000                 ;****************************************
0000                 ; 6800 binary counter routine, uses 6821
0000                 ; PIA port A (address 8004)
0000                 ; negative edge triggered via CA1
0000                 ; (using polling of interrupt flag).
0000                 ;****************************************
0000                 ;
0000          DRA    EQU    $8004       ;PIA base address
0000          DDRA   EQU    DRA         ;data direction reg.
0000          CRA    EQU    DRA+1       ;control reg.
0100                 ORG    $0100
0100                 ;
0100 4F              CLRA               ;select DDR
0101 B7 80 05        STAA   CRA
0104 43              COMA               ;invert A
0105 B7 80 04        STAA   DRA         ;port A all outputs
0108 86 04           LDAA   #4          ;use 06 for positive edge
010A B7 80 05        STAA   CRA         ;select DRA
010D 4F              CLRA               ;zero count
010E B7 80 04        STAA   DRA         ;all LEDs off
0111 B6 80 04  FLAG  LDAA   DRA         ;read control reg A
0114 2A FB           BPL    FLAG        ;wait for flag set
0116 7C 80 04        INC    DRA         ;increment count
0119 20 F6           BRA    FLAG        ;wait for next transition
```

Example 4: Cause an LED connected to control line CA_2 to flash on and off at a 1 Hz rate (system clock approximately 614 kHz).

```
 0000                     ;***************************************
0000                     ; Routine to flash LED connected to
0000                     ; CA2 (output mode) of 6821 PIA
0000                     ; located at address $8004-7
0000                     ;***************************************
0000                     ;
0000              CRA    EQU     $8005        ;control reg. A
0100                     ORG     $0100
0100                     ;
0100 86 30               LDAA    #$30         ;control word
0102 B7 80 05     FLASH  STAA    CRA          ;send to control reg
0105 CE 95 E7            LDX     #$95E7       ;use X as time
0108 09           DELAY  DEX                  ;delay loop counter
0109 26 FD               BNE     DELAY
010B 88 08               EORA    #8           ;toggle b3 of A
010D 20 F3               BRA     FLASH
```

Problems

1 Explain how the following items may be directly interfaced to the data bus of a microcomputer:
   (a) A number of two-state input devices.
   (b) A number of two-state output devices.

2 Describe the function of the following components in an interfacing device:
   (a) Data output register.
   (b) Data direction register.
   (c) Control register.
   (d) Status flags.

3 With the aid of a block diagram, show how a PIA (or PIO) may be used to interface a parallel peripheral device to a microcomputer.

4 Demonstrate how a 6530 RRIOT may be configured such that bits 2, 3 and 7 of port A, and bits 1, 5 and 7 of port B act as outputs and all remaining bits act as inputs (assume that the RRIOT is located in the address range 1700_{16} to 1703_{16}).

5 The timer in a 6530 RRIOT is required to generate pulses on bit 7 of port B every 100 ms. Write a 6502 assembly language routine to show how the RRIOT should be configured and the timer loaded for this application (assume the RRIOT I/O section is located at addresses 1700_{16}, and the timer section is located in the address range 1704_{16} to $170F_{16}$.

6 A 6502 based microcomputer uses a 6522 VIA which is located in the address range $A000_{16}$ to $A00F_{16}$. Show how the 6522 VIA may be programmed to carry out the following operations:
(a) Generate a 1 kHz square wave output from CA_2.
(b) Generate a 1 kHz output from PB_7 using timer 1.
(c) Count a hundred input pulses applied to PB_6 using timer 2.

7 Explain how the timing of data transfers between a peripheral device and port A of a 6522 VIA may be controlled using CA_1 and CA_2.

8 Show how a Z80 microcomputer with an 8255 PPI may be programmed to enable the following operations to take place:
(a) Read data in from port A of the 8255, invert the data and send it back out via port C.
(b) Generate a 1 kHz output from bit 0 of port C using the bit set/reset facility.
(c) Increment the binary number indicated by eight LEDs connected to port A each time that STB A (PC_4) is activated.

9 A Z80 based microcomputer with an 8255 PPI has eight two-state input devices connected to port A. An active STB input is used to transfer data from these devices into the PPI and simultaneously initiates an interrupt.
(a) Draw a simple circuit to show how the Z80, 8255 PPI and the two-state devices are interconnected.
(b) Write a Z80 assembly language program to show how the 8255 PPI should be configured for this application.

10 A Z80 based microcomputer has a Z80 PIO which is I/O mapped at addresses 80_{16} to 83_{16}. Write Z80 assembly language routines to show how the following operations may be carried out:
(a) Read data from eight two-state devices connected to port B and send this data to eight two-state indicators connected to port A.
(b) Read data from four two-state devices connected to bits 0 to 3, and send this data out to bits 4 to 7 of the same port.
(c) Use bits 5 to 7 of port A as control inputs which cause an interrupt to be initiated when all three are active high. The Z80 MPU must be configured to accept mode 2 interrupts, and the ISR vector is assumed to be located at address $0D42_{16}$.

11 A Z80 based microcomputer has a Z80 PIO which is I/O mapped at

address 80_{16} has a single seven-segment LED connected to port A via a suitable interface circuit. A switch is connected to the remaining bit of port A, and is arranged so that the number on the seven-segment LED is incremented each time that the switch is closed.

(a) Draw a diagram to show how the seven-segment display and the switch may be connectd to the PIO.

(b) Write a Z80 assembly language routine to show how the PIO must be configured to enable the circuit to function as intended.

12 A 6800 based microcomputer has a 6821 PIA located in the address range 8004_{16} to 8007_{16}. Eight two-state input devices are connected to port A of the 6821, and eight two-state indicators are connected to port B. Write a 6800 assembly language routine to cause the data set up on the input devices to be displayed on the indicators each time that CA_1 becomes active (low).

13 A 6800 based microcomputer has a 6821 PIA located in the address range 8004_{16} to 8007_{16}. Eight two-state input devices are used to monitor an industrial process, and are connected to port A of the 6821. The two-state devices normally apply a logical 0 to each of the port inputs, but if a logical 1 is detected on any input, an LED connected to CA_2 is illuminated.

(a) Draw a diagram to show how the two-state input devices and the LED may be connected to the PIA.

(b) Write a 6800 assembly language routine to enable such a system to be implemented.

Chapter 6

Serial I/O controllers

Serial data transfers

The term *serial* when applied to data transfers usually means *bit-serial* in which the individual bits of data bytes are transferred in time sequence, one after another, as shown in Figure 6.1.

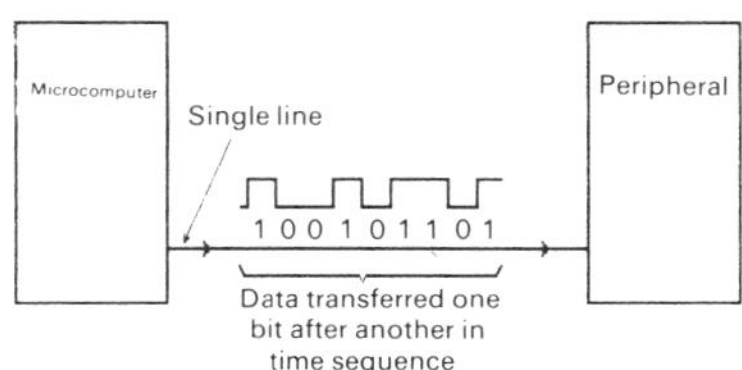

Figure 6.1

Serial data transfers are commonly used when peripheral devices are located at some distance from the microcomputer to which they are attached. A typical arrangement for serial data communications is shown in Figure 6.2.

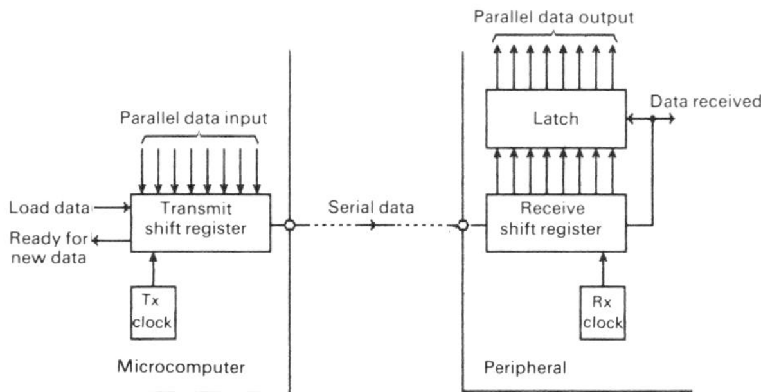

Figure 6.2

It can be seen from this diagram that the hardware required is relatively simple and cost effective, requiring only one wire or data channel (plus ground) for each data path. This has the advantage that connections between a peripheral (e.g., keyboard or printer) and a microcomputer can be made without resorting to bulky multicore or ribbon cables, and also avoids problems associated with interaction between adjacent signals when using long parallel conductors. Data transfers usually take place *asnychronously* so that it is not necessary for the MPU and peripheral to share a common clocking signal (although both clocks must operate at very similar rates if errors are to be avoided). In effect, each data word transferred carries its own synchronizing signal in the form of *start* and *stop* bits which are appended as shown in Figure 6.3.

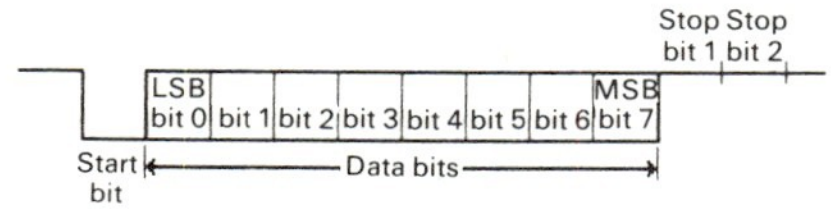

Figure 6.3

When receiving, a peripheral waits for the falling edge of each start bit before clocking in the serial data, therefore discrepancies in the clocking frequency are acceptable provided that clocking still occurs within the correct bit period. A progressive shift in clocking point is corrected when the next start bit appears, thus preventing accumulative effects from corrupting received data (see Figure 6.4).

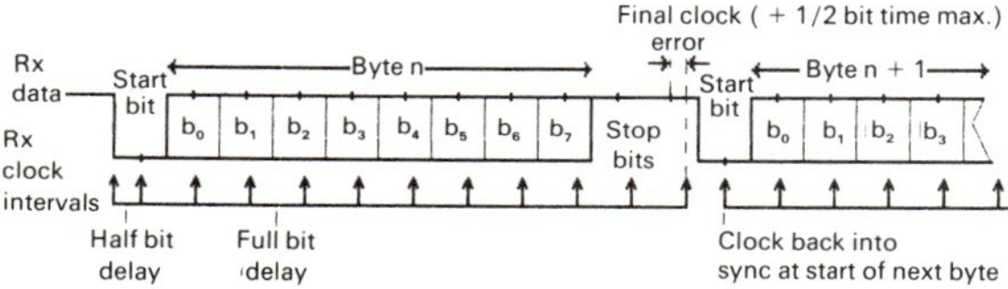

Figure 6.4

Baud rate

Since not all bits transferred in a serial system are actual data bits, expressing a data transfer rate in terms of *bits per second* may cause confusion. For example, if 8-bit data words are transferred at the rate of one word per second, the data transfer rate might be considered as 8 bits per second. However, since each word has a start and stop bit added, in order to transfer one word per second, the transfer rate must be 10 bits per second. This confusion is avoided by stating data transfer rates in terms of their *baud rate*. The baud rate is defined as:

$$\textbf{Baud rate} = \frac{\mathbf{1}}{\textbf{bit time}}$$

Thus at 2400 baud, the bit time is 1/2400 or 417 μs. Consider the following two transfer formats:

	(a)	*(b)*
Data bits	7	6
Start bit	1	1
Stop bits	2	1
Total bits	10	8

Assuming 2400 baud, the data transfer rates are:

(a) $$\frac{10^6}{10 \times 417} = 240 \text{ characters/second}$$

(b) $$\frac{10^6}{8 \times 417} = 300 \text{ characters/second}$$

Serial/parallel data conversion

Serial data transfers may take place using a single I/O line of a parallel interface device in conjunction with suitable software to perform the parallel/serial conversion, or by the use of dedicated serial I/O controllers, e.g. UART, ACIA or SIO. The first of these methods may be considered as implementing a UART in software and requires virtually no additional hardware. The second method does require additional hardware, but little extra in the way of software.

Software UART

This arrangement uses software to simulate the functions of a UART (*universal asynchronous receiver/transmitter*), and serial data is transferred via a single port line of a parallel I/O device. It is therefore readily adaptable for different baud rates, and in many cases, automatically adjusts itself to the correct rate after measuring the baud rate of incoming data. The hardware required for this system is shown in Figure 6.5.

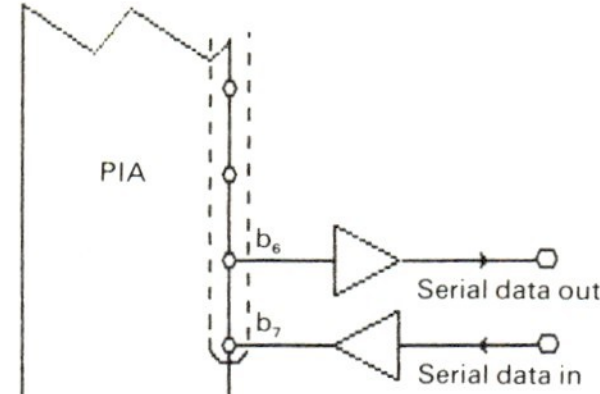

Figure 6.5

The software required depends upon the actual format used. The use of start and stop bits has already been discussed, and these must be added to data by the software prior to transmission. These extra bits must be detected and removed by the software used for reception. Figure 6.6 shows flowcharts for the transmission and reception processes which assume 8-bit data with the addition of a start bit and one stop bit.

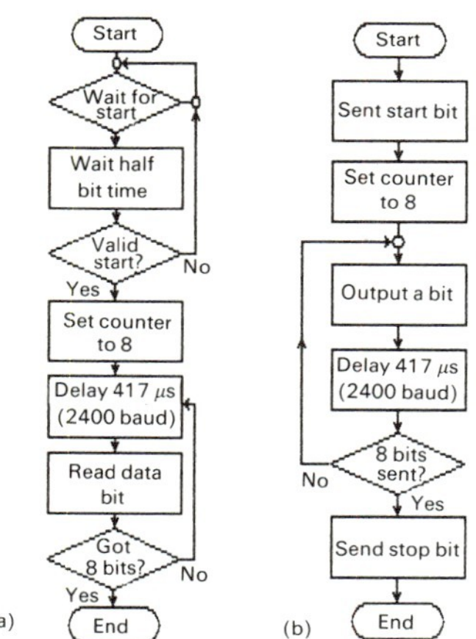

Figure 6.6

Sample software routines for the 6502, Z80 and 6800 MPUs are as follows:

6500 serial I/O routines

The following 6502 routines provide serial I/O from a 6530/6532 PIA, bits PB_0 and PA_7. The baud rate is determined by the 16-bit delay parameter stored in RAM locations $17F2 and $17F3.

```
0000                    ;************************************
0000                    ; Serial input routine for 6502 MPU
0000                    ; with 6530 RRIOT located $1740 - $1743
0000                    ; Return with character in Acc
0000                    ;************************************
0000                    ;
0000              PAD    = $1740
0000              PBD    = PAD+2
0000              CHAR   = $00FE
0000              LCONST = $17F2
0000              HCONST = $17F3
0000              TEMPH  = $17F4
1E00                   * = $1E00
1E00                    ;
1E00 A2 08         INCH  LDX    #08        ;set up 8 bit count
1E02 A9 01               LDA    #01
1E04 2C 40 17      IN1   BIT    PAD
1E07 D0 22               BNE    IN4        ;no character ready
1E09 30 F9               BMI    INCH       ;wait for start bit
1E0B 20 56 1E            JSR    FDEL       ;delay 1 bit time
1E0E 20 6D 1E      IN2   JSR    HDEL       ;delay 1/2 bit time
1E11 AD 40 17      IN3   LDA    PAD        ;read 8-bit port
1E14 29 80               AND    #$80       ;mask off low order
1E16 46 FE               LSR    CHAR       ;shift character right
1E18 05 FE               ORA    CHAR       ;combine with next bit
1E1A 85 FE               STA    CHAR       ;and update shift reg
1E1C 20 56 1E            JSR    FDEL       ;delay 1 bit time
1E1F CA                  DEX               ;decrement bit counter
1E20 D0 EF               BNE    IN3        ;get next bit
1E22 20 6D 1E            JSR    HDEL       ;wait for end of bit
1E25 A5 FE               LDA    CHAR       ;return char in Acc
1E27 29 7F               AND    #$7F       ;clear parity bit
1E29 60            IN4   RTS
1E2A                    ;
1E2A                    ;************************************
1E2A                    ; Serial output routine for 6502 MPU
1E2A                    ; with 6530 RRIOT located $1740 - $1743
1E2A                    ; Character for transmission in Acc
1E2A                    ;************************************
1E2A                    ;
1E2A 85 FE         OUTCH STA    CHAR       ;temp store character
1E2C AD 42 17            LDA    PBD        ;generate start bit
1E2F 29 FE               AND    #$FE       ;clear bit 0
1E31 8D 42 17            STA    PBD        ;to signal start
```

```
1E34 20 56 1E          JSR    FDEL       ;delay 1 bit time
1E37 A2 08             LDX    #$08       ;transmit 8 bits
1E39 AD 42 17    OUT1  LDA    PBD        ;get current port status
1E3C 29 FE             AND    #$FE       ;clear bit 0
1E3E 46 FE             LSR    CHAR       ;shift next bit into carry
1E40 69 00             ADC    #$00       ;and put carry into bit 0
1E42 8D 42 17          STA    PBD        ;and send it
1E45 20 56 1E          JSR    FDEL       ;delay 1 bit time
1E48 CA                DEX               ;count bits transmitted
1E49 D0 EE             BNE    OUT1       ;sent all 8 bits?
1E4B AD 42 17          LDA    PBD        ;if so, generate stop bit
1E4E 09 01             ORA    #$01       ;set bit 0 (stop)
1E50 8D 42 17          STA    PBD        ;and send it
1E53 20 56 1E          JSR    FDEL       ;hold stop for 1 bit period
1E55 60                RTS
                       ;
1E56                   ;************************************
1E56                   ; Time delay subroutine
1E56                   ; Sixteen bit time constant stored in
1E56                   ; memory determines baud rate.
1E56                   ;************************************
1E56                   ;
1E56 AD F3 17    FDEL  LDA    HCONST     ;get time const high byte
1E59 8D F4 17          STA    TEMPH      ;keep working copy
1E5C AD F2 17          LDA    LCONST     ;get time const low byte
1E5F 38          DLY1  SEC               ;decrement accumulator
1E60 E9 01       DLY2  SBC    #$01       ;by subtracting 1
1E62 B0 03             BCS    DLY3       ;gone past zero?
1E64 CE F4 17          DEC    TEMPH      ;if so, decrement high byte
1E67 AC F4 17    DLY3  LDY    TEMPH      ;high byte past zero?
1E6A 10 F3             BPL    DLY1       ;until count = 0
1E6C 60                RTS
1E6D                   ;
1E6D AD F3 17    HDEL  LDA    HCONST     ;get time const high byte
1E70 8D F4 17          STA    TEMPH      ;keep working copy
1E73 AD F2 17          LDA    LCONST     ;get time const low byte
1E76 4A                LSR    A          ;divide 16-bit time const
1E77 4E F4 17          LSR    TEMPH      ;by two (half delay)
1E7A 90 E3             BCC    DLY1       ;no carry high byte to low
1E7C 09 80             ORA    #$80       ;else correct low byte
1E7E B0 E0             BCS    DLY2       ; = branch always
```

Z80 serial I/O routines

The following Z80 routines provide serial I/O from an 8255 PPI, bits 0 and 7. The nominal baud rate is 2400, although this may be altered by making adjustments to the delay parameter in register D. It will be necessary to modify the value in D if a different MPU clock frequency is used.

```
                          ;**************************************
                          ; Read serial input data via
                          ; bit 7 of 8255 Port A
                          ; Baud rate is 2400, 8 bits, parity zeroed
                          ; bit time for 2400 baud is 417us
                          ; D=2DH gives bit time of 417us
                          ; D=44H gives bit time of 625us
                          ;**************************************
                          ;
2000                      ORG     2000H
0000 =           PORTA    EQU     0             ;8255 Port A
                                    ;
2000 0E00        SDATA:   LD      C,0           ;clear receive reg
2002 0608                 LD      B,8           ;read 8 bits
2004 DB00        FSTART:  IN      A,(PORTA)     ;read serial port
2006 CB7F                 BIT     7,A           ;wait for stop bit
2008 20FA                 JR      NZ,FSTART     ;
200A DB00        START1:  IN      A,(PORTA)     ;wait for start bit
200C CB7F                 BIT     7,A           ;(input goes to '1')
200E 28FA                 JR      Z,START1      ;
2010 1644                 LD      D,44H         ;1.5 bit time delay
2012 CD3820               CALL    DELAY         ;
2015 AF          RDBIT:   XOR     A             ;clear C flag
2016 DB00                 IN      A,(PORTA)     ;read serial port
2018 CB7F                 BIT     7,A           ;and if a zero is
201A 2001                 JR      NZ,BIT0       ;read, then shift a 1
201C 37                   SCF                   ;into the receive
201D CB19        BIT0:    RR      C             ;shift register (C)
201F 1602                 LD      D,2D H        ;1 bit delay
2021 CD3820               CALL    DELAY         ;
2024 10EF                 DJNZ    RDBIT         ;stop after 8 bits
2026 CBB9                 RES     7,C           ;and zero parity bit
2028 79                   LD      A,C           ;transfer data to Acc
2029 C9                   RET
                          ;
```

```
                          ;**********************************
                          ; Serial output routine for Z80
                          ; MPU with 8255 PPI PORT A address 0
                          ; Data output from bit 0
                          ; Character for transmission in A
                          ;**********************************
                          ;
202A 060A       OUTCH:    LD      B,10          ;counter (10 bits)
202C B7                   OR      A             ;clear carry for start
202D 17                   RLA                   ;move carry to A bit 0
202E D300       SHIFT:    OUT     (PORTA),A     ;send 1 bit to ser. port
2030 CD3820               CALL    DELAY         ;delay 1 bit time
2033 1F                   RRA                   ;get next bit ready
2034 37                   SCF                   ;set carry for stop bit
2035 10F7                 DJNZ    SHIFT         ;all bits sent?
2037 C9                   RET
                          ;
                          ;*************************************
                          ; Bit timing for serial data
                          ; time = [10+(16 x D)] x 0.5586us
                          ; Clock = 1.79 MHz (D=contents of D reg.)
                          ;*************************************
                          ;
2038 15         DELAY:    DEC     D             ;delay set
2039 20FD                 JR      NZ,DELAY      ;set by D reg
203B C9                   RET
```

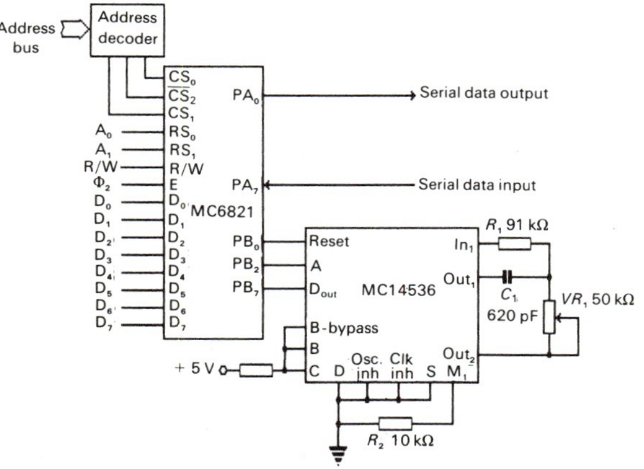

Figure 6.7

6800 serial I/O routines

An interface circuit of the type shown in Figure 6.7 may be used to provide serial I/O for peripheral devices.

The baud rate of the serial data is determined by the MC14536 device whose timing is controlled by an external *RC* network (R_1, C_1 and VR_1). Adjustment of the 50 kΩ variable resistor (VR_1) is used to set the baud rate. The operation of this circuit comes under the control of the serial I/O software via port B bits 0, 2 and 7. The following software routines may be used for serial data transfers:

```
0000                 ;************************************
0000                 ; Serial input routine for 6800 MPU
0000                 ; with 6821 PIA located $8004 - $8007
0000                 ; Return with character in Acc A
0000                 ;************************************
0000                 ;
0000            PAD  EQU    $8004
E100                 ORG    $E100
E100                 ;
E100 CE 8004    INCH LDX    #PAD
E103 A6 00      IN1  LDA A  0,X       ;look for start bit
E105 2B FC           BMI    IN1
E107 6F 02           CLR    2,X       ;set counter for half bit
E109 8D 29           BSR    HDEL      ;start timer
E10B 8D 22           BSR    DEL       ;delay half-bit time
E10D C6 04           LDA B  #4        ;set del for full-bit time
E10F E7 02           STA B  2,X
E111 58              ASL B            ;set up counter with 8
E112 8D 1B      IN2  BSR    DEL       ;wait one char time
E114 0D              SEC              ;mark com line
E115 69 00           ROL    0,X       ;get bit into carry
E117 46              ROR A            ;carry into acc
E118 5A              DEC B            ;dec bit counter
E119 26 F7           BNE    IN2       ;got all 8 bits?
E11B 8D 13           BSR    DEL       ;wait for stop bit
E11D 84 7F           AND A  #$7F      ;reset parity bit
E11F 39              RTS
E120                 ;
E120                 ;************************************
E120                 ; Serial output routine for 6800 MPU
E120                 ; with 6821 PIA located $8004 - $8007
E120                 ; Character for transmission in Acc A
E120                 ;************************************
E120                 ;
```

```
E120  C6 0A        OUTCH LDA B   #0A        ;set up counter (10 bits)
E122  6A 00              DEC     0,X        ;set start bit
E124  8D 0E              BSR     HDEL       ;start timer
E126  8D 08        OUT1  BSR     DEL        ;delay one-bit time
E128  A7 00              STA     0,X        ;put out one data bit
E12A  0D                 SEC                ;set carry bit
E12B  46                 ROR A              ;shift in next bit
E12C  5A                 DEC B              ;dec bit counter
E12D  26 F7              BNE     OUT1       ;sent all bits?
E12F  39                 RTS
E130                     ;
E130                     ;************************************
E130                     ; Bit timer for serial data transmit
E130                     ; and receive routines
E130                     ;************************************
E130                     ;
E130 6D 02         DEL   TST     2,X        ;check for time up
E132 2A FC               BPL     DEL        ;if not - wait
E134 6C 02         HDEL  INC     2,X        ;reset timer
E136 6A 02               DEC     2,X
E138 39                  RTS
```

Shift register (in VIA)

Some parallel I/O devices, e.g. 6522 VIA, contain shift registers which may be used for transmission/reception of serial data. The 6522 VIA contains an 8-bit shift register which may be used to shift serial data into or out of the CB_2 pin under the control of an internal modulo-8 counter. The rate at which data is transferred may be controlled by either the MPU clock $\phi 2$, interval timer 2 (*one-shot* or *free-run* modes), or by an external clock connected to CB_1. The source of shift pulses and the direction of serial data is determined by the contents of the auxiliary control register (ACR), as shown in Figure 6.8, and Table 6.1.

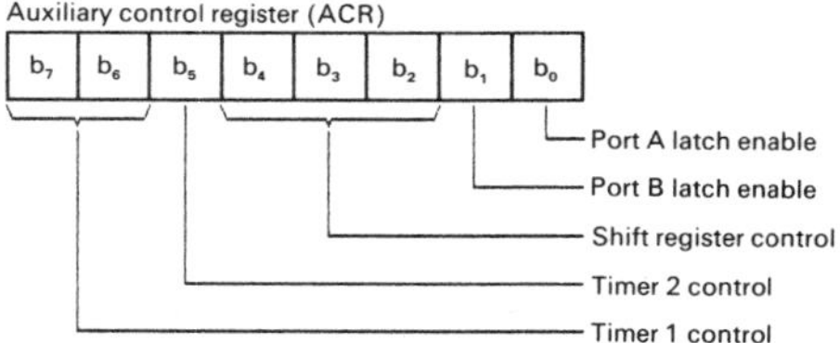

Figure 6.8

Table 6.1

PORT A LATCH ENABLE	
ACR0 = 1	Port A latch is enabled to latch input data when CA1 Interrupt Flag (IFR1) is set
= 0	Port A latch is disabled, reflects current data on PA pins
PORT B LATCH ENABLE	
ACR1 = 1	Port B latch is enabled to latch the voltage on the pins for the interrupt lines or the ORB contents for the output lines when CB1 Interrupt Flag (IFR4) is set.
= 0	Port B latch is disabled, reflects current data on PB pins.
SHIFT REGISTER CONTROL	
ACR4 ACR3 ACR2	MODE
0 0 0	Shift Register Disabled
0 0 1	Shift in under control of Timer 2
0 1 0	Shift in under control of Φ2
0 1 1	Shift in under control of external clock
1 0 0	Free running output at rate determined by Timer 2
1 0 1	Shift out under control of Timer 2
1 1 0	Shift out under control of Φ2
1 1 1	Shift out under control of external clock
TIMER 2 CONTROL	
ACR5 = 0	T2 acts as an interval timer in the one-shot mode
= 1	T2 counts a predetermined number of pulses on PB6
TIMER 1 CONTROL	
ACR7 ACR6	MODE
0 0	T1 one-shot mode -- Generate a single time-out interrupt each time T1 is loaded. Output to PB7 disabled.
0 1	T1 free-running mode -- Generate continuous interrupts. Output to PB7 disabled.
1 0	T1 one-shot mode -- Generate a single time-out interrupt and an output pulse on PB7 each time T1 is loaded.
1 1	T1 free-running mode -- Generate continuous interrupts and a square wave output on PB7.

A 6502 assembly language routine required for serial data output from CB_2 is as follows:

```
0000                    ;*****************************
0000                    ;Serial data output from CB2 of
0000                    ;a 6522 VIA
0000                    ;Clock source: MPU ϕ2
0000                    ;*****************************
0000                    ;
0000                    ACR = $A00B
0000                    SR  = $A00A
0000                    BUFF= $0080
0200                       *= $0200
0200                    ;
0200  A9 00             LDA   #0
0202  8D 0B A0          STA   ACR
0205  A9 18             LDA   #$18        ;select shift out
0207  8D 0B A0          STA   ACR         ;under control of ϕ2
020A  A5 80             LDA   BUFF        ;get parallel data
020C  8D 0A A0          STA   SR          ;shift out serial
....  .. .. ..
....  .. .. ..
```

The $\phi 2$ shift out mode is selected by loading ACR with 18_{16} which puts the binary combination 110_2 into bits 4, 3 and 2. The shift register is loaded with data from memory location 0080_{16} and this action automatically starts the shifting operation at a rate determined by $\phi 2$. The program should wait until all eight bits have been shifted out before loading the shift register with new data. The 6522 VIA automatically sets bit 2 of the interrupt flag register (IFR) once all eight bits have been shifted out, and the state of this flag should be tested to determine when the shift register may be reloaded. Bit 2 of the IFR is cleared by writing new data into the shift register.

The following 6502 assembly language routine reads in serial data from CB_2:

```
0000                    ;*****************************
0000                    ;Serial data input from CB2 of
0000                    ;a 6522 VIA
0000                    ;Clock source: MPU ϕ2
0000                    ;*****************************
0000                    ;
0000                    ACR = $A00B
0000                    SR  = $A00A
```

```
0000                IFR = $A00D
0000                BUFF= $0080
0200                  *= $0200
0200                ;
0200  A9 00                 LDA   #0
0202  8D 0B A0              STA   ACR         ;clear shift reg
0205  A9 0C                 LDA   #$0C        ;select shift in
0207  8D 0B A0              STA   ACR         ;under control of ϕ2
020A  AD 0D A0      FLAG    LDA   IFR         ;read 8-shifts flag
020D  29 04                 AND   #04         ;mask unwanted flags
020F  F0 F9                 BEQ   FLAG        ;all 8 shifts done?
0211  AD 0A A0              LDA   SR          ;read shift reg
0214  85 80                 STA   BUFF        ;save data in memory
....  .. .. ..
....  .. .. ..
```

Reading the parallel data from the shift register automatically clears bit 2 of the IFR and initiates another shift-in sequence. In both of these examples, shift pulses generated internally are available as output from CB_1 for controlling external circuits.

Dedicated serial I/O controllers

Dedicated serial I/O controllers are available in most MPU families, each performing similar functions but allocated a name peculiar to each manufacturer, for example:

1 UART – universal asynchronous receiver/transmitter.
2 USART – universal aynchronous/asynchronous receiver/transmitter.
3 DART – dual asynchronous receiver/transmitter.
4 ACIA – asynchronous communications interface adapter.
5 SIO – serial input/output.

As an example of a typical dedicated serial I/O controller, the operation of the Motorola 6850 ACIA is now considered.

Motorola 6850 ACIA

The 6850 ACIA (asynchronous communications interface adapter) provides data formatting and control to interface serial asynchronous signals to an MPU bus system. A block diagram of this device is shown in Figure 6.9(a) and (b).

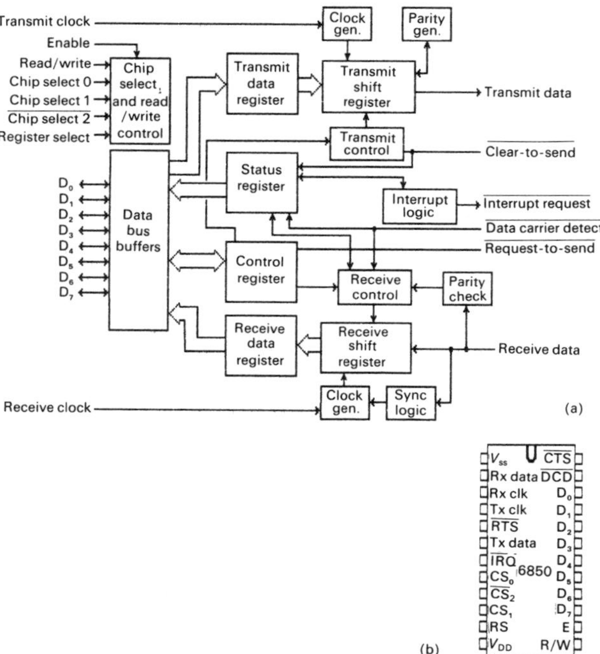

Figure 6.9

The 6850 appears to the programmer as two addressable locations, at which are located four registers, two read-only and two write-only. The read-only registers are *status* and *receive data*; the write-only registers are *control* and *transmit data*. The receive and transmit sections may be separately clocked so that different baud rates can be used for reception and transmission of data.

Transmission of data

A character may be written into the *transmit data register* if the TDRE (transmit data register empty) bit in the status register indicates that it is empty. This character is transferred to the *transmit shift register* where it is serialized and transmitted via the *transmit data* output, preceded by a start bit, and followed by one or two stop bits. A parity bit (odd or even) may also be optionally added at this stage. Once the first character has been transferred to the shift register, the TDRE bit may again be tested, and if the transmit data register is empty, a further character may be loaded while the preceding character is still being transmitted (double buffering). This second character will automatically be transferred to the shift register once transmission of the preceding character has been completed.

Reception of data

Serial data is received from a peripheral device through the *receive data* input. The receive clock is synchronized (with the aid of internal ÷16 and ÷64 dividers) using the high to low transition of the start bit of the received data. Received data is then clocked into the *receive shift register* at approximately the mid-point of each bit time. As the character is being received, an internal parity check is carried out and any error is reported by a bit in the status register. Other forms of error such as *framing error*, *overrun error* and *receive data register full* are also reported in a similar manner. Once assembled, the received character is transferred to the *receive data register* and the *receive data register full* (RDRF) bit in the status register is set to indicate this has taken place. A further character may now be clocked into the *receive shift register*. The data in the *receive data register* may be put onto the MPU data bus by performing a read operation which automatically clears the *receive data register full* bit in the status register.

6850 control register

The ACIA control register is an 8-bit write-only buffer, the contents of which control the user-selectable options such as number of data and stop bits, parity, clock divide ratio and interrupt status as shown in Table 6.2.

Table 6.2

Status register

bit 7	bit 6	bit 5	bit 4	bit 3	bit 2	bit 1	bit 0
Interrupt Request (IRQ)	Parity Error (PE)	Receive Overrun (OVRN)	Framing Error (FE)	$\overline{\text{Clear to Send}}$ (CTS)	$\overline{\text{Data Carrier Detect}}$ (DCD)	Transmit Data Register Empty (TDRE)	Receive Data Register Full (RDRF)

6850 status register

The ACIA status register is an 8-bit read-only register which indicates the current state of the transmitting and receiving processes (including modem), reports any errors detected while receiving data, and shows the current interrupt request status. The interrupt request status bit may be polled in non-interrupt I/O systems to determine whether a character is ready for transmission or reception. The function of each bit in the status register is shown in Table 6.3.

Table 6.3

Control register

CR1	CR0	Function
0	0	÷ 1
0	1	÷ 16
1	0	÷ 64
1	1	Master reset

CR4	CR3	CR2	Function
0	0	0	7bits+Even Parity+2 Stop bits
0	0	1	7bits+Odd Parity+2 Stop bits
0	1	0	7bits+Even Parity+1 Stop bit
0	1	1	7bits+Odd Parity+1 Stop bit
1	0	0	8bits+2 Stop bits
1	0	1	8bits+1 Stop bit
1	1	0	8bits+Even Parity+1 Stop bit
1	1	1	8bits+Odd Parity+1 Stop bit

CR6	CR5	Function
0	0	RTS=Low, Transmitting Interrupt Disabled
0	1	RTS=Low, Transmitting Interrupt Enabled
1	0	RTS=high, Transmitting Interrupt Disabled
1	1	RTS=Low, Transmitting a Break Level on the Transmit Data Output, Transmitting Interrupt Disabled

Interfacing a 6850 ACIA to the MPU buses

A 6850 ACIA may be connected to the bus system of a microcomputer as shown in Figure 6.10.

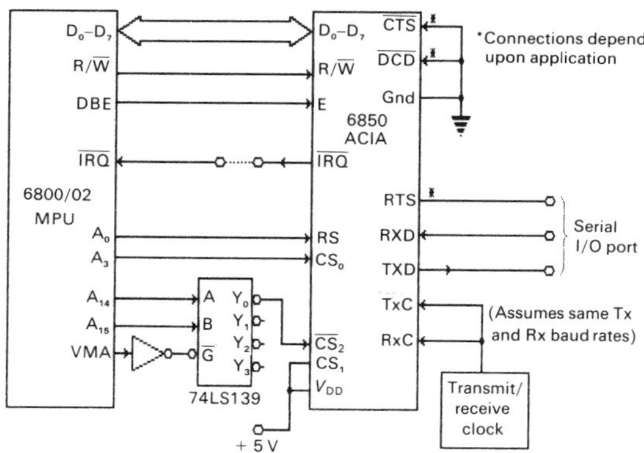

Figure 6.10

Software routines

Although the 6850 originates from the 6800 MPU family, it is a very flexible device which may be operated under a variety of different conditions and is therefore often encountered in systems which use other types of MPU. The following software routines demonstrate how simple serial I/O may be achieved.

(a) 6502

```
0000                      ;***************************************
0000                      ; 6502 subroutines to transmit and receive
0000                      ; data through a 6850 ACIA located at
0000                      ; memory addresses 0E800H & 0E801H
0000                      ;***************************************
0000                      ;
0000           ACIAC   =       $0E800          ;ACIA control reg.
0000           ACIAD   =       ACIAC+1         ;ACIA data reg.
0200                  *=       $0200
0200                      ;
0200                      ;***************************************
0200                      ; Subroutine to initialise ACIA
0200                      ; control register
0200                      ;***************************************
0200                      ;
0200 A9 03     INIT    LDA     #3              ;master reset
0202 8D 00 E8          STA     ACIAC           ;word for ACIA
0205 A9 11             LDA     #$11            ;8-bit, no parity
0207 8D 00 E8          STA     ACIAC           ;2 stop, non int.
020A 60                RTS                     ;serial I/O
020B                      ;
020B                      ;***************************************
020B                      ; Subroutine to read in data byte
020B                      ; from ACIA
020B                      ;***************************************
020B                      ;
020B AD 00 E8 CONIN    LDA     ACIAC           ;test RDRF bit=1
020E 29 01             AND     #1              ;(char. ready)
0210 F0 F9             BEQ     CONIN           ;wait until full
0212 AD 01 E8          LDA     ACIAD           ;read in data
0215 29 7F             AND     #$7F            ;mask parity bit
0217 60                RTS
0218                      ;
0218                      ;***************************************
0218                      ; Subroutine to send  ASCII character
0218                      ; in X to ACIA
0218                      ;***************************************
0218                      ;
0218 AD 00 E8 CONOUT   LDA     ACIAC           ;test TDRE bit = 1
```

```
021B 29 02              AND     #2              ;(ready to send)
021D F0 F9              BEQ     CONOUT          ;wait until ready
021F 8A                 TXA                     ;put char, into A
0220 8D 01 E8           STA     ACIAD           ;and sent it to
0223 60                 RTS                     ;ACIA data reg.
```

(b) Z80

```
                        ;****************************************
                        ; Z80 subroutines to transmit and receive
                        ; data through a 6850 ACIA located at
                        ; memory addresses 0E800H & 0E801H
                        ;****************************************
                        ;
E800 =          ACIAC   EQU     0E800H          ;ACIA control reg.
E801 =          ACIAD   EQU     ACIAC+1         ;ACIA data reg.
1800                    ORG     1800H
                        ;
                        ;****************************************
                        ; Subroutine to initialise ACIA
                        ; control register
                        ;****************************************
                        ;
1800 3E03       INIT:   LD      A,3             ;master reset
1802 3200E8             LD      (ACIAC),A       ;word for ACIA
1805 3E11               LD      A,11H           ;8-bit, no parity
1807 3200E8             LD      (ACIAC),A       ;2 stop, non int.
180A C9                 RET                     ;serial I/O
                        ;
                        ;****************************************
                        ; Subroutine to read in data byte
                        ; from ACIA
                        ;****************************************
                        ;
180B 3A00E8     CONIN:  LD      A,(ACIAC)       ;test RDRF bit=1
180E E601               AND     1               ;(char. ready)
1810 CA0B18             JP      Z,CONIN         ;wait until full
1813 3A01E8             LD      A,(ACIAD)       ;read in data
1816 E67F               AND     7FH             ;mask parity bit
1818 C9                 RET
                        ;
```

```
                        ;****************************************
                        ; Subroutine to send  ASCII character
                        ; in C to ACIA
                        ;****************************************
                        ;
1819 3A00E8   CONOUT: LD      A,(ACIAC)        ;test TDRE bit = 1
181C E602             AND     2                ;(ready to send)
181E CA1918           JP      Z,CONOUT         ;wait until ready
1821 79               LD      A,C              ;put char. into A
1822 3201E8           LD      (ACIAD),A        ;and sent it to
1825 C9               RET                      ;ACIA data reg.
```

(c) 6800

```
0000                    ;****************************************
0000                    ; 6800 subroutines to transmit and receive
0000                    ; data through a 6850 ACIA located at
0000                    ; memory addresses 0E800H & 0E801H
0000                    ;****************************************
0000                    ;
0000          ACIAC     EQU     $0E800          ;ACIA control reg.
0000          ACIAD     EQU     ACIAC+1         ;ACIA data reg.
0200                    ORG     0200H
0200                    ;
0200                    ;****************************************
0200                    ; Subroutine to initialise ACIA
0200                    ; control register
0200                    ;****************************************
0200                    ;
0200 86 03    INIT      LDAA    #3              ;master reset
0202 B7 E8 00           STAA    ACIAC           ;word for ACIA
0205 86 11              LDAA    #$11            ;8-bit, no parity
0207 B7 E8 00           STAA    ACIAC           ;2 stop, non int.
020A 39                 RTS                     ;serial I/O
020B                    ;
020B                    ;****************************************
020B                    ; Subroutine to read in data byte
020B                    ; from ACIA
020B                    ;****************************************
020B                    ;
020B B6 E8 00 CONIN     LDAA    ACIAC           ;test RDRF bit=1
020E 84 01              ANDA    #1              ;(char. ready)
```

```
0210 27 F9              BEQ     CONIN           ;wait until full
0212 B6 E8 01           LDAA    ACIAD           ;read in data
0215 84 7F              ANDA    #$7F            ;mask parity bit
0217 39                 RTS
0218                    ;
0218                    ;****************************************
0218                    ; Subroutine to send  ASCII character
0218                    ; in Acc B to ACIA
0218                    ;****************************************
0218                    ;
0218 B6 E8 00 CONOUT    LDAA    ACIAC           ;test TDRE bit = 1
021B 84 02              ANDA    #2              ;(ready to send)
021D 27 F9              BEQ     CONOUT          ;wait until ready
021F 17                 TBA                     ;put char. into A
0220 B7 E8 01           STAA    ACIAD           ;and sent it to
0223 39                 RTS                     ;ACIA data reg.
```

RS-232 serial communications

The Electronic Industries Association (EIA) Recommended Standard (RS) RS-232 contains a specification for the interconnection between two systems to allow them to communicate in a serial manner. This standard defines the permissible voltage levels, control lines and physical connectors. It does not concern itself with such items as number of bits, baud rate and other factors related to the speed of the serial data. Most peripheral devices such as printers, VDUs or keyboards are available with RS-232 compatible I/O and this simplifies the connection of such peripherals to a microcomputer. Typically peripheral devices may be located at distances of up to 20 metres when using this standard.

EIA RS-232 standards

In order to minimize the effects of electrical noise upon serial data signals, the RS-232 standard specifies voltage levels of between + 3 V and + 25 V for

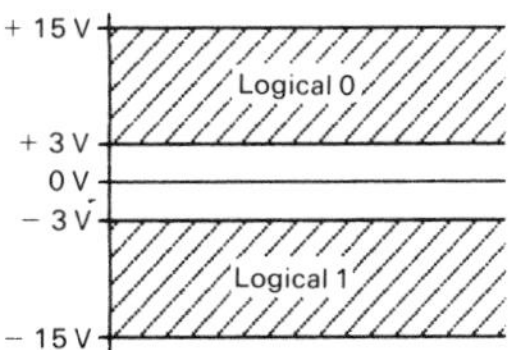

Figure 6.11

logical 0, and between − 3 V and − 25 V for logical 1. The later RS-232C standard is universally used nowadays in which the voltage levels are reduced to + or − 15 V, as shown in Figure 6.11 (note signal inversion, logical 1 being negative with respect to logical 0).

Most practical implementations use + 12 V for logical 0 and − 12 V for logical 1.

RS-232 signals

The RS-232 standard specifies a 25 pin 'D' connector (Figure 6.12), with signals as shown in Table 6.4.

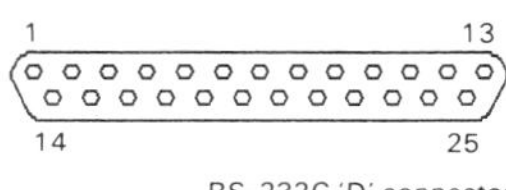

Figure 6.12

Table 6.4

Pin	*Description*	*Name*	*RS-232*
1	Protective ground	Prot	AA
2	Transmitted data	XMT	BA
3	Received data	RCV	BB
4	Request to send	RTS	CA
5	Clear to send	CTS	CB
6	Data set ready	DSR	CC
7	Signal ground	Com	AB
8	Data carrier detect	DCD	CF
9	—		
10	—		
11	Select XMT frequency	STF	CG
12	Secondary DCD	dcd	SCF
13	Secondary CTS	cts	SCB
14	Secondary XMT	xmt	SBA
15	Transmit clock	Xclk	DB
16	Secondary RCV	rcv	SBB
17	Receive clock	Rclk	DD
18	—		
19	Secondary RTS	rts	SCA
20	Data terminal ready	DTR	CD
21	Signal quality	SQ1	CG
22	Ring indicator	RI	CE
23	Data rate select	DRS	CH
24	External transmit clock	—	DA
25	Busy – standby	BY	—

Most implementations of RS-232 do not make use of all of these signals, and some are specifically for use with modems. A simple RS-232 link may use only three conductors, XMT, RCV and Com. Descriptions of the most commonly used pins are as follows:

Protective ground (*Prot*): This pin usually connects to the metal chassis of one device, and is connected via the cable to the corresponding connection on the other device.

Transmitted data (*TXD*): This pin provides an output signal which transfers serial data from one RS-232 device to another, provided that the *Clear to send* (CTS) signal is active.

Received data (*RXD*): This pin accepts serial input data which has been transmitted by some other RS-232 device.

Request to send (*RTS*): This pin provides an output logic level which indicates that an RS-232 device is ready to transmit serial data. The state of this signal is tested by the receiving device so that it knows when to expect more data.

Clear to send (*CTS*): This pin provides an output logic level which indicates that an RS-232 receiving device is ready to accept data via its *Received data* input. It thus provides a signal to the transmitting device which inhibits the transfer of data until the receiving device is ready.

Data set ready (*DSR*): This pin provides an output logic level which indicates that an RS-232 receiving device is ready for operation (i.e., switched on or operational).

Signal ground (*Com*): This provides a common reference or ground for all input and output signals.

Data terminal ready (*DTR*): This pin provides an output logic level which indicates that the RS-232 transmitting device is ready for operation (i.e., switched on or operational).

Although it is possible to transfer data using only two lines (signal plus ground), it is usual to make use of 'handshake' signals such as RTS and CTS, to enable the receiving device to control the flow of data. This arrangement avoids the receiving device from being presented with more data if it is still busy processing previous data, thus avoiding data loss.

RS-232 interconnections

The type of interconnection required between two devices depends upon the nature of the devices and the form of handshaking used. If one of the devices is a *modem* (modulator/demodulator) which is used for long distance communications, typically via the public telephone system, then *one-to-one* cables may be used, i.e., each pin at one end connected to corresponding pins at the other end. Often this is not the case, for example an RS-232 link may be used to connect a microcomputer to a printer. In such cases it may be necessary to 'cross-over' the pin 2 and pin 3 connections, since the *serial output* (TXD) of the microcomputer must be connected to the *serial input* (RXD) of the printer. In effect, the cable must be wired as a *null-modem* as shown in Figure 6.13.

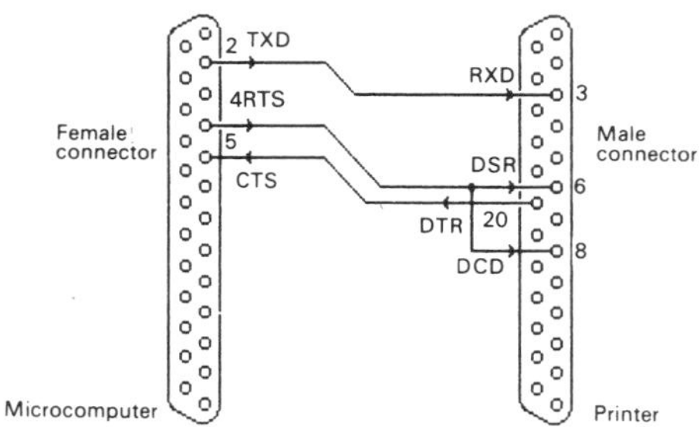

Figure 6.13

TTL/RS-232 interfaces

Since RS-232 voltage levels are incompatible with TTL levels, some form of interface circuit is required to provide voltage level conversion. In addition, the logic levels must be inverted (see Figure 6.14).

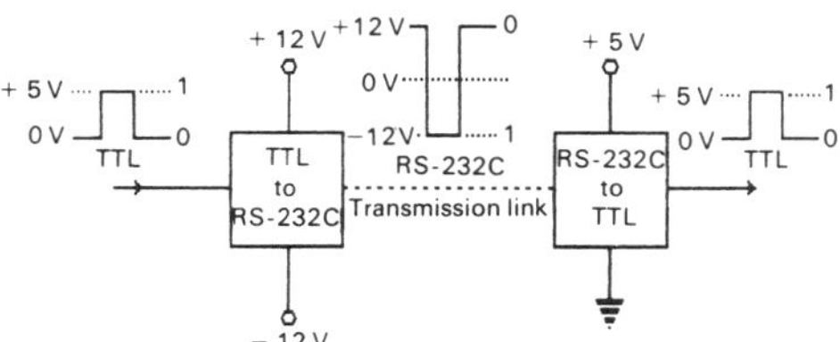

Figure 6.14

Interface circuits may be constructed from discrete components, or may make use of purpose built interface devices such as the 1488 and 1489 chips.

When receiving data, conversion of RS-232 signals to TTL voltage levels is relatively straightforward, requiring only limiting the swing of input signal between 0 V and + 5 V, followed by signal inversion. Suitable circuits for this purpose, using both discrete and integrated solutions are shown in Figure 6.15(a) and (b).

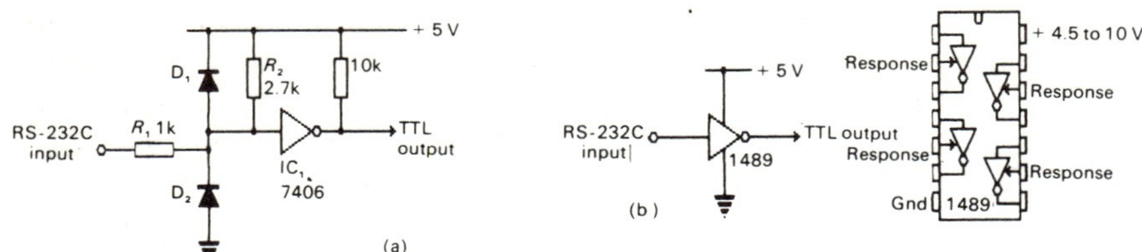

Figure 6.15

The discrete component version shown in Figure 6.15(a) uses two 'catching'diodes, D_1 and D_2 in conjunction with R_1 to prevent the incoming RS-232 signal from exceeding the maximum permissible TTL input voltages. Signal inversion is provided by IC_1, the 7406 inverter.

The integrated 1489 version of the circuit is shown in Figure 6.15(b). This device automatically limits its output voltage swing to that of its power supply. A *CR* network may be connected to the 'response' pin to allow the user to determine the threshold levels of the incoming signals and to provide a degree of noise filtering. In non-critical applications it is usual to leave the response pin unconnected.

When transmitting data, the conversion of TTL signals to RS-232 levels is slightly more complicated, since in addition to inversion, it also requires the generation of opposite polarity signals at (usually) higher voltage levels. Typically the $\pm$ 12 V levels of RS-232C are used. Suitable circuits for this purpose, using both discrete and integrated solutions are shown in Figure 6.16(a) and (b).

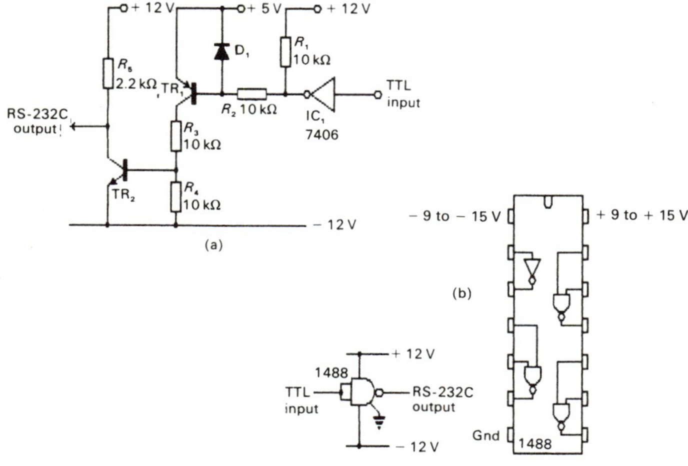

Figure 6.16

The discrete version shown in Figure 6.16(a) uses a 7406 'open-collector' IC to invert the TTL level source. The output signal may swing between 0 V and + 12 V, and is applied to the base of TR_1. Owing to the presence of D_1 and R_2, the base of TR_1 may swing approximately $\pm$ 0.6 V positive or negative with respect to the + 5 V supply line. This is sufficient to cause TR_1 collector to switch between + 5 V and − 12 V. The voltage level available at the junction of R_3/R_4 biases the base of TR_2 so that its collector potential switches between + 12 V and − 12 V, i.e, RS-232C levels.

The integrated 1488 version of the circuit is shown in Figure 6.16(b). This device contains three NAND gates and an inverter, and provided that pins 1 and 14 are connected to appropriate positive and negative supplies, it automatically converts TTL level signals at its inputs into RS-232 output levels.

ASCII codes

Although not mandatory, serial data transfers usually take place using ASCII (American Standard Code for Information Interchange) codes. Up to 128 different characters and control codes are represented using 7-bit binary codes from 00_{16} to $7F_{16}$. An eighth bit may be used as a parity bit for error checking purposes, or for other special purposes, e.g. for a limited range of graphics codes. Standard ASCII codes are shown in Table 6.5.

Table 6.5

b	b	b	b	0	0	0	0	1	1	1	1	← b6
3	2	1	0	0	0	1	1	0	0	1	1	← b5
↓	↓	↓	↓	0	1	0	1	0	1	0	1	← b4
0	0	0	0	NUL	DLE	SP	0	@	P	'	p	
0	0	0	1	SOH	DC1	!	1	A	Q	a	q	
0	0	1	0	STX	DC2	"	2	B	R	b	r	
0	0	1	1	ETX	DC3	#	3	C	S	c	s	
0	1	0	0	EOT	DC4	$	4	D	T	d	t	
0	1	0	1	ENQ	NAK	%	5	E	U	e	u	
0	1	1	0	ACK	SYN	&	6	F	V	f	v	
0	1	1	1	BEL	ETB	'	7	G	W	g	w	
1	0	0	0	BS	CAN	(	8	H	X	h	x	
1	0	0	1	HT	EM	)	9	I	Y	i	y	
1	0	1	0	LF	SUB	*	:	J	Z	j	z	
1	0	1	1	VT	ESC	+	;	K	[	k	{	
1	1	0	0	FF	FS	,	<	L	\	l	|	
1	1	0	1	CR	GS	—	=	M	]	m	}	
1	1	1	0	SO	RS	.	>	N	↑	n	~	
1	1	1	1	SI	US	/	?	O	←	o	DEL	

Problems

1 (a) With the aid of a diagram representing letter 'A', describe the format used for serial data transfers.
(b) Explain why '*start*' and '*stop*' bits are required in serial data transmissions.

2 (a) Explain the term '*baud rate*'.
(b) Each character in a serial data transfer system consists of 7-bit data, no parity and single start/stop bits. If data is transferred at the rate of 1068.4 characters per second, calculate the baud rate.

3 (a) With the aid of a diagram, show the main features of a serial data transfer system.
(b) Describe two methods which may be used to perform parallel to serial or serial to parallel data conversion.

4 (a) With the aid of a block diagram, describe the main features of an ACIA (UART).
(b) Explain the advantages of using '*double buffering*' in an ACIA.

5 (a) List the advantages of using a serial data communications standard.
(b) Describe the main features of the RS-232 standard.

6 (a) Explain how problems associated with errors in Rx clock frequency of an ACIA (UART) are dealt with when receiving asynchronous serial data transmissions.
(b) What factor determines the maximum acceptable error.

7 Draw a circuit to provide an interface between an RS-232C transmit/receive link and a microcomputer data bus.

Chapter 7

Dedicated I/O controllers

Most of the I/O devices discussed so far have been general purpose and not dedicated to one specific application. Provided that the timing parameters of a particular application are within the capabilities of a selected MPU, then general purpose I/O devices in conjunction with suitable software may be used to implement all aspects of a system. Whether it is advisable to implement a complete system in this manner depends upon many different factors and is the subject of hardware–software *trade off* considerations during the system design phases. Improved performance may be obtained at relatively little extra cost by using dedicated I/O devices for such purposes as keyboard encoding, VDU timing signals, or floppy disk drive control.

Keyboard encoding

Keyboards are commonly used for data entry in all types of microcomputer or microcontroller system and two types of keyboard may be encountered:

1 Hex keypad.
2 ASCII (QWERTY) keyboard.

Hex keypad interface

A hex keypad usually consists of sixteen key switches organized in the form of a 4 × 4 matrix to reduce the number of I/O lines required (see Figure 7.1).

Such a keypad allows entry of hexadecimal numbers 0 to 9 and A to F, although the key legend may often be altered to cater for more specific system orientated inputs. When a key is pressed, the corresponding row and column lines are connected together, and by scanning rows and columns this key may

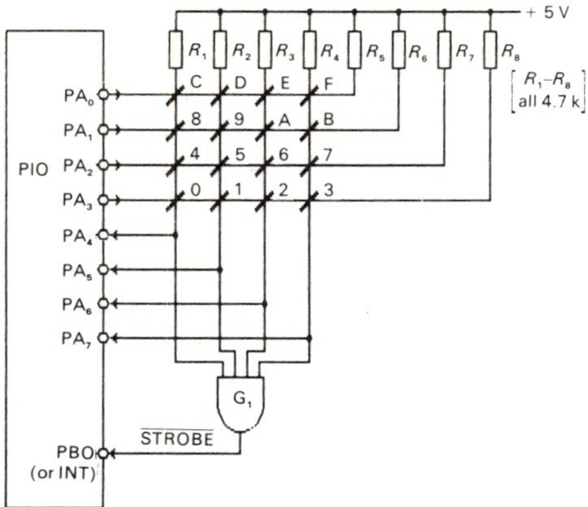

Figure 7.1

be identified and an equivalent binary code generated. The scanning and encoding may be accomplished using either software or hardware.

Software scanning

A hex keypad is often encoded by means of a software scanning routine which applies a logical 0 to each row input in sequence ('walking 0'), and checks each column output for key closure by checking for a column line at logical 0. As the complete keyboard is scanned, a key counter is incremented by one for each key tested. Scanning ceases once a key closure is detected and the value in the counter identifies the key pressed. Software routines to perform this task are as follows:

(a) 6502

```
0000                     ;*********************************
0000                     ;hexadecimal keypad scan subroutine
0000                     ;Exit: keycode in A
0000                     ;X and Y are preserved
0000                     ;Port configured b0-b3 outputs
0000                     ;b4-b7 inputs
0000                     ;*********************************
0000                     ;
0000           KEYCNT  = $0090          ;keycounter
0000           PAD     = $1700          ;I/O port
03F0                  *= $03F0
03F0                     ;
03F0 98        INKEY   TYA
03F1 48                PHA              ;preserve Y
```

```
03F2 8A              TXA
03F3 48              PHA             ;preserve X
03F4 A9 00    SCAN   LDA  #0         ;clear key counter
03F6 85 90           STA  KEYCNT
03F8 A2 F7           LDX  #$F7       ;X=row pattern
03FA A0 04    NEWROW LDY  #4         ;Y=column counter
03FC 8E 00 17        STX  PAD        ;send row pat to keypad
03FF AD 00 17        LDA  PAD        ;read columns into A
0402 0A       SHIFT  ASL  A          ;shift col data into carry
0403 90 0C           BCC  FOUND      ;exit with key code if closed
0405 E6 90           INC  KEYCNT     ;advance key count if no key
0407 88              DEY             ;move to next column
0408 D0 F8           BNE  SHIFT      ;all 4 columns checked?
040A 8A              TXA             ;shift row pattern right
040B 4A              LSR  A          ;one place for next row
040C AA              TAX             ;and check for last row
040D B0 EB           BCS  NEWROW     ;C=0 if all 4 sent
040F 90 E3           BCC  SCAN       ;no key, so keep scanning
0411 68       FOUND  PLA
0412 AA              TAX             ;restore X
0413 68              PLA
0414 A8              TAY             ;restore Y
0415 A5 90           LDA  KEYCNT     ;key code into A
0417 60              RTS
```

(b) Z80

```
                    ;*********************************
                    ;Hexadecimal keypad scan subroutine
                    ;Exit: keycode in a
                    ;Other registers preserved
                    ;Port configured b0-b3 outputs
                    ;b4-b7 inputs
                    ;*********************************
                    ;
0005 =      PORT    EQU     5
0EBE                ORG     0EBEH
                    ;
0EBE C5     INKEY:  PUSH    BC              ;preserve BC
0EBF D5             PUSH    DE              ;and DE
0EC0 0E05           LD      C,PORT          ;access I/O via C
0EC2 AF     SCAN:   XOR     A               ;clear key counter
0EC3 1EF7           LD      E,11110111B     ;E=row pattern
0EC5 0604   NEWROW: LD      B,4             ;B=column counter
0EC7 ED59           OUT     (C),E           ;send rwpat to keypad
```

```
0EC9 ED50              IN      D,(C)            ;read columns into D
0ECB CB22     SHIFT:   SLA     D                ;test col bit in CFlg
0ECD 3009              JR      NC,FOUND         ;exit with keycode
0ECF 3C                INC     A                ;advance count if no key
0ED0 10F9              DJNZ    SHIFT            ;all 4 cols checked?
0ED2 CB2B              SRA     E                ;test row bit in CFlg
0ED4 38EF              JR      C,NEWROW         ;4 row patterns sent?
0ED6 30EA              JR      NC,SCAN          ;no key, keep scanning
0ED8 D1       FOUND:   POP     DE               ;restore DE
0ED9 C1                POP     BC               ;and BC
0EDA C9                RET
```

(c) 6800

```
0000                   ;**********************************
0000                   ;hexadecimal keypad scan subroutine
0000                   ;Exit: keycode in accumulator A
0000                   ;B and X are preserved
0000                   ;Port configured b0-b3 outputs
0000                   ;b4-b7 inputs
0000                   ;**********************************
0000                   ;
0000          KEYCNT   EQU  $0090        ;keycounter
0000          COLCNT   EQU  $0091        ;column counter
0000          DRA      EQU  $8004        ;I/O port
01DD                   ORG  $01DD
01DD                   ;
01DD 37       INKEY    PUSH B            ;preserve B
01DE 7F 00 90 SCAN     CLR  KEYCNT       ;clear key counter
01E1 C6 F7             LDAB #$F7         ;B=row pattern
01E3 86 04    NEWROW   LDAA #4
01E5 97 91             STAA COLCNT       ;init column count
01E7 F7 80 04          STAB DRA          ;send row pat to keypad
01EA B6 80 04          LDAA DRA          ;read columns into A
01ED 48       SHIFT    ASLA              ;shift col data into carry
01EE 24 0D             BCC  FOUND        ;exit with keycode if closed
01F0 7C 00 90          INC  KEYCNT       ;advance count if no key
01F3 7A 00 91          DEC  COLCNT       ;move to next column
01F6 26 F5             BNE  SHIFT        ;all 4 columns checked?
01F8 54                LSRB              ;shift row pattern right
01F9 25 E8             BCS  NEWROW       ;repeat for all 4 rows
01FB 20 E1             BRA  SCAN         ;keep scanning if no key
01FD 33       FOUND    PULB              ;restore B
01FE 96 90             LDAA KEYCNT       ;keycode into A
0200 39                RTS
```

Dedicated encoder IC

Although software scanning routines are relatively simple, a system designer may prefer to make use of a hardware encoding device. One such device which is readily interfaced to the data bus of a microcomputer is the 74C922 (see Figure 7.2).

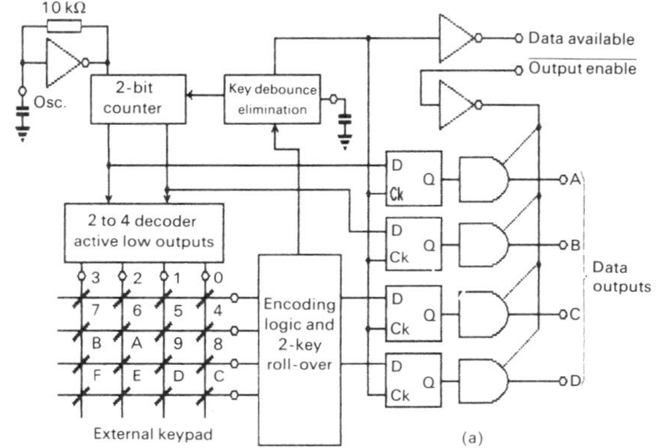

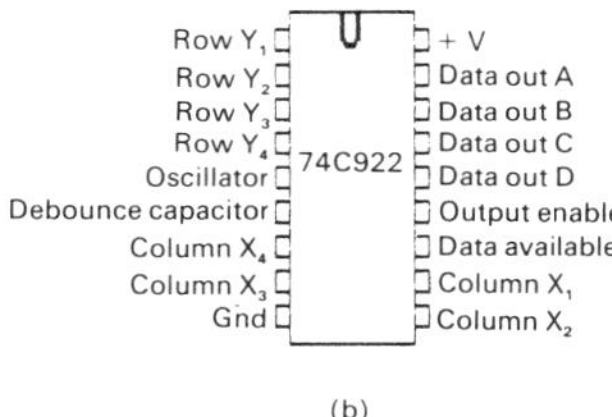

Figure 7.2

Scanning of the rows and columns takes place in a similar manner to that used for the software examples using either an internal or an external clock oscillator. An external oscillator may be connected to pin 5 for applications that require the scanning to be synchronized to some external event, otherwise a 100 nF capacitor may be connected between this pin and ground to activate an internal oscillator. The switch bounce delay period is controlled by a capacitor (typically 10 μF) connected between pin 6 and ground. When a key press is detected, the DA (data available) pin goes high and the key code is latched into an internal register. Tristate outputs from this register allow simple interfacing to an MPU data bus to be achieved, as shown in Figure 7.3.

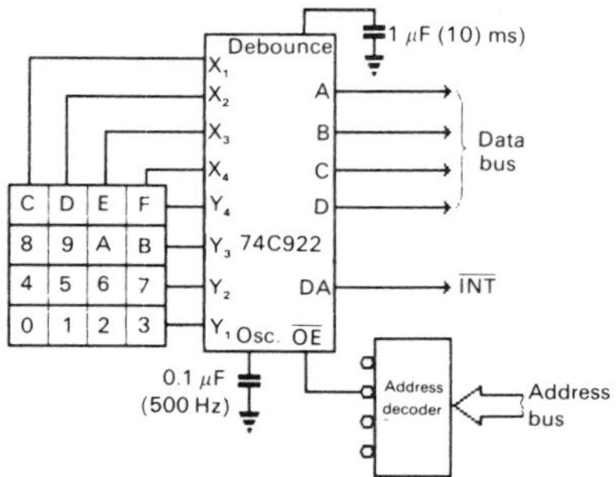

Figure 7.3

ASCII (QWERTY) keyboard interface

Microcomputer systems may require full textual input, e.g. for word processing, and in such cases will normally make use of a QWERTY keyboard (so named because of the order of the top row of letters on the keyboard). The

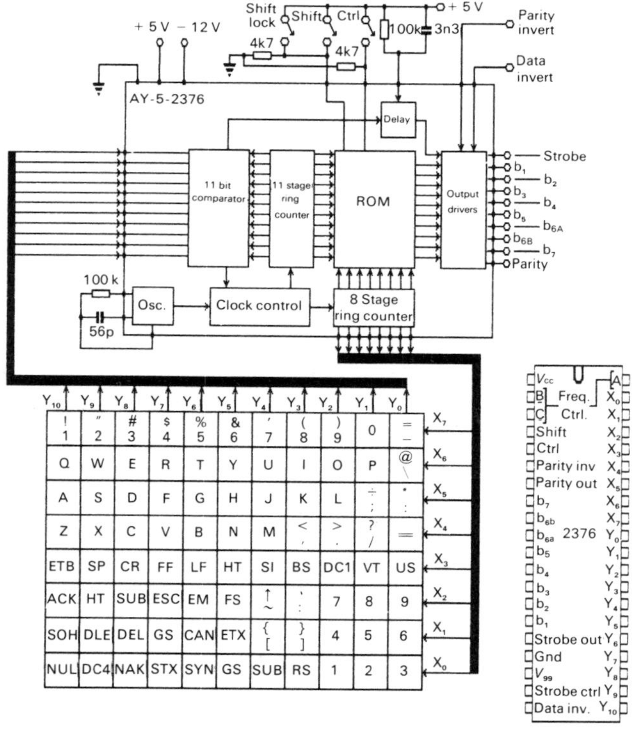

Figure 7.4

output from this type of keyboard usually takes the form of ASCII codes as described in Chapter 6. Key switches are arranged in the form of a matrix as for the hex keypad, although the total number of switches is obviously much larger. It is possible to also use software scanning with this type of keyboard although this task would take more time due to the extra keys, therefore a hardware keyboard encoder is more likely to be used. A typical encoder is the GI 2376 as shown in Figure 7.4.

ASCII codes are stored in an internal ROM which is addressed by the X and Y outputs from the 2376. These X and Y outputs are provided by two ring counters, eight bits for the rows (X) and eleven bits for the columns (Y). For each row input the eleven columns are scanned by comparing their outputs with the eleven bit output of the ring counter. Scanning ceases when key closure is detected and code conversion is achieved by addressing the ROM. This particular device does not have tristate outputs therefore it must be interfaced to a microcomputer via an I/O port otherwise tristate buffers must be added. Often with keyboards of this type a serial interface will be implemented.

VDU interface

The visual display unit (VDU) is a commonly used microcomputer output peripheral device which is fast in operation and flexible in terms of its display. It allows a wide range of alphanumeric and graphic characters to be displayed and gives a virtually instantaneous response to changes made by the operator and is sufficiently fast to provide animated (moving) displays.

Principle of operation

The VDU display operates in a similar manner to that of a conventional TV receiver. A cathode ray tube (CRT) is used in which a fine beam of electrons is acccelerated towards a phosphor coated screen by a very high positive potential (10 to 25 KV), and causes the phosphor to emit light from the point of impact. The brightness of this light output may be controlled by adjusting the intensity of the electron beam. A magnetic deflection system which takes the form of two sets of coils at right angles to one another is fitted around the neck of the CRT. Current is passed through these coils which causes the electron beam to be deflected from its central position in both horizontal and vertical directions. Sawtooth shaped deflecting currents are used in both sets of coils, and the frequency of the horizontal deflection current is made approximately 300 times that of the vertical deflection current so that the CRT screen is completely 'scanned' (see Figure 7.5).

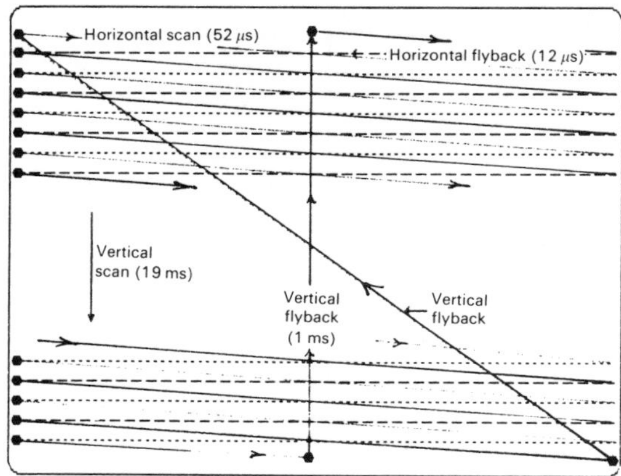

Figure 7.5

The human eye is unable to follow the rapidly moving point of light but instead perceives a patch of light which covers the entire CRT screen. If the intensity of the electron beam is modulated while scanning takes place, an image is built up momentarily on the CRT screen. This image may be displayed constantly by repeating the whole process 50 times per second with a small vertical displacement on alternate scans so that consecutive vertical scans 'interlace' (this reduces flicker).

Each complete scan of the CRT must be in an identical position on the screen otherwise the image would appear fragmented. This is achieved by the use of horizontal and vertical synchronizing pulses as shown in Figure 7.6.

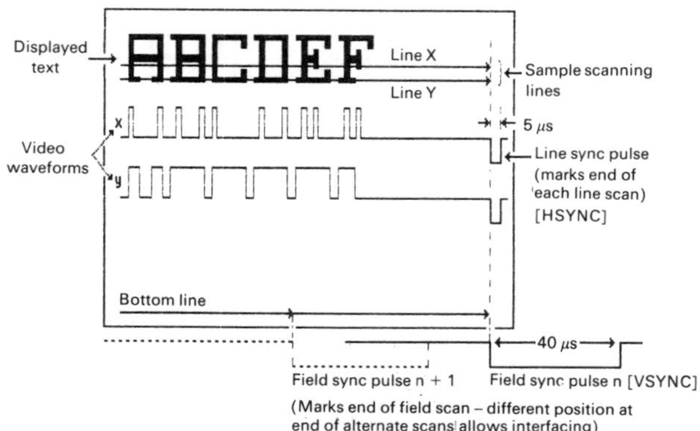

Figure 7.6

Forming characters on the CRT screen

Characters for display on the CRT screen are stored in a *screen memory* as ASCII codes. This memory forms part of the MPU memory system but is distinguished by being jointly accessible by the MPU and the CRT controlling circuits (i.e., *shared memory*). These ASCII codes must be converted into character display codes as shown in Figure 7.7.

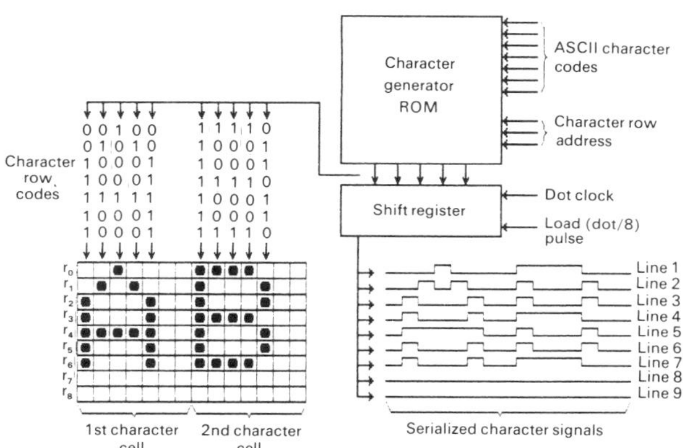

Figure 7.7

It can be seen that although each screen character is represented by a single ASCII code, seven (or more) display codes are required to form the actual display. These display codes are stored in a *character generator* ROM which must be addressed to obtain the correct character code. The ROM address consists of the ASCII code plus the character line address. Therefore to display a complete line of text on the CRT, the same sequence of screen memory locations must be addressed repeatedly, once for each line in the character display, before moving on to the next line of text.

In addition, each characteı code must be serialized in order to modulate the CRT electron beam. This requires some form of parallel to serial converter such as a shift register.

Cathode ray tube controller devices

From the previous descriptions it can be seen that the implementation of a VDU requires the generation of a large number of timing and control signals, which owing to their high speeds are unlikely to be provided by the MPU itself. Discrete logic may be used for this purpose but does require a rather

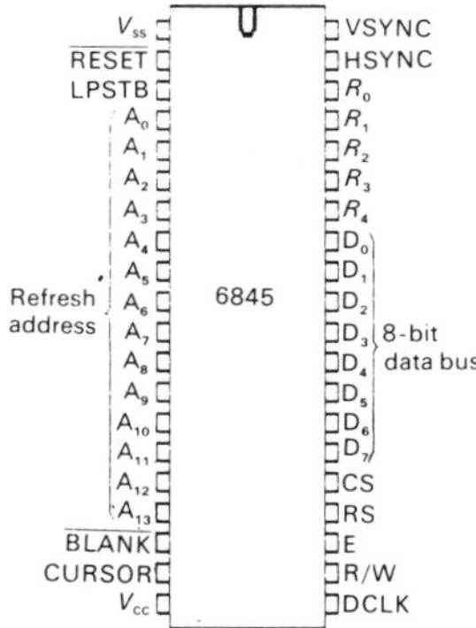

Figure 7.8

large number of counter and logic ICs (perhaps 30 or 40). For this reason, special cathode ray tube controller (CRTC) devices have been developed, many of which may be software controlled to enable the user to define various parameters such as number of characters per line, cursor positioning, etc. The 6845 is a typical CRTC and its pin-out is shown in Figure 7.8.

This particular device consists of horizontal and vertical counting circuits, display address generator, cursor register and comparator, and light pen register. The following descriptions define the function of each of the signals associated with this device:

A_0—A_{13}: These fourteen output lines provide refresh addresses for the screen RAM. Up to 16K bytes of RAM may be accessed for display, starting at an address determined by the contents of the 'start address' register. Multiplexers are used to isolate the screen memory from the MPU address bus, but still permit MPU access for updating the display. The CRTC provides full screen refresh without using the MPU.

D_0—D_7: These eight data lines interface directly to the MPU data bus and allow data to be transferred between the MPU and the CRTC registers.

HSYNC: This output provides synchronizing pulses for the horizontal scan timebase generator in the VDU and ensures that the CRT electron beam scans in step with the CRTC screen memory access. The position and width of these pulses are software controllable by the contents of registers within the CRTC.

VSYNC: This output provides synchronizing pulses for the vertical scan timebase generator in the VDU, indicating completion of a vertical scan and initiating a return to the top of the VDU screen.

BLANK: This output blanks the VDU electron beam during flyback, i.e., when beam is deflected back for the start of a further horizontal or vertical scan. This prevents unwanted flyback traces from appearing on the VDU screen.

CURSOR: This output marks the position on the screen where the next character sent to the VDU will appear. The cursor itself is a patch of light on the screen which can be made to blink (fast or slow). Both the cursor size and fast/slow/non-blink options are programmable by the contents of registers within the CRTC.

DCLK: This is the 'dot' clock input to the CRTC which derives its signal from an external clock oscillator. This signal determines the rate at which the electron beam in the VDU may be modulated and hence determines the definition of each character. For a given horizontal scanning rate, the frequency of the dot clock is determined by the number of characters displayed on each line. This is typically 6 MHz for 40 characters/line (40 column) and 12 MHz for an 80 column display.

RS: This is a *register select* input which is normally connectd to address line A_0. The 6845 contains two directly addressable locations only. The lower address (RS = 0) contains a 5-bit write-only register which specifies the data register that can be accessed at the higher address (when RS = 1). The 6845 contains eighteen registers which are accessible through this single address (see Table 7.1).

LPSTB: This is an input which accepts a signal from a 'light pen'. A light pen has a photosensitive tip which may be placed on the VDU screen in any desired position. When the electron beam in the VDU scans past this position, the logic output from the light pen changes momentarily and is detected by the CRTC. During the display of a screen full of characters, counters are maintained within the CRTC which record the actual screen position being scanned at any instant. An active signal from a light pen causes this count to be transferred into the 16-bit light pen register in the CRTC. This information may be subsequently used by the software to allow control by the light pen, e.g. menu selection or drawing.

MISC: The remaining inputs (RESET, CS, E and R/W) function in the normal manner and are not considered further.

6845 registers

The 6845 is a programmable device which permits a wide range of display standards to be selected. For example, American (525 line) or European (625 line) standards may be selected, synchronizing parameters, numbers of characters per row and number of rows per screen are all selectable. Full details are shown in Table 7.1.

Table 7.1

CRTC register	*Description*
R_0 Horiz. total chars.	Total of displayed and non-displayed characters minus 1 per horizontal line.
R_1 Horiz. displayed chars.	The number of characters actually displayed on each horizontal line.
R_2 Horiz. sync position	The character position on the horizontal line where the horizontal sync occurs. For a normally centred screen an equal number of non-displayed character positions should appear either side of the displayed characters. As the value in R_2 increases towards R_0 value, the display moves to the right. As the value in R_2 decreases towards the value in R_1, the display moves to the left.
R_3 VSYNC, HSYNC widths	Widths of the horizontal and vertical sync pulses as defined below: b_7 b_6 b_5 b_4 b_3 b_2 b_1 b_0 8 4 2 1 8 4 2 1 VSYNC pulse width (number of scan lines) (b_7–b_4); HSYNC pulse width (number of char. clock periods) (b_3–b_0)
R_4 Vertical total rows	A 7-bit value containing the total number of character rows, minus one, in a field (= 1572/vert scan freq).
R_5 Vertical total adjust	A 5-bit value containing the number of additional scan lines needed to complete an entire vertical scan.
R_6 Vertical displayed rows	A 7-bit value which determines the number of displayed character rows in each vertical scan.
R_7 Vertical sync position	A 7-bit value which defines the character row at which vertical sync occurs. This must be greater than R_6 and less than or equal to R_4. As R_7 increases, the display moves up the screen. As R_7 decreases the display moves down.
R_8 Mode control	Interlace/non-interlace.
R_9 Scan line	This byte defines the total number of lines per character row.
R_{10} Cursor start line	Defines start line for cursor and type of cursor display (steady, slow or fast blink).
R_{11} Cursor end line	Defines last line for cursor display.
R_{12} Display start address (H) R_{13} Display start address (L)	Location of VDU screen RAM in memory.
R_{14} Cursor position address (H) R_{15} Cursor position address (L)	Address in screen RAM of initial cursor position.
R_{16} Light pen register (H) R_{17} Light pen register (L)	Address in screen RAM corresponding to current position of light pen on VDU screen.

VDU block diagram

The block diagram of a VDU which uses a 6845 CRTC is shown in Figure 7.9.

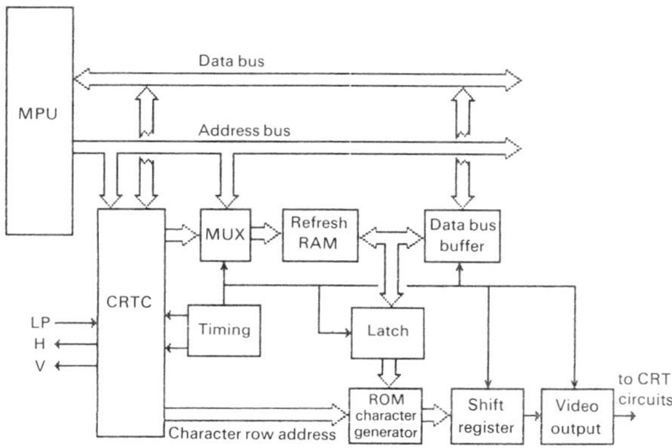

Figure 7.9

Floppy disk controllers

A floppy disk is commonly used for backing storage in a microcomputer system. It consists of a plastic disk, commonly $5\frac{1}{4}$ in or $3\frac{1}{2}$ in diameter which is coated with a fine magnetic material (see Figure 7.10).

The disk is rotated in a drive unit at approximately 300 rev/min and digital data is transferred to or from the magnetic surface of the disk via a read/write head. The information stored on the disk is organized in the form of tracks

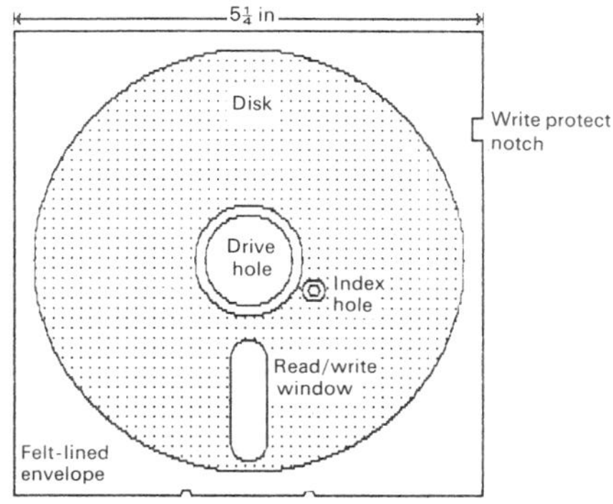

Figure 7.10

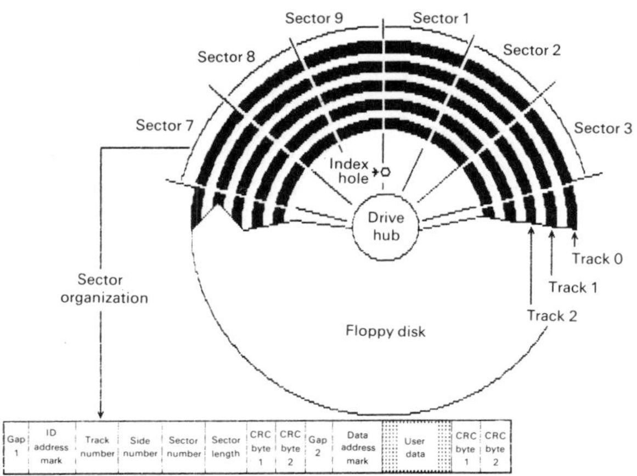

Figure 7.11

and sectors as shown in Figure 7.11 (the exact number of tracks and sectors varies from one system to another).

A disk drive unit is a complex system consisting of a mixture of electronic and mechanical components which must be controlled by the microcomputer which uses it for data storage. Basically a microcomputer must be able to step the read/write head from track to track and identify sector positions on the disk so that data may be correctly stored and retrieved, i.e., the microcomputer must know the exact position of the read/write head at all times. This can only be achieved if a disk is *formatted* before use, i.e., tracks and sectors are already marked out on the disk surface together with appropriate identification (ID) marks. The microcomputer must also be able to manage the actual data transfer to and from the disk, although conversion of data bytes into bit serial format recording currents and vice versa is carried out by the disk drive electronics. Although a disk drive may be controlled from the parallel I/O ports of a microcomputer, it is more usual to make use of a dedicated floppy disk controller (FDC) IC which also carries out the formatting process. The block diagram and pin-out of a typical FDC chip is shown in Figure 7.12(a), (b) and (c).

FDC block functions

The function of each block in Figure 7.12(a) may be summarized in the following manner:

Data shift register: This is an 8-bit shift register which converts serial input data from the read/write head into parallel form during disk read operations,

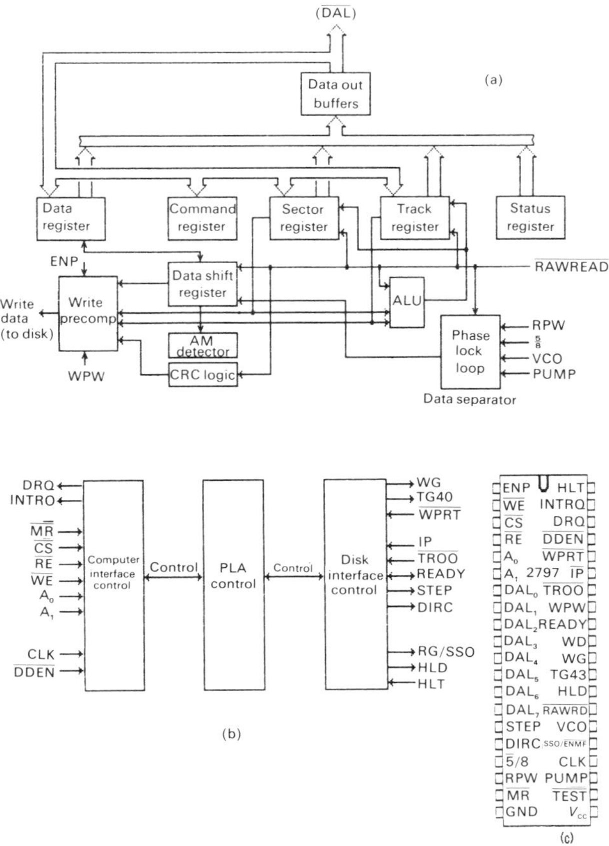

Figure 7.12

and converts parallel data into serial data for the read/write head during disk write operations.

Data register: This is an 8-bit register which holds data for transfer to or from the data access lines (DAL) during disk read and disk write operations. When reading the disk, assembled data in the data shift register is transferred in parallel into the data register. When writing to the disk, data is transferred from the data register into the data shift register. When seeking a certain track on the disk, the desired track number must be loaded into this register before executing a 'seek' command.

Track register: This is an 8-bit register which holds the track number corresponding to the current position of the read/write head. The contents of this register are incremented by one each time that the read/write head is stepped in (towards the disk centre) and decremented by one each time that the read/write head is stepped out. The contents of this register are compared with the track number recorded in the disk ID field during read, write and verify operations. During a seek operation, stepping pulses are issued in the appropriate direction until the contents of the track register equal the contents of the data register.

Sector register: This is an 8-bit register which is loaded via the data access lines with the number of the required sector for read or write operations. The contents of this register are compared with the sector number recorded in each ID field on the disk, thus enabling the required sector to be located.

Command register: This 8-bit register holds the code of the command currently being executed. Eleven commands are available as shown in Table 7.2.

Status register: This is an 8-bit register which holds device status information relating to read/write errors, drive busy, disk write protected, head load, track 0 and index pulse (see manufacturer's data sheet for full information).

CRC logic: This logic is responsible for generating or checking the 16-bit cyclic redundancy code. This code is used to check for errors when recovering

Table 7.2

				Bits				
Command	*7*	*6*	*5*	*4*	*3*	*2*	*1*	*0*
Restore	0	0	0	0	h	V	r1	r0
Seek	0	0	0	1	h	V	r1	r0
Step	0	0	1	T	h	V	r1	r0
Step-in	0	1	0	T	h	V	r1	r0
Step-out	0	1	1	T	h	V	r1	r0
Read sector	1	0	0	m	L	E	U	0
Write sector	1	0	1	m	L	E	U	a0
Read address	1	1	0	0	0	E	U	0
Read track	1	1	1	0	0	E	U	0
Write track	1	1	1	1	0	E	U	0
Force interrupt	1	1	0	1	I3	I2	I1	I0

r1/r0 = Stepping motor rate
V = Verify flag (1 = verify)
h = Head load flag (1 = load at beginning)
a0 = Data address mark (1 = deleted DAM)
L = Sector length flag
E = 15 ms delay (1 = delay, 0 = no delay)
U = Update SSO (1 = update to 1)
I0 = 1 interrupt – drive has become ready
I1 = 1 interrupt – drive has become not ready
I2 = 1 interrupt at each index hole
I3 = 1 immediate interrupt, requires a reset
I3–I0 = 0 terminate with no interrupt (INTRQ)

data from the disk. Two checks are made, one on the sector ID information and the second on the actual data stored in the sector.

ALU: The arithmetic and logic unit (ALU) is used to perform all increment, decrement and compare operations required for updating registers within the FDC and for comparisons with the IDs recorded on the disk.

AM detector: This section detects the presence of address marks which are used to indicate the start of each sector, start of the ID sequence and start of data record. Address marks are clock/data bit patterns which are not repeated elsewhere in the remainder of the ID or data field.

Write precomp: This section allows the width of write pulses to be controlled by external compensation components.

Data separator: This is a phase lock loop circuit which enables data and clock pulses to be separated when reading from the disk. The 5/8 input allows the voltage controlled oscillator (VCO) frequency to be adjusted to provide separation for $5\frac{1}{4}$ in or 8 in disk standards.

Interfacing to MPU buses

An FDC device may be used to interface a disk drive to the buses of a microcomputer as shown in Figure 7.13.

The control lines are divided into two groups which interface:

1 The FDC chip to the microcomputer buses.
2 The disk drive to the FDC chip.

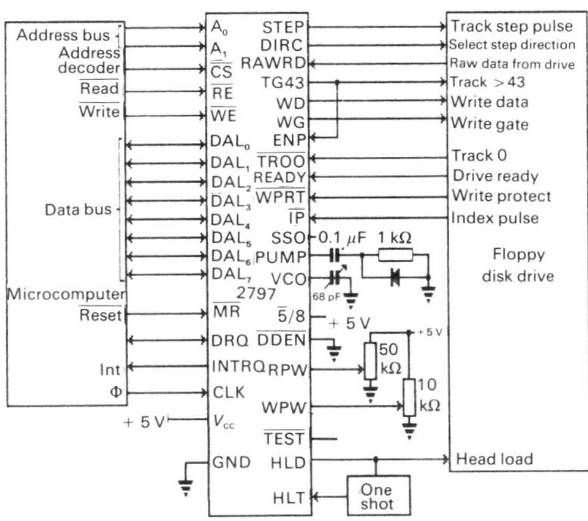

Figure 7.13

The control lines which interface the FDC to an MPU are similar to those used for most other types of device already encountered, the exception being DRQ (data request) which indicates that the data register contains assembled data during disk read operations, or is empty during disk write operations. This output may be used to interrupt the MPU, or alternatively, bit 1 of the status register may be polled since this contains a copy of DRQ during read and write operations. The function of each of the control lines which interface the disk drive to the FDC are as follows:

$\overline{\text{MR}}$ (master reset): A logic low on this input resets the FDC device and pre-loads the command and sector registers.

STEP: This output becomes active in response to a 'step command', and delivers one stepping pulse to the read/write head stepper motor of the drive causing it to move to the next track position. The directon of step is the same as that used for a previous step command, and the track register is automatically updated.

DIRC: This output determines the direction of stepping of the read/write head. A logical 1 causes the read/write head to step in towards the centre while a logical 0 causes the head to step out.

$\overline{5}$|8: This input selects the internal VCO frequency for use with either $5\frac{1}{4}$ in drives (logical 0) or 8 in drives (logical 1).

RPW: This is the 'read pulse width' pin. The slider of an external potentiometer is connected to this pin to control the operation of the data separator to obtain correct phasing of the read data pulse.

$\overline{\text{TEST}}$: A test input which may be forced low to enable external components to be correctly adjusted. Also, in conjunction with MR (master reset), selects either internal or external data separation.

PUMP: An output signal which consists of negative and positive pulses whose duration depends upon the phase relationship between the incoming data and the VCO (voltage controlled oscillator) frequency. The pulses are converted into a slowly changing DC potential which is used to control the frequency of the VCO. Forms part of the data separation circuit.

SSO: This is the 'side select output' which is controlled by the 'S' flag during read and write operations. It may be used to control 'double sided' disk drives.

VCO (voltage controlled oscillator): This is a pin to which an external capacitor is connected to adjust the frequency of the internal VCO.

RAWREAD: This input accepts data directly from the read/write head of the disk drive (after suitable amplification). This data consists of negative-going pulses for each transition in recorded flux.

HLD: This is the 'head load' output which is used to energize a solenoid on the disk drive and allows the read/write head to contact the disk surface.

TG43 (track greater than 43): This output becomes active when the read/write head is positioned between tracks 44 to 76 (the innermost tracks). It is valid only during read or write operations and may be connected to the ENP input to alter the write precompensation on these tracks.

WG (write gate): This output is activated to allow current to flow into the read/write head for writing to the disk. To prevent corrupt data being recorded, this output is not activated until the first byte has been written to the data register. Writing is inhibited if the 'write protect' input is held at logical 0.

WD (write data): This output provides data for writing to the disk in the form of 250 ns (MFM) or 500 ns (FM) pulses per flux transition. WD provides data, clock and ID information for both FM (single density) or MFM (double density) formats.

READY: This input accepts a signal from the disk drive which indicates its state of readiness. If the READY input is low, read and write operations do not take place and an interrupt is generated. An inverted copy of READY is available in bit 7 of the status register.

WPW (write precompensation width): An external potentiometer may be connected to this pin to control the delay when using write precompensation.

$\overline{\text{TR00}}$ (track 00): This input from the disk drive informs the FDC that the read/write head is positioned over track zero, and an inverted copy of this bit is available in bit 2 of the status register after step, seek and restore commands. It is used to preset the read/write head to a known position to provide a reference for subsequent step operations.

$\overline{\text{IP}}$ (index pulse): This input accepts index pulses from the disk drive which indicate the start of the first record on each track. The pulses are generated each time that a single hole in the disk lines up with a corresponding hole in the outer envelope. Disk sectors are numbered from this reference point. An inverted copy of IP is available in bit 1 of the status register during step, seek and restore commands.

$\overline{\text{WPRT}}$ (write protect): This input is sampled whenever a write command is received. If a logical 0 is detected at this input the write command is terminated and the write protect status bit is set. The signal is generated by the disk drive by sensing whether the write protect notch in the disk envelope has been covered.

$\overline{\text{DDEN}}$ (double density): This input selects either single density (logical 1) or double density (logical 0) operation. Single density used FM recording and double density uses MFM recording as shown in Figure 7.14.

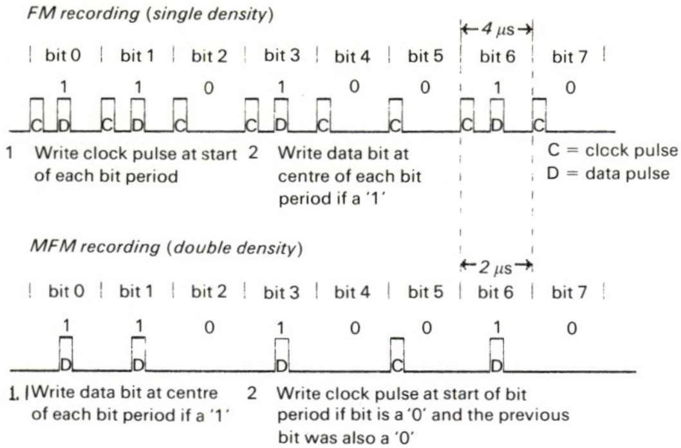

Figure 7.14

It can be seen in Figure 7.14 that double density recording is achieved by using fewer pulses for each byte of information, i.e., using the same number of pulses in MFM recording results in twice the number of bytes recorded.

ENP (enable precompensation): A logical high on this input enables write precompensation to be used.

Index

6500 serial I/O software, 148
6522:
  configuring, 119
  peripheral control register, 116
  VIA, 115
6530:
  direction control registers, 110
  I/O facilities, 109
  RRIOT, 108
  timer, 111
6800 serial I/O software, 153
6821:
  PIA, 135
  PIA configuring, 139
    control registers, 136
    data direction registers, 136
    output registers, 135
6845:
  CRTC, 180
  registers, 181
6850:
  ACIA, 157
  control register, 159
  receive data register, 159
  receive shift register, 159
  software routines, 160
  status register, 159
  transmit data register, 158
  transmit shift register, 158
8255:
  PPI, 121
  configuring, 123
  operating modes, 121
  single bit control, 125
  status word, 125

A to D conversion, 48
ACIA, 157
Active filters, 13
ADC interfacing, 54
Amplification, 1
ASCII (QWERTY) keyboard interface, 176
  codes, 169

Band-pass filters, 15
Baud rate, 146
Binary:
  counter ADC, 49
  weighted DAC, 23
Bipolar:
  DAC, 30
  transistor, 76
Buffer memory, 74
Buffering, 71
Bus structure, 70

Cathode ray tube controller (CRTC), 179
Character generator ROM, 179
Common mode rejection, 8
Control register, 104, 106
Conversion time (ADC), 54
CMRR, 3
CRT scanning, 177
Cut-off frequency, 12

D to A conversion, 23
DAC:
  applications, 33
  interfacing, 31
Darlington driver, 77
Data:
  acquisition system, 82
  direction register, 106
  input register, 104
  logger, 82
  output register, 104, 105
  transfers, 70
Dedicated I/O controllers, 171
Differential amplifier, 8
Differential linearity (ADC), 54
Direct memory access (DMA), 71, 74
Double buffering (of ACIA), 158

Electrical:
  buffering, 76
  isolation, 89
End of conversion (EDC), 49

FDC interfacing, 187
Filtering, 1, 11
Flash converter, 51
Floppy disk controller (FDC), 183

Gain, 29
Gain error, 53

Handshaking, 71, 72
Hex keypad interface, 171
High-pass filter, 11

Index

IEEE-488 bus, 85, 87
Inductive loads, 79
Interrupts, 71, 73

Keyboard:
  encoder IC, 175
  encoding, 171

Linearization, 1
Linearity, 10, 30
  ADC, 53
Listener, 87
Low-pass filter, 11

Missing codes, 52
Monotonicity, 28
Motor control, 42
Multiplexed:
  displays 82
  inputs, 82
Multiplexing, 81

Null modem cable, 167

Offset, 29
Offset-null, 10
Offsetting, 1, 9
Operational amplifiers, 2
Opto-isolator, 89

Panel meter control, 42
Parallel:
  flash converter, 51
  I/O controllers, 93
  to serial conversion, 80
Passive filters, 12
Polling, 71
Ports, 107
Programmable I/O devices, 104

Quantizing error, 52

R-2R resistor DAC, 26
Ramp waveform, 33
Resolution, 28, 54
RS-232, 164
  interconnections, 166
  signals, 165
  standards, 164

Scaling, 63
Scaling algorithm, 64
Serial:
  I/O controllers, 145, 157
  data, 70
  data transfers, 145
  to parallel conversion, 80
Settling time, 30
Shift register, 154
Signal:
  conditioning, 1
  conversion, 23
Sine waveshape, 35
Software:
  ADC conversion, 58
  filtering, 15
  scanning (of keyboard), 172
Standard buses, 85
Start:
  bit, 146
  of conversion (SDC), 49
Status flags, 107
STD bus, 85
Stop bit, 146
Successive approximation, 50
Switch debouncing, 79
Synchronisation (of data), 71

Talker, 87
Timing, 70
Tracking converter, 50
TTL:
  input port, 93
  logic inverter, 77
  output port, 97
  to RS-232 interface, 167

UART:
  hardware, 157
  software, 147

VDU:
  block diagram, 183
  interface, 177
VMOS FET driver, 78
Voltage gain, 3

Waveform synthesis, 33

Z80 PIO: 126
  configuring, 129
  input/output select register, 128
  mask control register, 128
  mask register, 128
  mode control register, 128
  serial I/O software, 151
Zero transition, 53